The GOOD RESORT Guide

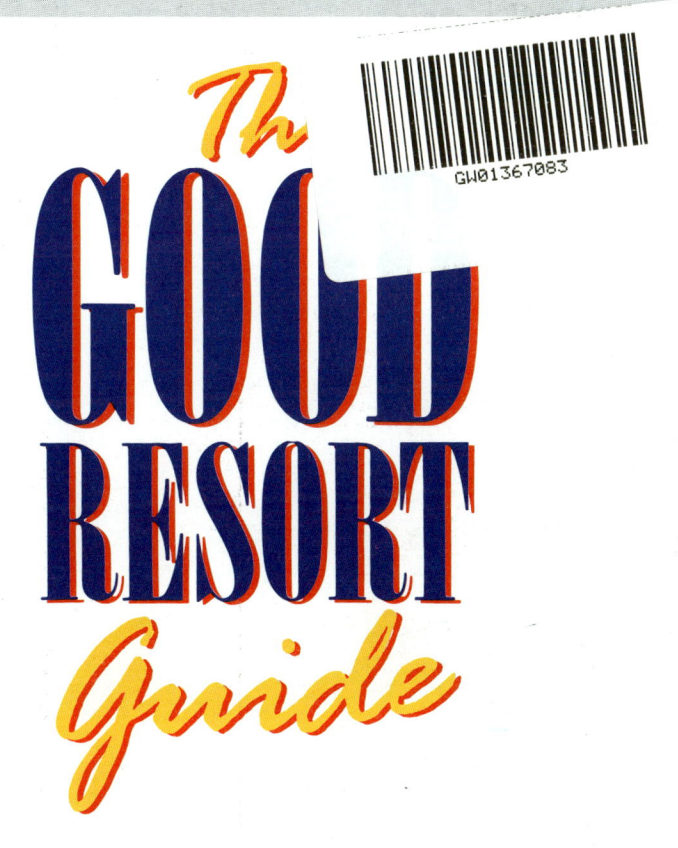

The BBC Breakaway Book of top European resorts.

Introduced by Roger Macdonald

Published by Pickfords Travel.
By arrangement with BBC Publications, a division of BBC Enterprises Ltd.

©1987 PICKFORDS TRAVEL SERVICE LTD
ISBN 1 870330 00 5

CONTENTS

INTRODUCTION	4

CANARY ISLES	6
TENERIFE	8
GRAN CANARIA	14
LANZAROTE	18
FUERTEVENTURA	21

MOROCCO	24
AGADIR	25
TANGIER	29

TUNISIA	34
PORT EL KANTAOUI	36
SOUSSE	36

CYPRUS	42

GREECE	48
HALKIDIKI	51
CRETE	56
RHODES	62
CORFU	68

YUGOSLAVIA	74
DALMATIAN RIVIERA	76
ISTRIAN RIVIERA	80

CONTENTS

ITALY — 86
NEAPOLITAN RIVIERA	88
ADRIATIC RIVIERA	92
VENETIAN RIVIERA	97
SARDINIA	99
SICILY	103

MALTA — 108

FRANCE MEDITERRANEAN — 116

SPAIN — 126
MAJORCA	127
MINORCA	133
IBIZA	137
FORMENTERA	143
COSTA BRAVA	146
COSTA DORADA	153
COSTA BLANCA	159
COSTA DE ALMERIA	166
COSTA DEL SOL	170

PORTUGAL — 178
ALGARVE	180
ESTORIL COAST	187

CHANNEL COAST — 192
FRANCE	193
BELGIUM	196
HOLLAND	199

DENMARK — 202

INDEX — 210

CREDITS — 214

THE GOOD RESORT GUIDE

INTRODUCTION

Choosing the right holiday can be the most difficult task of the year. If you make a serious mistake, there is no real remedy, and often twelve months to brood on what went wrong. A holiday, once taken, cannot be repaired, or altered, or sent back to the shop for a refund. Few people would dream of buying a house without expert advice, or a car without careful examination; but holidays, which can cost as much as either of these on an annual basis, are sometimes booked in haste and repented at leisure. Until now, holidaymakers planning a trip to one of the major resort areas in and around Europe, have had to rely largely on tour operators' brochures to make their choice — brochures which, after all, are produced to sell holidays not to highlight their occasional shortcomings.

4 THE GOOD RESORT GUIDE

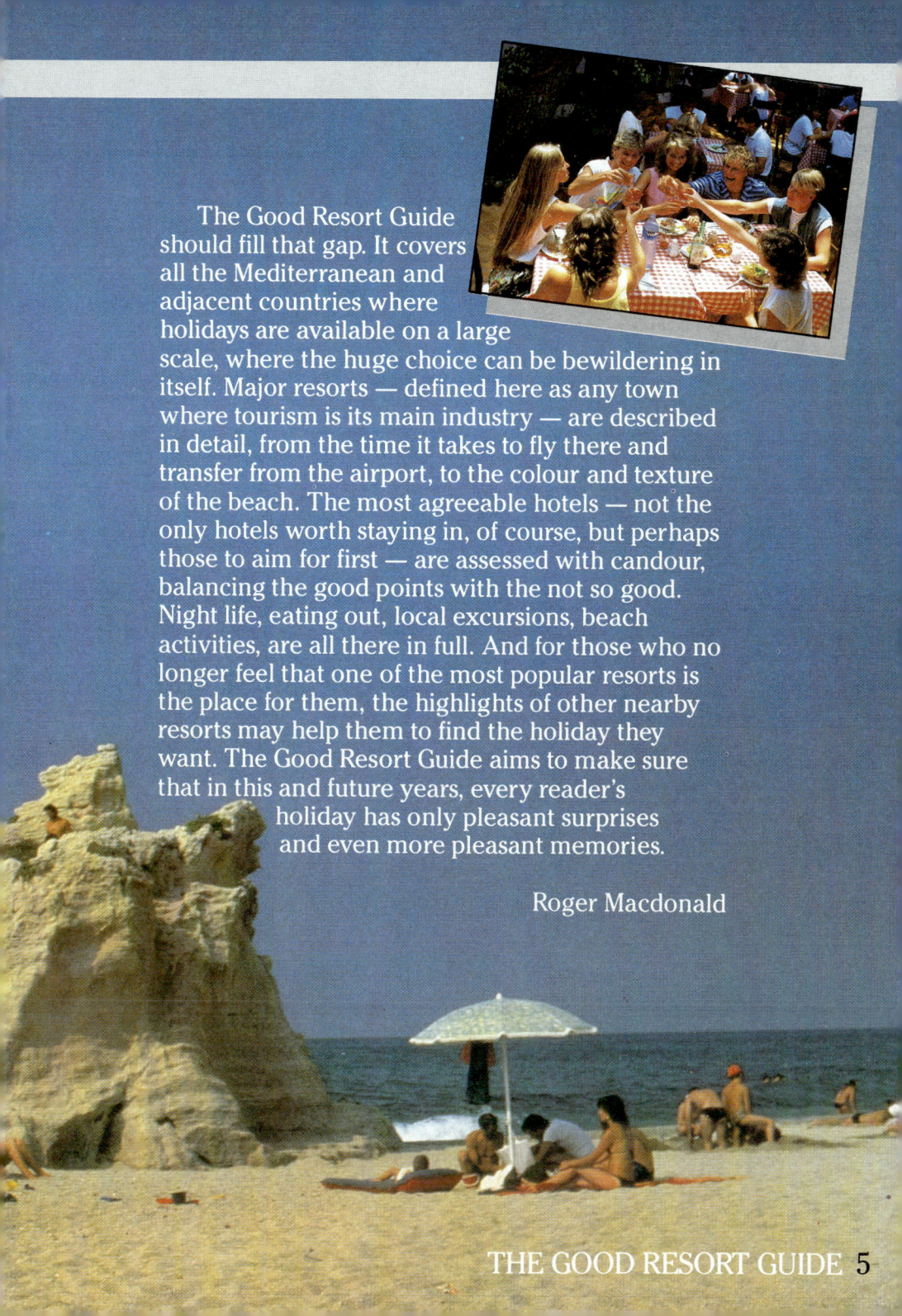

The Good Resort Guide should fill that gap. It covers all the Mediterranean and adjacent countries where holidays are available on a large scale, where the huge choice can be bewildering in itself. Major resorts — defined here as any town where tourism is its main industry — are described in detail, from the time it takes to fly there and transfer from the airport, to the colour and texture of the beach. The most agreeable hotels — not the only hotels worth staying in, of course, but perhaps those to aim for first — are assessed with candour, balancing the good points with the not so good. Night life, eating out, local excursions, beach activities, are all there in full. And for those who no longer feel that one of the most popular resorts is the place for them, the highlights of other nearby resorts may help them to find the holiday they want. The Good Resort Guide aims to make sure that in this and future years, every reader's holiday has only pleasant surprises and even more pleasant memories.

Roger Macdonald

CANARY ISLES

Tenerife	8
Gran Canaria	14
Lanzarote	18
Fuerteventura	21

6 THE GOOD RESORT GUIDE

CANARY ISLES

The islands came first, not the birds, though no one knows exactly how the canaries got there. When they were first exported to Europe, in the sixteenth century, canaries were pure white: it was cross-breeding that added their colour. Not even cross-breeding, however, could make the females sing.

For centuries the Canaries were known as the Fortunate Islands, and sailors who thought themselves unlucky to be shipwrecked quickly discovered that they were indeed fortunate to find such a friendly native population and such an agreeable climate. The Canaries lie on the same latitude as Florida, and are spread across 300 miles of the Atlantic, but come as close as 60 miles to the African coast. In all there are six substantial and seven small islands, plus the island of San Borondin; but regard with suspicion anyone who claims to have been there, because it was invented by superstitious Canarians to avoid unlucky thirteen!

Their climate is the key to the Canaries' success as a tourist destination, especially in the winter months. From November to May, the temperature on the warmer coasts is invariably between 68 and 77 degrees. Even at the height of summer, it never goes above the mid eighties, cooled by the ocean currents of the Canary Stream that run south-west along the coast of Africa. Not that the sea itself is cold: in the winter, the sea temperature reaches around

Sunset in the Canary Isles

THE GOOD RESORT GUIDE 7

TENERIFE

65 degrees, rising to around 75 in the summer months.

However, contrary to popular opinion, the Canaries are not free of rain in the winter. On the contrary, from late October to early March, several continuous days of cloud or rain are quite common, especially in the northern parts of all the islands. December, January and February are the wettest months: while June, July and August have virtually no rain at all. It follows that while the Canaries may offer the greatest contrast to British temperatures in the winter, only at the height of their summer is sunshine virtually guaranteed.

TENERIFE

Tenerife, the largest and most popular of the major Canary Islands, has breathtaking natural beauty. The north is a fertile sub-tropical landscape, with banana plantations and citrus trees. The south is closer to the moon, incredible rock formations surrounding lifeless plateaux of cooled lava which remind visitors of Tenerife's volcanic origins. This apparently impossible contrast is explained by a mountain ridge dividing the island, and dominated by the towering peak of Mount Teide, rising 12,000 feet above the sea.

PLAYA DE LAS AMERICAS

As only a few holidaymakers are prepared to return home without evidence of exposure to the sun, the rest will want to know that Playa de las Americas offers the best prospect of sunshine combined with many other amenities, though it lacks the nightlife of Puerto de la Cruz (see page 10). Playa de las Americas, on the south coast of the island, is a purpose-built resort in which the building is likely to continue for several years in both coastal directions, south-eastwards to the fishing harbour of Los Cristianos, and north towards Torviscas, San Eugenio and a brand new marina. If cranes and girders bring you out in a rash, this is not a place to choose.

Bulldozers are not confined to the building sites. They have also been at work blending yellow Saharan sand with the original black sand that covers the island. The result in Playa de las Americas is a kind of grey wash to the beach, frankly off-putting at first, though after a time you get used to it and begin to appreciate its fine texture and gentle slopes into the sea. While the beach is protected by breakwaters, when the wind comes up, big waves can be

Beach at Playa de las Americas

THE GOOD RESORT GUIDE

TENERIFE

offputting for small children. These very same conditions, of course, add spice to the windsurfing available, though even that is considerably outclassed by the facilities at nearby Los Cristianos. You can also fish or play tennis, provided you bring your own equipment.

Playa de las Americas has no natural centre. Modern complexes of shops, restaurants, bars (including British-style 'pubs') and discos have sprung up in a haphazard fashion along the sea road behind the pleasant promenade. However, for the moment at least, the bigger hotels can be reasonably confident of keeping your business in the evenings.

Excursions

Visiting the other islands is one of the most popular activities. There are four hydrofoil services most days between Santa Cruz and Las Palmas in Gran Canaria, the journey taking under 1½ hours. It takes the same time from Los Cristianos by ordinary ferry to reach the tiny island of Gomera to the south-west, still almost entirely unspoilt. The roads consist of unrelenting hairpin bends and the ground is so formidably steep that the islanders have invented a language of high pitched whistles to pass messages from peak to peak.

Cabaret entertainment, Puerto de la Cruz

THE GOOD RESORT GUIDE 9

TENERIFE

From Gomera, Mount Teide back on Tenerife dominates the skyline, seeming to rise directly out of the waves, an extraordinary sight. Visiting the mountain is a complete day out from almost anywhere on Tenerife, but guaranteed to be a experience recalled long after the beach holiday or the night life are confused and forgotten. A cable car carries visitors to Teide, which rhymes with lady, almost to the very top; buffeted by the slightest breeze, it is not an experience for the nervous passenger. A short walk to the actual summit remains, but far from being an easy climb, it takes a tremendous effort in the thin atmosphere. The view, though, is supremely worthwhile, back down to the black hole of the dormant volcano, and around 360 degrees to pick out the other Canaries scattered across the Atlantic. On an exceptionally clear day, using a telescope or powerful binoculars, even the African coast is said to be a smudge on the horizon.

Because it is almost impossible to strike the correct balance between the best beaches and the best night life, organised excursions do well, especially those that take visitors round a series of shows and nightclubs: they can always come back independently to the one they like best. Puerto de la Cruz (see Other Resorts) has a small casino in the Taoro Park; one of, if not the best, nightclubs is the Tablao Martianez, renowned for its flamenco; and among the discos, Bentley's and Joy stay open until the last person leaves. For a particularly spectacular night out, try La Cueva, whose dinner dance takes place in an enormous volcanic cave, with an exceptional African cabaret. In most instances, the price of eating and drinking on a night out will be significantly lower than in mainland Spain.

The island's capital, Santa Cruz, is a pleasant if nondescript town on the north-east coast; shopping excursions are common.

Lido at Puerto de la Cruz

TENERIFE

Bird park, Puerto de la Cruz

Tenerife is more than simply a duty-free zone — it's been that for over a century — it practises free trade on a massive scale, so very few items imported are subject to tax. As a result, shop prices are extremely competitive, especially jewellery, leather goods, perfume, alcohol, tobacco, and electronic goods. However, if you buy a watch or a tape recorder, a camera or a calculator, remember that if it does go wrong, you can scarcely pop back to the shop.

PLAYA DE LAS AMERICAS HOTELS

Conquistador ★★★★ the pool is its pride and joy, a series of little lagoons linked by bridges with a tropical bar at its centre. The hotel is horseshoe-shaped, and overlooks a small, rocky beach. The main Playa is a good 15 minutes' walk away. Restaurant with mixed waiter and buffet service, good facilities for children, disco, live music four nights a week. Squash, but bring your own racket. 522 rooms on 7 floors (5 lifts).

Tenerife Sol ★★★★ a double hotel of more or less identical blocks linked by rather cramped public areas and a fine, split level swimming pool. Convenient for shops and night life, overlooking the sea, but still 5 minutes from the main sandy beach. Ideal for families with supervised playroom, paddling pool, playground, early suppers, high chairs and cots. Most of the 522 rooms on ten floors (4 lifts) have a kitchenette and refrigerator.

Tenerife Princess ★★★★ a good 15 minutes from the beach and the centre, modern, sister hotel to the Conquistador. Imaginative, stepped design to give the maximum number of rooms a sea view, hour-glass shaped pool, spanned by a rope bridge. Good facilities for children, including a large paddling pool. Tennis courts. 370 rooms on 7 floors (3 lifts).

Gran Tinerfe ★★★ well established, mature gardens, three swimming pools, and even a special terrace where you can go topless (what happens if you go topless elsewhere is not quite clear). The hotel overlooks the sea, but the nearest beach, reached by a footpath, is a mixture of sand and rock. The main Playa is still ten minutes' away. Wide choice of food. 349 rooms on 11 floors (3 lifts).

OTHER RESORTS

PUERTO DE LA CRUZ

Still the largest and most popular resort in Tenerife, though fast losing ground to Playa de las Americas, Puerto de la Cruz is sophisticated, lively and beautifully situated in the midst of lush green scenery on the northern coast. That, however, is the sum total

Puerto de la Cruz

of its considerable advantages; its disadvantages are considerable, too. First, its distance from the airport, a transfer time of 1½ hours at least. A few years back, many flights arrived at the old airport (Los Rodeos, now used almost entirely for domestic charter flights from the Spanish mainland) a mere eight miles away. Second, the principal reason why the new airport was built in the south: flying conditions are consistently superior there. Cloudy weather is quite common in Puerto de la Cruz, and while it passes quickly, it returns just as quickly, too. Third, the only beach, Playa

THE GOOD RESORT GUIDE 11

CANARY ISLES

TENERIFE

CANARY ISLES

Martianez, lies well away from the centre, is tiny and as black as soot, a legacy of lava from the extinct volcanoes. Even swimming is not without its risks because of strong, unpredictable currents.

To give the resort credit, Puerto de la Cruz has tackled the problem of the beach (the others being beyond their control) with considerable imagination and skill. In the centre of town, like a series of sapphire stepping stones to the ocean, lies the Lido, a succession of inter-connecting sea water swimming pools and sun terraces, with changing rooms, restaurants and bars, all provided for an extremely modest admission fee. Children have their own special pool and a playground. Between the Lido and the Playa Martianez is a fine, palm-lined promenade.

Puerto de la Cruz is not, obviously, strong on water sports. However it offers tennis, horseriding nearby, and a considerable 18-hole golf course at Los Rodeos, eight miles away. The shops are excellent, the night life (see Excursions) formidable. But can you risk going home without a tan?

EL MEDANO

This resort, located on the sunny south coast, has the best beach on the island, soft golden sand sloping gently into the sea. It even boasts

Fishing boats at Los Cristianos

of a hotel that has been partly constructed on pylons sunk into the sand, like some refugee British pier, and you cannot get much closer to the beach than that. However the centre of the resort is a rather gloomy village with

Las Canadas crater

12 THE GOOD RESORT GUIDE

TENERIFE

practically no night life. Ideal, you might think, for a quiet holiday... except that El Medano beach is directly on the flightpath from the nearby Reina Sofia airport.

PLAYA DE LAS AMERICAS FACTS

Your journey

	Hours
From Bristol, Cardiff, Heathrow	4
From Gatwick, Luton	4¼
From Birmingham, East Midlands, Manchester, Stansted	4½
From Newcastle	4¾
From Glasgow	5

Playa de Las Americas is 25 minutes by coach from Reina Sofia airport.

Shopping
Most shops open 0900 to 1300 and again from 1700 to 2000, although shops away from the main resorts tend to take a shorter lunch break and close earlier.

Money matters
Most banks open from 0900 to 1400 Mondays to Fridays and from 0900 to 1300 on Saturdays.

Banks are closed on January 1, January 6, Good Friday, May 1, July 25, August 15, October 12, December 8, December 25. However Tenerife has a particularly large number of other festivals, including a winter carnival (first 10 days in February), a flower festival on Corpus Christi (May or June), the ox-cart processions of San Isidro (June) and San Benito (July), and the fireworks of the Fiestas of San Juan (June), Del Mar (July) and Asuncion (August), when banks delight in closing early or simply not opening at all.

Many businesses, not just travel agencies, offer currency exchange as a sideline but give a poorer rate than the banks. Credit cards are accepted in most hotels and shops but their use is less widespread than in mainland Spain.

Weather

Averages	Jan	Feb	Mar	Apr	May	Jun	Jul	Aug	Sep	Oct	Nov	Dec
Temperature	70	70	71	73	75	79	83	85	82	79	75	71
Sun hours	6	7	7	8	9	10	11	10	8	7	7	6
Rain days	4	4	3	2	1	1	0	1	1	3	4	3
Sea temp.	68	64	66	68	68	70	72	73	72	72	68	66

These figures are for the resort areas in the south. The northern resorts are colder and wetter in the winter months, as these figures suggest:

Averages	Jan	Feb	Mar	Apr	May	Jun	Jul	Aug	Sep	Oct	Nov	Dec
Temperature	64	62	64	64	68	71	74	75	74	70	69	64
Rain days	7	7	5	3	1	0	0	1	2	6	7	6

Local transport
Although car hire is not exempt from VAT, rates are slightly cheaper than mainland Spain. Taxis have posted fixed prices in some resorts, meters in others; but expect to agree a rate for a long journey: four sharing often works out cheaper than four coach excursion tickets. Local bus services are cheap and usually reliable.

Plugs
Beware some older hotels whose plug sockets cater only for 110 volts, rather than the usual 220 volts. Your own appliances can easily blow a fuse — if there is one.

GRAN CANARIA

GRAN CANARIA

The third largest of the Canary Islands behind Tenerife and Fuerteventura, Gran Canaria makes up in scenery what it lacks in size. Almost circular in shape, lying south-east of Tenerife, the island has a similar though smaller mountain peak, with cliffs and valleys that drop sheer into the sea. In the north, fertile fields of bananas, sugar-cane and vines give way to soft green slopes of pines. In the south, a desert of sand dunes backed by harsh mountain peaks provides the setting for a series of popular resorts, favoured by the higher temperatures and consistent sunshine which the northern coast can only envy. And everywhere are sad little signs of the Guanches, the original peoples of the islands. before the Spanish conquistadores sold them into slavery or put them to the sword.

MASPALOMAS

In the extreme south of the island, stretching across more than five miles of coastline, is the multiple resort of Maspalomas. It takes its name from Maspalomas village, which these days is little more than a road sign on the route to Puerto Rico. Playa Maspalomas is at the western end of the resort, on a well laid out headland free of through traffic and much the quietest section in consequence. Its beach is truly extraordinary, mile upon mile of dunes running into firm, white sand. Apart from the slightly polluted river mouth, down by the lighthouse, bathing is attractive and safe; you can go horse-riding on the beach, too. Most of

14 THE GOOD RESORT GUIDE

GRAN CANARIA

the shops and the night life in this area are centred on the hotels.

An 18-hole golf course separates Playa Maspalomas, sometimes called Playa El Oasis because its palm trees make it look like a desert watering hole, from Playa del Ingles. While the southern end of this part of the resort still has a splendidly broad beach backed by sand dunes, to return to your hotel after paddling in the sea sometimes can resemble a forced route march uphill. Many of the hotels are located close to the main road behind the resort, and while minibuses shuttle holidaymakers back and forth to the beach, queues can be long and the walk still longer. If the architecture was attractive, the effort might be worthwhile, but Playa del Ingles is an ugly, sprawling, high-rise concentration of concrete with as much charm as a cement mixer. Shopping precincts such as the Cita and the Casbah (where you can bargain furiously) are relentlessly efficient but supremely soulless, not helped by the fact that the shopkeepers seem far more fluent in German than they are in English. Still, Playa del Ingles offers plenty to do in the evenings, from a stroll along the promenade with its bars and restaurants, to a visit to the bright lights of night clubs and discos led by the Lido and Aladino's; or even, believe it or not, a floodlit greyhound track.

San Agustin, a little to the north-east, is the oldest part of the resort with some pleasant residential roads, but slightly greyer sand. While the main beach, Playa de las Bumas, offers facilities for windsurfing, it is much narrower than elsewhere and interrupted by patches of rock. Immediately to the rear lies a casino, next door to the Tamarindos Sol hotel: you need your passport to gamble. La Gruta Pirata is a notable night club. All three parts of the resort are within easy striking distance of 'Sioux City', a wild west show that the children will love but probably has Buffalo Bill Cody turning in his grave.

Cathedral at Las Palmas

Excursions

Day or overnight trips by air are readily available from the airport 14 miles away, including, remarkably, the Gambia, Marrakesh (see Morocco, page 28) and the Spanish Sahara. Tenerife is half an hour's flying time, Lanzarote five minutes more. With Gran Canaria itself, the most popular trip is to the capital, Las Palmas, situated in the far north-east of the island. Its tax free status makes shopping cheap and attractive, and it has an interesting old quarter. In the centre of the island is an extraordinary crater, the Caldera Bandama, almost a perfect circle, created in the days of thundering volcanoes, but now safe enough for farms to have sprung up at its bottom. The Tejada Cross offers the traditional

Beach at Maspalomas

THE GOOD RESORT GUIDE

GRAN CANARIA

lookout point, and a mid-morning traffic jam; independent travellers may prefer to try the Pozo de las Nieves, at almost 6,496ft the highest point on the island, sometimes snow-capped, almost always providing epic views.

However the most satisfying day out may well be by boat on a deep-sea fishing expedition, for which Gran Canaria is famous. Many species of fish can be caught off the island, and several world records have been broken. Some hotels will actually cook your catch (it saves them ingredients, after all!): ask them to serve it up with papas arrugadas, whole potatoes cooked in their skins, and a deliciously sharp local sauce called mojo.

MASPALOMAS HOTELS

Costa Canaria ★★★★ on a slip road south of the main street in San Agustin, with elegant, spacious gardens leading directly on to the beach. Your sun bed near the swimming pool is allocated on arrival and reserved for you throughout your stay. Particularly suitable for children, with family rooms, children's pool, children's playground and special meals. Air-conditioned dining room with wide choice. Night club/disco in the basement. 173 rooms on seven floors (2 lifts).

Dunamar ★★★ unlike many Playa del Ingles hotels, within 5 min walk of the beach, which is just across the promenade. As the hotel is built on the side of a hill, the swimming pool is on the first floor and reception on the seventh. With rooms in one section going up as high as the 14th floor (3 lifts), it is therefore a very oddly-shaped hotel indeed. However a relaxed, sophisticated environment, not really ideal for children. 184 rooms, most with sea view.

Palm Beach ★★★ a quiet residential road is all that separates it from the Playa Maspalomas, 1 minute away. The hotel, in a central position in the resort, has lavish sub-tropical gardens

Sand dunes, Gran Canaria

16 THE GOOD RESORT GUIDE

GRAN CANARIA

and a large swimming pool. Some family rooms, and a children's playground, but not really ideal for children. Live music most evenings. Fluency in German an advantage. 358 rooms on seven floors but no sea views below the third.

Ifa Beach ★★★ close by the San Agustin beach, a few steps from the sun terraces surrounding the two swimming pools, one of which is heated in the winter months. The children can not only eat supper early: they have their own restaurant. 203 rooms on six floors (2 lifts).

Parque Tropical ★★★ interesting architecture, in Spanish hacienda style with heavy wooden balconies on three sides of a square. The fourth leads directly by way of some steps to a small beach, not part of the Playa del Ingles proper, part sand, part pebble. Although situated in the resort centre, the hotel gardens are secluded and relaxing, with a series of pools and waterfalls crossed by little bridges. Dangerous for small children; ideal for the rest. 235 rooms, mainly on four floors.

Street cafés, Las Palmas

MASPALOMAS FACTS

Your journey

	Hours
From Heathrow	4
From Gatwick	4¼
From Birmingham, Manchester	4½
From Glasgow	5
From Heathrow (via Bilbao)	5¼

Gando Airport is located on the east coast, midway between Las Palmas in the north and the southern resort areas. Transfer time to Maspalomas resorts is 45 minutes.

Shopping

Shops usually open 0900 to 1300 and 1600 to 2000 Monday to Friday; on Saturdays some may open 0900 to 1300 only. However shops catering principally for tourists stay open all day. Many shops are closed on January 1, January 6, Good Friday, May 1, July 25, August 15, October 12, December 8, December 25. Gran Canaria also largely closes down for the Festival of Our Lady of the Snows in August, the Festival of Our Lady of the Pines in September, and the Festival of Our Lady of Light in October, when Las Palmas produces some scintillating fireworks.

Money Matters

The larger banks open 0900 to 1400 Monday to Friday and 0900 to 1300 Saturdays; closed Sundays. However smaller branches have quite eccentric hours and may reopen in the early evening. Exchange bureaux are widely available in the principal resorts and charge a commission only slightly inferior to many banks. Credit cards and travellers cheques are accepted almost everywhere. The rate of exchange given in hotels for cash or travellers cheques can, however, be extortionately low.

Plugs

Beware some older hotels whose plug sockets cater only for 110 volts, rather than the usual 220 volts. Your own appliances can easily blow a fuse — if there is one.

THE GOOD RESORT GUIDE   17

GRAN CANARIA/LANZAROTE

Weather

Averages	Jan	Feb	Mar	Apr	May	Jun	Jul	Aug	Sep	Oct	Nov	Dec
Temperature	70	70	72	74	76	79	83	85	82	80	75	72
Sun hours	6	6	7	8	9	10	11	10	8	7	6	6
Rain days	1	2	2	2	1	0	0	0	0	1	2	3
Sea temp.	64	64	64	64	66	68	70	72	72	72	70	66

These are figures for the southern resort area. As with Tenerife, the north of the island (which includes Las Palmas, which has a good beach but strictly speaking is not a resort) is considerably cooler and wetter:

Averages	Jan	Feb	Mar	Apr	May	Jun	Jul	Aug	Sep	Oct	Nov	Dec
Temperature	62	62	62	64	66	69	72	73	73	71	67	63
Rain days	1	3	3	3	1	0	0	0	0	2	4	5

However, even the north of Gran Canaria is drier than the south of Tenerife. Air temperatures on the two islands are similar, but the sea around Tenerife is slightly warmer.

Local transport

A regular bus service runs between the lighthouse at Playa Maspalomas, along the main road of Playa del Ingles and San Agustin, all the way to Las Palmas, a further hour's journey. To avoid friction with the locals, remember to queue at a bus stop on the reverse side to the UK, that is, facing the direction in which you intend to travel. Keep your ticket, as they are inspected regularly.

Plugs

Beware some older hotels whose plug sockets cater only for 110 volts, rather than the usual 220 volts. Your own appliances can easily blow a fuse — if there is one.

LANZAROTE

The closest Canary Island of any substance to the continent of Europe, Lanzarote was also the first to be conquered. Early in the fifteenth century, the Norman knight Jean de Bethencourt, in the service of the King of Castille, subdued the island. When the fighting was over, he celebrated by snapping his lance, throwing the pieces into the air, and shouting 'Lanza rota' ('broken lance'). This was how Lanzarote got its name, or if it wasn't then it's still a good story...

Bethencourt's followers could be forgiven for wondering what all the fuss was about. They had become rulers of a land of jagged black lava, pock-marked and pitted by the last convulsions of extinct volcanoes. Much to their surprise, the volcanic ash held water through the driest months, acting as a perfect sponge,

18 THE GOOD RESORT GUIDE

LANZAROTE

Puerto del Carmen, Lanzarote

and stimulating the crops. Melons, tomatoes and grapes thrive in this bizarre environment.

Lanzarote has changed little over the centuries. Even the onslaught of tourism has left its villages and villagers largely to lead their own separate lives, and the construction of hotels and self-catering apartments has been carefully and tastefully planned.

PUERTO DEL CARMEN

The principal resort, Puerto del Carmen, with its backcloth of black hills, lies on the east coast some six miles from the Arrecife airport. It was once known as La Tinosa or 'stained beach', a singularly unattractive description but by no means inaccurate as the main beach does indeed consist largely of dark volcanic sand. It has been renamed Playa Blanca, 'white beach', emphasizing how the Trades' Description Act has yet to touch the Spanish tourist industry. Still, the beach is pleasant enough, rarely crowded, sloping gently into the sea. It stretches from Playa Los Fariones, named after hotel Los Fariones (see below), to the less developed Playa de los Pocillos at the eastern end of the resort. Windsurfing and scuba diving (you need a certificate of competence) are the principal water sports offered here, though Puerto del Carmen also has a lavish sports centre, Viajes Insular Sports Club, with tennis courts, squash courts and a splendid swimming pool; it is open to visitors.

During the day Puerto del Carmen seems a rather characterless resort, but in the evening it comes into its own. Along the waterfront of the fishing village in the old quarter the bars begin to fill and the restaurants open up. Sea food is their speciality, local varieties called Sama and Vieja; there is also a local wine, Malvasia, which can charitably be described as an acquired taste. Carmen is the centre of Lanzarote's night life, with several exuberant discos, including Joker, Palm Beach and Wilson. At the Playa de los Pocillos end, a British pub called the Bristol pulls the pints.

THE GOOD RESORT GUIDE

LANZAROTE

Excursions

Land Rovers are more common and practical than large coaches in order to reach the rougher roads of Lanzarote's lunar landscape. But you may end the day riding a camel imported from the Sahara, on the last leg of a visit to the Fire Mountain, a stunning yet chilling wilderness of red-tipped rock formations and deep black lava. This excursion also visits the green and turquoise lagoon at El Golfo and the salt flats at Janubio, on the western coast.

In the north of the island, visit the caves of Los Verdes, which stretch for more than four miles; you can see only a little more than a mile, in a visit lasting just over an hour. The steep path is not really suitable for toddlers or old people. Not far away is another cave, Jameos del Agua, which in the evening becomes a rather jolly night club, full of coach parties. The usual entertainment is some local folk dancers, disco dancing around an underground lake, and a buffet dinner.

From the northernmost peak of Mirador del Rio, you can see far into the Atlantic and pick out some of the tiny islands around Lanzarote. The nearest, La Graciosa, is inhabited by fishermen, who will sometimes take you across (in about an hour) from the tiny port of Orzola.

Camel trekking on Fire Mountain

PUERTO DEL CARMEN HOTELS

Los Fariones ★★★★ central, colourful, comfortable, overlooking a sandy beach (see page 19) reached directly through the gardens and down a series of steps. Sea water swimming pool, set in delightful terraces; separate pool for children. Suitable for young families, with large family rooms available. Tennis, mini-golf. Disco. 243 rooms on four floors (2 lifts).

San Antonio ★★★★ two miles outside the centre of Puerto del Carmen, right beside the Playa de los Pocillos, reached through extensive gardens. The dark sand gives way to rocks at the water's edge. Large swimming pool, paddling pool for children, whose other special facilities include a playground, babysitters (local girls), and early suppers. Public rooms a little cramped. Disco beach club open nightly. 327 rooms (many ideal for families with interconnecting doors) on four floors (5 lifts).

PUERTO DEL CARMEN FACTS

Your journey

	Hours
From Gatwick	4¼
From Manchester	4½

Transfer time from Arrecife Airport is around 25 minutes.

Shopping

Most shops are open 0900 to 1300 and 1600 to 1800 Monday to Friday. On Saturday they open 0900 to 1300 and on Sunday, not at all. Tourist shops please themselves.

Money matters

Banks open Monday to Friday 0900 to 1400 and until 1300 Saturday. All banks are closed on January 1, January 6, Good Friday, May 1, July 16, July 25, August 15, October 12, December 8, December 25.

Expect erratic opening hours when a carnival takes place in the capital, Arrecife, at the end of February. From mid-August until the end of the month, Arrecife also plays host to the Fiesta de San Gines, with firecrackers, competitions and camels on parade.

CANARY ISLES

20 THE GOOD RESORT GUIDE

LANZAROTE/FUERTEVENTURA

Weather

Averages	Jan	Feb	Mar	Apr	May	Jun	Jul	Aug	Sep	Oct	Nov	Dec
Temperature	70	70	72	75	75	78	82	85	81	80	78	72
Sun hours	7	8	8	8	9	10	11	10	8	6	6	6
Rain days	3	3	4	3	2	1	0	0	0	1	2	4
Sea temp.	67	67	67	67	69	71	73	75	75	75	73	69

The resorts, mainly self-catering, on the south coast are slightly drier, especially in the spring. Temperatures are however consistently high throughout the island the whole year round.

Local transport

Most hire car companies are closed on Sundays. Taxis are cheap and plentiful in the main resort areas. A bus service runs hourly along the east coast between Puerto del Carmen and Arrecife.

FUERTEVENTURA

Sahara by the sea, a narrow desert island barely 60 miles from the African coast, Fuerteventura offers breathtaking beaches, unlimited sunshine, endless opportunites for solitude, but little else. A recent addition to the package tour programme, it is not a destination for holidaymakers who like variety in their night life and sophisticated sight seeing.

The beaches here are quite simply outstanding, mile upon mile of soft white sand running into a vivid blue sea. Behind the dunes are low, rather desolate hills, for the shortage of fresh water has meant a constant battle for survival among the tiny island population. Ironically their life actually became more arduous after the introduction by Europeans of goats, who ruined the pastureland. The island's capital used to be called Puerto Cabra, Port of the Goat. It has been changed to Puerto del Rosario to make the place more attractive to tourists, a lost cause if ever there was one, for it is difficult to find a more one-horse (or one-goat) town in the whole of the Canary Islands.

The tourist industry consists of half a dozen hotels and a number of apartment complexes scattered around Fuerteventura in an entirely haphazard development. Virtually all their supplies have to be imported, including fresh water, which makes the fresh water swimming pool of one hotel near the northern fishing village of Corralejo an unimaginable extravagance. Corralejo has a few bars and restaurants, and even a disco, but by and large night life is confined to the hotels.

Windsurfing is the principal sport, and at Caleta de Fuste, a hotel minibus ride from Playa de Corralejo, is the El Castillo school, which specialises in courses for beginners. It may also have occurred to some would-be visitors that the best conditions for windsurfing may simultaneously be the worst for sun-bathing on the beach, which is completely exposed (like many of the tourists, for that matter). However the wind does moderate the temperatures, on an island that thinks nothing of seeing the sun 350 days a year.

THE GOOD RESORT GUIDE

FUERTEVENTURA

Beach at Fuerteventura

Excursions

Rather in the way that a dinner party for Man Friday would have been the height of excitement for Robinson Crusoe, excursions which seem acceptable on Fuerteventura would be dismissed out of hand elsewhere. The most pleasant trip is undoubtedly to los Lobos Island, two miles north of Corralejo, which has a tiny fishing village and some delightfully secluded beaches. The fishing is outstanding and there are opportunities for snorkelling with harpoon or camera. A rough, tough road through the centre of the island leads to the earlier capital, Betancuria, little white houses on a little patch of green surrounded by hostile hills. Its church, rebuilt in the 17th century, is surprisingly grand, because this was once the home of the bishop of all the Canary Islands, presumably because the town was thought too far from the sea to be a target for pirates. They were wrong: in 1539 the Berbers trekked

FUERTEVENTURA

across the mountains and burned the cathedral to the ground. Around the coast, the roads are rather better, and jeeps can be hired with tyres suitable for the sands. There is, however, one hazard: groups of Spanish soldiers on training exercises, although their favourite assault course seems to be a lilo by the sea.

FUERTEVENTURA HOTELS

Tres Islas★★★★ three miles from Corralejo, in the north east of the island, next to a superb sandy beach. Some guests, however, may not get beyond the huge, elegant swimming pool surrounded by gardens and terraces. The hotel provides tennis (four floodlit courts), billiards, bowling, rifle shooting and gymnastics. Two restaurants, but eating out can be a problem, Not ideal for children, despite its position. 356 rooms on six floors (4 lifts). Transfer time: 45 minutes.

Oliva Beach★★★ overlooking Corralejo beach, close to Tres Islas Hotel, less sophisticated but friendly. Swimming pool, sauna, good variety of evening entertainment. Children well catered for with separate pool, playground, and early meals. Food generally good but by no means inspired. 386 rooms on eight floors (3 lifts). Transfer time: 45 minutes.

Los Gorriones Sol★★★ near Jandia, in the south east of the island, a hotel completely isolated among large sand dunes. Guests are however comfortably insulated from external inconvenience by two swimming pools, tennis courts, a paddling pool, mini-golf and several shops. There is no reason to leave the grounds, which is just as well, in view of the lack of alternative local amenities and the fact that the sea is 500 yards. away. Transfer time: 1¾ hours. 309 rooms on eight floors (3 lifts).

Betancuria

Parador Nacional★★★ rather quaintly described as 108 nautical miles from Las Palmas, rather a long swim, this government-run hotel lies at the southern end of the splendid east coast beach of Playa Blanca, two miles south of Puerto del Rosario. The airport is equally close, which might become a problem when the number of flights increases. Swimming pool, pleasant garden. 50 rooms. Transfer time: 10 minutes.

Hotel pool, Fuerteventura

FUERTEVENTURA FACTS

Your journey

	Hours
From Gatwick	4
From Gatwick (via Tenerife)	6

Tenerife, 45 minutes by ferry, which comes in conveniently close to the Tres Islas and Oliva Beach hotels, can be used as the gateway from many other UK airports. Transfer times to Puerto del Rosario Airport on Fuerteventura are given under each hotel entry.

Weather

Refer to figures for Tenerife, as climate is almost identical.

MOROCCO

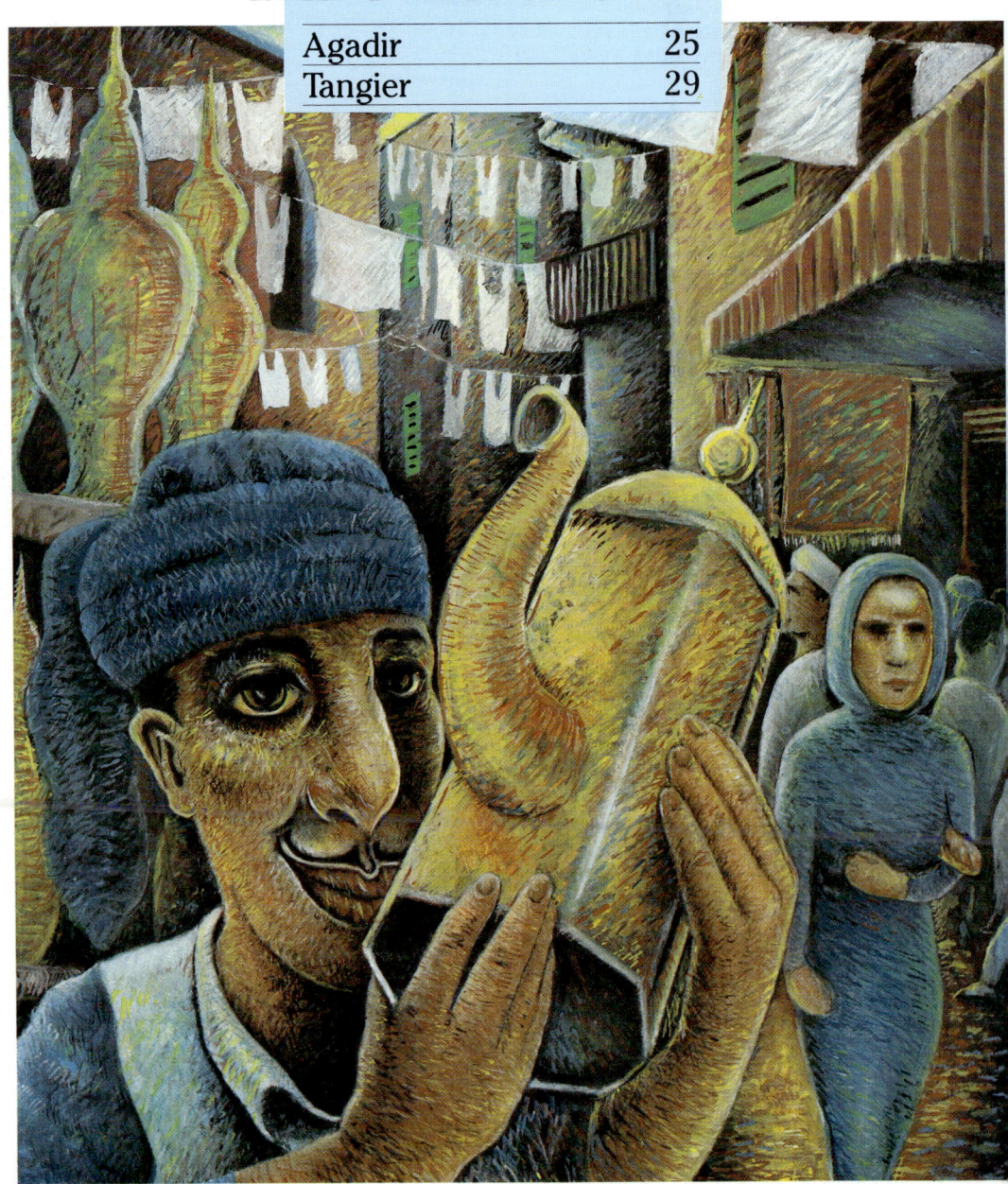

Agadir	25
Tangier	29

24 THE GOOD RESORT GUIDE

AGADIR

In modern Morocco, one thousand and one nights are no longer the fables of Islam but rather the weekly occupancy rate of a large hotel. Extensive tourist development has turned what was once a remote and medieval kingdom into a major holiday destination, offering the thrill of escaping from Europe without arduous travelling or significant time changes; sustained winter sunshine; and beautiful beaches combined with exotic inland cities. For this is the land where the Rifs laid ambush to the luckless columns of the French Foreign Legion; and these are the mountains where Atlas held the world on his shoulders. Except of course when Hercules took over, while Atlas fetched the golden apples of the Hesperides, then tricked him into taking back his burden: probably the only time in history that a Moroccan has not had the best of a bargain.

AGADIR

Agadir, whose name means fortress, was flattened a quarter of a century ago by a devastating earthquake in which only the Kasbah survived. The rest of the old city was completely abandoned for fear of further tremors, and a modern city built nearby in its place. The intricate honeycomb of narrow streets gave way to wide, tree-lined avenues, illuminated at night. Indeed technology has permeated even the most traditional customs: when the priests incantations beckon the faithful to prayer, the sound is projected on modern amplifiers.

Agadir has one fixed price centre with traditional Moroccan handicrafts for sale, called Coopartim. As its prices are extremely

Agadir beach

THE GOOD RESORT GUIDE 25

AGADIR

low, this is an ideal yardstick for bargaining in the bazaar. For bargain you will have to, like it or not: in Morocco, only someone with more money than sense pays the asking price. In shops, you will have done badly if you pay more than half the starting figure. Even if credit cards are accepted, use them as part of the bargaining process: when a figure is agreed, produce a card, then bargain down further for cash. Although of course it is unwise to carry large sums about with you to buy expensive items such as carpets, cash, especially dollars or deutschmarks, seems to have a beneficial effect on the final price. Remember also that there appears to be no word in Morocco for 'change', and few Moroccans understand the concept.

Fez market

For services rendered, however, everyone expects and accepts tips. This can put the price of almost every activity up by at least ten per cent, especially for sporting activities, which in Agadir include golf, tennis, riding and by the sea, water-skiing, windsurfing and sailing. The beach, five miles of superb sand, is less safe than it looks for small children. Despite a protective barrier, large waves roll dangerously close to the shore when the wind and the tide are high, and the Atlantic has a strong undercurrent further out.

Life guards always seem to be off duty when they are needed. In the same way, hotel beach patrols, supposedly charged with the task of keeping away unwanted beach sellers, are nowhere to be seen in the early afternoon. Resign yourself to being offered ice creams, jewellery and doughnuts, all of doubtful origin. If they have British newspapers for sale, scan the date carefully: young boys have been known to pick up a discarded pile of ancient editions at the wholesalers, and be far away before the unsuspecting British tourist discovers it was a paper delivered back home the week before for a fraction of the price.

Beach shoes, however, do well as a sales item. Many a bold tourist has stridden barefoot across the road from his hotel to pick his way painfully past wild shrubs and piles of rubble. Agadir's promenade is in the planning stage, where it has remained for more than a decade.

On the beach or in the bar, you do not fly the Flag but drink it: it is the best local beer. Local wine is cheap and pleasant, but expect to find a lot of sediment at the bottom of the bottle; the corks are often cheap and crumbling.

If you plan to eat out economically, beware the prices displayed outside an Agadir restaurant. Invariably the 15% tax and 10-15% service charge will not be included, which can put the price up by as much as a third. The favourite Moroccan dish is couscous, boiled baby lamb or chicken complete with the day's vegetables and decorated with semolina pellets. Or you could try a tasty if rather thick soup called harira, or bstill, a pastry where the filling is pigeon, a marginal improvement on four and twenty blackbirds. Not surprisingly, European restaurants, especially French and Italian do well with visitors, although those who sample the Chinese and Vietnamese restaurants available are rarely disappointed. In the port itself, the fish restaurants provide marvellous crayfish and lobster almost straight from the boats. However to get by the outside gate, you need to take your passport.

For a rather safer four-course Moroccan meal, try a 'Berber' evening, where visitors to the chief Berber's kasbah are entertained by long-gowned locals and by traditional music. The wine flows too freely for you to recall that far from receiving such renowned hospitality, in the bad old days affluent travellers ended the evening with their money stolen and their throats cut.

26 THE GOOD RESORT GUIDE

AGADIR

Wool dyer's souk, Morocco   Inset: Moroccan carpet shop

THE GOOD RESORT GUIDE 27

MOROCCO

AGADIR

After a meal in downtown Agadir, you may fancy a drink in a local cafe, but do not be surprised to find them all shut after 10pm. Only the more expensive bars catering mainly for tourists stay open after midnight. Discotheques stay open more or less until everyone leaves (though the last couple may be gently nudged). Most of them are based in hotels, such as Sahara, at, surprise, surprise, the Sahara Hotel, and King Bird, under the same management as the nearby Hotel Tagadirt.

Interior of spice shop

Excursions

Marrakesh is an arduous trip but a truly memorable experience. Once foreigners ventured here at their peril, and even today, the ambience of its huge central square, the Place Djenaa El Fna, owes nothing to the modern tourist. It is the heart and spirit of the imperial city, scarcely changed from the days when men rode for days on camel to sample its marvels. And marvels they are: magicians who hold burning coals between their toes, or pour scalding water over their arms, or eat their way through a meal of glass, all with no apparent injury; black-garbed acrobats like cousins of the ninja who seem to suspend the laws of gravity; father and son teams of snake-charmers, establishing the existence of its deadly fangs by enticing the snake to strike fatally at some harmless caged rodent at the start of the show. No wonder the fortune teller's predictions are nearly always gloomy.

If you intend to stray far from the main square, a guide is essential to penetrate the confusing alleyways of the old quarter, the medina. A likely lad may also be useful in getting rid of his contemporaries, who otherwise will pester you for money here to the point of exhaustion — yours, not theirs. Even outside the gates, there is little prospect of relief, unless you get up on a camel or ride around the outside walls in a horse and carriage. A green oasis in a desert of dust and mountains. Marrakesh remains almost unchanged after a thousand years of history.

AGADIR HOTELS

Sahara★★★★ if only it were closer to the beach, this hotel would be ideal. It is spacious, attentive, superb Moroccan styles inside and out. The amenities are impressive: two swimming pools, including one for children; five tennis courts; free Turkish bath; nightclub, disco, four restaurants, including one with strong claims to serve the best Moroccan meal in town. 286 rooms, with full air-conditioning.

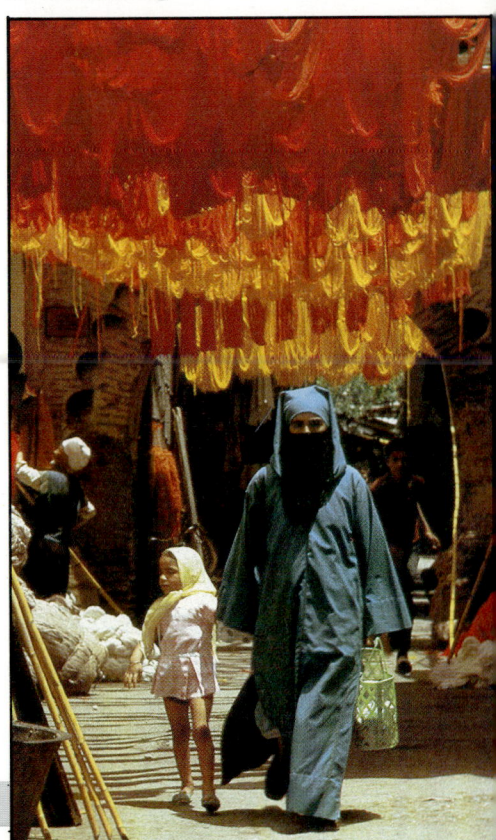

Wool market at Marrakesh

THE GOOD RESORT GUIDE

AGADIR/TANGIER

Beach at Tangier   Inset: Tangier

Salam★★★ you need to be fit to stay here as the hotel is located well back from the beach, on a nearby hill. To reach it you must climb thirty formidable steps, a tough task on a really hot day. Still, you can always cool down in the delightful swimming pool surrounded by agreeable gardens. The children's pool, however, is a potential hazard for the very young as it is by no means shallow. The main hotel has 150 rooms.

Tagadirt★★ designed like a Moroccan village, this hotel and apartment complex really fails to satisfy either category. The elevated passageways may look attractive, but visitors soon tire of the steps and rather cramped accommodation. The pool, too, is small but at least the beach is close, reached by a bridge across the main road in front of the hotel. 145 rooms.

TANGIER

Tangier is sold as a beach resort by some tour operators, and it must be said bluntly that holidaymakers for whom the beach is a firm priority would be better off elsewhere. Only with independent transport is it possible to find an entirely satisfactory beach several miles out, and then it will be almost empty, lacking any kind of amenity. (Just one exception: the Arabian Sands holiday village, see page 31) Tangier's own beach, to the south-west, has no shortage of sand but some of it is a disagreeable grey colour. Nor, unfortunately, is there a natural explanation: it is simply dirty. At the western end the risk of pollution from the port is considerable, and at the further east the beach is scruffy, stony and shelves too steeply for comfort. For the most of its length

MOROCCO

THE GOOD RESORT GUIDE   29

TANGIER

the shoreline is separated from the hotels by a busy road and by a railway line; although rail traffic is almost exclusively freight wagons, the number of safe crossing points is inevitably restricted. There are, however, some advantages: a number of good beach restaurants and many activities including watersports, tennis and horse-riding.

A steep hill divides the beach area from much of the town, where some of the hotels are located in a modern, rather uninspired sector of Tangier: very few are close to the old quarter, which is where Tangier really comes to life. The medina is a maze of narrow streets and gloomy passages, looking much more sinister than they are in fact, and packed with tiny shops offering an abundance of jewellery, leather goods, textiles and carpets which, if you believe the proprietor, will relieve you of the need to return home on the charter flight. Although the techniques for bargaining in shops or dealing with persuasive passers-by are much the same in Agadir or Marrakesh (see page 28), it must said that in Tangier, people with something to sell can be particularly persistent. As far as touts are concerned, the only advice must be: do not agree to go anywhere with them, especially at night, or part with any money. In shops, spend a good deal of time comparing prices before entering into a serious bargaining session. However, do not be put off: the atmosphere is marvellous, shopping can be enormous fun, and if you need a breather, the Petit Socco in the centre of the medina has several cafes in an agreeable square.

The kasbah is not part of the medina but at the top of the hill behind. This is where the great Sultan, Moulay Ismail, had his fortress palace, now a museum, almost impregnable in its time from land or sea. You can see the beautiful interior marble courtyard, the Sultan's garden and the treasury, where boxes of gold coins used to be thrown carelessly in a heap. Here, too, the Sultan had his harem, which was evidently kept busy, as he is reliably reported to have fathered several hundred children.

In the evening you can eat a Moroccan meal in the heart of the kasbah and then visit a Tangier night club. Most of them cater

TANGIER

specifically for tourists but are no less entertaining for that: expect to see belly dancers, snake charmers, incredible acrobats and tribal dancing to the sound of the Saharan drums. Resist the temptation to do your own thing. At best, you will be exploited and be less well entertained; at worst, you may be attacked and robbed. Women should recognise that strolling about alone at night, particularly in what Moslems might regard as provocatively revealing clothes, is to invite unwelcome attentions. Part of the attraction of Tangier is its reputation as a slightly wicked, slightly dangerous city. Do not go out of your way to prove it.

Excursions

Deep in the Rif mountains lies the town of Chaouen, which thirty-odd years ago was still a Spanish possession. The result is a fascinating blend of Moorish and Spanish architecture, a Spanish plaza and a Moorish medina, red tile roofs typical of southern Spain enclosing an ancient kasbah with a wonderfully peaceful garden. Behind it all, a dramatic mountain backcloth, with perilous narrow passes where the Rifs melted away whenever a well-armed force ventured into their lair. Many trips to Chaouen pass through Tetouan, which has its own teeming medina: keep a good grip on your wallet or handbag here.

A day in Gibraltar, only an hour away by hydrofoil, is a popular excursion. In summer, expect the last surviving British possession on the Continent of Europe to be extremely crowded and resign yourself to traffic jams. Since the border was fully re-opened, the Spanish, who have bigger cars than the local British, seem to be doing their best to bring the place to a complete standstill.

TANGIER HOTELS

Alhomades ★★★★ opposite the best part of the beach but still, for all that, separated from it by road and railway. Indoor and outdoor swimming pools. Own disco, on the roof of the hotel so the noise is not really a problem. Restaurant has superb views, which gives you something to do while waiting for the food. 150 rooms.

Arabian Sands ★★★ Holiday village ten miles west of Tangier, a series of white Moorish apartments built into the rocks and overlooking the sea. For once no reservations about the beach: mile upon mile of clean golden sand. Two restaurants, disco, swimming pool next to the beach, children's paddling pool and playground, baby-sitting. Ideal for families, though they have to pay to go on the village coach to Tangier.

Continental ★★ if you want an authentic atmosphere, this is it: a hotel at least 100 years old, that you can walk straight into from the maze of the medina. Packed with antiques, some of them even genuine, perched on a ledge overlooking the harbour. The view from its 36 rooms may compensate for the lack of amenities.

Rif ★★★★ once one of the great hotels of the world, but despite its spacious public rooms, it no longer achieves an official five-star rating. Its position on the main sea road still leaves the railway line to cross to get to the beach, and the traffic noise is considerable. The restaurant is partly indoors, partly outdoors, and when you

High Atlas, little mosque

THE GOOD RESORT GUIDE

AGADIR/TANGIER

Tangier

want one the waiters always seem to be in the other half to you. 130 rooms on 7 floors (2 lifts).

Solazur ★★★ circular, large, modern hotel, like many others separated from the beach by road and railway and in a drab, undeveloped part of town with indifferent transport to the medina. Double half-moon swimming pool, part shallow for children, in pleasant gardens. 358 rooms on ten floors (2 lifts).

Tarik ★★★ four miles outside Tangier, but this can be an advantage for sea bathing, and the hotel gardens lead directly on to the beach, mainly pebbles, but some sand. Disco. Swimming pool, tennis courts and many other sports facilities. Shuttle bus to centre of Tangier does not run at night. 154 rooms on 7 floors. (1 lift).

MOROCCO FACTS

Your journey

To Agadir	Hours
From Gatwick	3¾
From Manchester	4
To Tangier	
From Gatwick, Luton	2¾
From Manchester	3¼

Transfer time from Agadir airport, which is five miles to the south, is 20 minutes; from Tangier, eight miles south west, 45 minutes. However on a bad day, expect immigration to take an hour in itself. A British Visitor's Passport is not acceptable; you must have a full passport. Immigration may also take exception to 'family' passports containing two adults and their children. Adults are encouraged to have separate passports, and children travelling with their parents on a parent's passport must have their photograph added to that passport. You will also have to complete an immigration form three times, on arrival, at the hotel and on departure. Vaccination certificates are not required, but cholera, typhoid and polio vaccinations are nevertheless recommended, together with malaria tablets, which should be taken before and after as well as during the holiday.

Shopping

In Agadir, most shops open around 0830 until 1200, then again from 1530 to 1830, Monday to Friday, though some re-open earlier in winter.

32 THE GOOD RESORT GUIDE

AGADIR/TANGIER

As in the UK, local chemist shops run a rota for opening in the evenings and at weekends to deal with emergencies; which can include tourists who eat snacks from street traders or drink anything other than mineral water.

In Tangier, many shops close on Fridays, the Moslem holy day, but are open all day Saturday. In the medina, expect to find shops open every day, all day, and until quite late at night.

Money matters

In summer, most banks open 0815 to 1130 and again 1615 to 1800, Monday to Thursday. Morning opening times on Fridays are 0815 to 1200; afternoon times the same.

In winter, most banks open 0830 to 1130 and 1430 to 1630, Monday to Friday.

All banks are closed on March 3, July 9, November 18, and on the Islamic religious festivals such as Ramadan, which occur on different dates each year. Check with your hotel. Moroccan dirhams cannot legally be imported or exported, and receipts must be produced on departure at one of the airport banks to convert any dirhams you have left back into foreign currency. Be resigned to the fact that the banks will sometimes not have enough sterling and expect to be given some French francs or German marks.

Some hotels are approved banks and offer the same exchange rate, but enforce a fifty pound limit on each transaction.

Weather
Agadir:

Averages	Jan	Feb	Mar	Apr	May	Jun	Jul	Aug	Sep	Oct	Nov	Dec
Temperature	68	70	73	73	75	79	81	81	81	79	75	70
Sun hours	8	8	8	10	10	10	9	9	9	8	8	7
Rain days	4	3	3	2	1	0	0	0	1	2	3	4
Sea temp.	63	63	64	64	66	66	72	72	72	72	70	64

Tangier:

Averages	Jan	Feb	Mar	Apr	May	Jun	Jul	Aug	Sep	Oct	Nov	Dec
Temperature	59	61	63	66	70	75	79	81	77	72	64	61
Sun hours	4	5	6	7	10	11	11	9	8	6	5	4
Rain days	10	11	13	9	6	4	1	1	3	7	9	11
Sea temp.	63	63	63	64	68	68	72	73	72	72	68	64

Tangier is decidedly chilly between November and March, when it is often warmer in the sea than on land. Agadir has an agreeable temperature all the year round, with a sea breeze cooling the summers. On odd days, however, when the wind comes from the desert, it can be dramatically warmer: 118 degrees has been recorded in July. Inland temperatures in summer are almost unbearable in Morocco in the winter months, but Tangier is roughly twice as wet as Agadir. Evenings can be quite cold, especially in the winter.

Local transport

Because of the distance travelled on longer excursions, hiring a car is expensive and not a realistic alternative unless you plan to stay overnight, as no-one unfamilar with the route can compete. In the resorts, little cars with the sign 'Petit Taxi' are metered and cheap, though they charge much more after dark.

Duty-free

Spirits and cigarettes are cheaper at Agadir Airport than in town, but the duty-free shop is about the size of a tobacco kiosk, with limited choice. Tangier Airport's duty-free shop also has a limited number of items.

THE GOOD RESORT GUIDE

TUNISIA

Port El Kantaoui	36
Sousse	36

34 THE GOOD RESORT GUIDE

TUNISIA

Stretching from Mediterranean beaches in the north to desert steppes in the south, Tunisia is truly a land of intimate contrasts. Medieval strongholds share the shore with splendid hotels; veiled Arab women in white flowing robes barter with shifty traders alongside smart European ladies; French and Arabic are spoken equally, and often fluently, by the same Tunisian.

But for all the increasing spontaneity of its society, Tunisia has unconsciously taken a good deal of enjoyment out of its holiday industry. Far too many of its resorts are separate from the towns that gave them their identity, leaving the occupants hotel bound, with little opportunity for a casual stroll to a cafe. Although Tunisia has its tourist attractions, from the ancient city of Carthage to the seemingly boundless Sahara desert, they are thinly spread and hugely over-organised. In the summer, too, the heat can be unbearable away from the sea. Visitors are also unusually vulnerable to stomach upsets, especially those who go boldly into restaurants where no non-Arab has been before. What redeems Tunisia as a popular destination is its uncrowded beaches, mile upon mile of bleached sand, lapped by the southern Mediterranean sea.

The Gulf of Hammamet, with its fertile flowered landscape and sweeping groves of citrus trees, has been a favourite place for rest and recreation since the time of the Carthaginians and the Romans, and probably before that. Its position in the most southerly

Beach at Hammamet

THE GOOD RESORT GUIDE 35

SOUSSE/PORT EL KANTAOUI

TUNISIA

part of Tunisia, shielded from the last momentum of mid-Atlantic weather by Cape Bon, ensures long sustained periods of fine weather. The expansion of Tunisia's package tour industry has also made it a far from arduous destination, not much more than three hours flying time to Tunis or Monastir.

Souk, souvenir seller

SOUSSE/ PORT EL KANTAOUI

Of all the gulf resorts, Sousse has the richest promise of the kind of holiday sought by most visitors to Tunisia, a beach resort within striking distance of old Arabia. The beach resort, known as Port El Kantaoui, lies outside the old town, four miles to the north. Constructed entirely for one purpose, the enhancement of Tunisia's tourist industry, it has succeeded — just — in avoiding the impression of being a kind of leisure playground on the moon, the risk of all new projects that end abruptly at the edge of the desert. Port El Kantaoui has begun to straggle, and thereby to become more credible. Most of the unplanned development stems from the inevitable cottage industries that follow in the footsteps of big new hotels, a kind of modern camp follower, offering all the goods and services a hotel guest would like at a bargain price. As an unforeseen consequence, Port El Kantaoui no longer looks entirely like a Moorish Lego kit, in which all the pieces have been immaculately shaped, though as a marina, it still lacks the creative flair of Port Grimaud on the French Riviera or Puerto Banus near Marbella. The centre, built around the principal moorings, has some lovely houses and maisonettes in typical Arabic architecture, and some assorted bars and boutiques, which display acceptable credit cards with a relish that should send alarm bells ringing in every value-seeker's head. The hotels, in the main now complete, are a good walk from this main complex and from the original port.

With a rather strange sense of priorities, El Kantaoui left improvements to its northern beach extremely late, but has now removed many of the bumps and rubble that ruined the sandy surface. Despite their efforts, however, a familiar problem with Tunisian beaches, seaweed on the water, constantly reappears, a clammy shock for swimmers who reach the high water mark. South of the marina, the beach has also been cleaned up, but with heavy marine traffic in and out of the nearby port, the suspicion of pollution remains.

Sousse itself has its share of seaweed, all that mars an exceptionally good beach running for four miles from the north of the town, divided though it is by a railway line that turns towards the sea. Fortunately, however, it is some way from the hotels and the frequency of trains is in any case a fraction of those in Estoril or the Costa Dorada. On the firm sand, the more energetic tourist can try his or her hand on a horse or a camel.

There is plenty to do in Sousse, the third biggest town in Tunisia, with some elegant shops along the tree-lined avenue of Habib Bourgiba. Most people however are content to wander in the maze of little streets and squares (including the courtyard of the Grand Mosque) that make up the old walled quarter close to the port, where salesmen are plentiful but bargains hard to come by. To see the strangely cubic quality of Sousse, as its houses have scarcely a curve between them, go into training and climb the tight spiral staircase to the top of the minaret tower on the ribat, a fortified monastery where the Moslem knights once prayed for victory in battle.

THE GOOD RESORT GUIDE

SOUSSE/PORT EL KANTAOUI

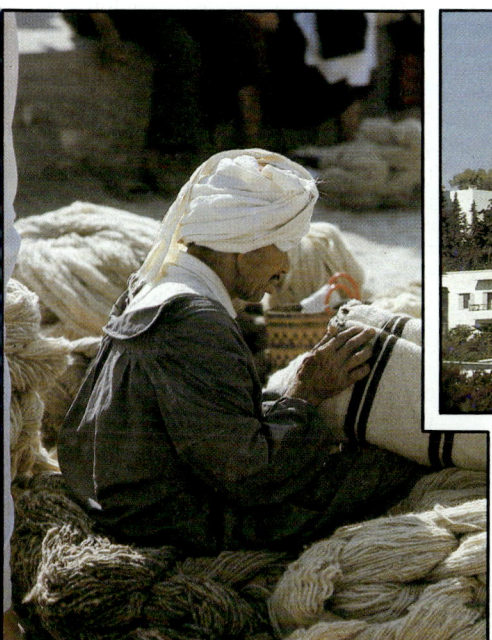

Carpet seller, Tunisian market

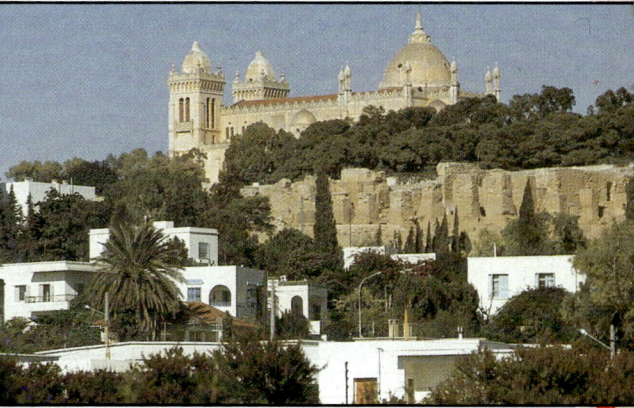

Carthage

All this exercise is certain to add spice to the appetite, and probably to the meal, for Tunisian food is frequently prepared with peppers fierce enough to put your throat on fire. Mechouia, a mixture of tunny fish, hard-boiled eggs, lemons, onions, tomatoes and hot peppers all cooked in olive oil provides one appetiser that will give you a good idea what you are in for. Then you may be offered doigts de Fatima, Fatima's fingers, not a dish for cannibals but a sausage-like pastry called brik filled with mincemeat and fried in olive oil. Next, couscous, rather tastier than in Morocco (see page 24), and finally degla mehcheya, sweetened dates stuffed with almonds and sealed in rose water. Do not, however, make the mistake of trying to wash it down with thibarine, a date liqueur that tastes like cointreau but with an effect not far short of a swig of methylated spirits.

Excursions

Echoes of the Foreign Legion abound in Tunisia, and none more so than in the deep south at Kebili, where on an overnight trip, you can spend the night in an old Legion fort. Far from being deserted, Beau Geste fashion, it has been turned into a quite presentable establishment, unrecognisable as the spartan barracks where the legionnaires were rudely woken up at dawn for a dangerous desert patrol. Kebili is an oasis on the edge of Chott el Djerid, a huge and desolate salt lake, where even the bedouin move with caution, a place whose dried bleached bones still indicate where man and beast tried to beat the desert and paid for their folly.

Also on the edge of the Sahara, but in far more hospitable surroundings, stands Gabes, a settlement of a dozen villages linked by a winding forest road. The most popular means of local transport, apart, that is, from the ubiquitous camel, is the caleche, a horse-drawn carriage with no apparent springs. Arab women, however, still go on foot, deeply veiled and carrying those impossibly huge water jars on their shoulders. Emancipation has not yet crept up on Tunisia, it seems.

Closer to Sousse, but directly to the west, Kairouan rises dramatically before your eyes from the steppes of the desert, as though by magic. An Islamic stronghold created literally in an empty land back in the seventh century, it still uses camel power to turn the pumping machinery for the water supply, though whether this is cheaper than a generator or for the benefit of tourists is not entirely clear. A succession of camels, blindfolded to prevent dizziness, walk around in a circle to pull the levers.

To the south of Sousse, El Djem offers an equally dramatic approach, a prodigiously

THE GOOD RESORT GUIDE 37

SOUSSE/PORT EL KANTAOUI

TUNISIA

straight Roman road leading directly to the amphitheatre, one of the biggest ever built in the Roman Empire. Like the Colosseum in Rome, it once staged huge battles between teams of gladiators and was flooded for sea fights that were sometimes larger than the events they were intended to depict. The ruins of Carthage, a few miles outside Tunis on the north-east coast, are a reminder of the time when the authority of Rome counted for little here, and the Carthaginians were a proud independent people. The Baths of Antoninus, hundreds of rooms providing sauna, swimming and massage, can be clearly identified, an indication of the sophistication and relaxed durability of their civilisation. The Romans won in the end of course, ejecting the Carthaginians from their capital, which over the centuries was progressively dismantled to build Tunis nearby. A substantial part of it can be seen in the north wall of the old quarter, whose structure supports the more precarious fabric of tiny shops bidding energetically for

business, just as they have done for centuries. Tunis, after all, has had its tourists long before charter flights, if only to gaze in awe on the Grand Mosque, the focal point of North African society for more than a thousand years.

Roman amphitheatre, at El Djiem   Above: Ruins at Carthage

38 THE GOOD RESORT GUIDE

SOUSSE/PORT EL KANTAOUI

SOUSSE/PORT EL KANTAOUI HOTELS

Diar El Andalous★★★★ in Port El Kantaoui, leading directly on to the sand dunes behind the less appetising northern beach, about 1½ miles from the marina. Circular pool with central bar, not ideal for heavy nocturnal drinkers. Several restaurants. Children's playground and cinema. 300 rooms, all air-conditioned.

El Kanta★★★★ in Port El Kantaoui, part of the marina development, an ingenious and elegant building with arcaded balconies, set in beautiful gardens. Large swimming pool, five minutes' walk to the beach, though you have to cross a busy main road. 250 rooms on seven floors (2 lifts), with full air-conditioning in the warmer months.

Marhaba Beach★★★★ in Sousse, two miles north-west of the centre, Arabic architecture with a particularly attractive swimming pool. Right next to a superb beach, ideal for children, who also have their own playground. However, despite the presence of a night-club, rather short on entertainment. 254 rooms on 5 floors (2 lifts), air-conditioning only in high season.

Tour Khalef★★★ in Sousse, next door to the Marhaba Beach hotel with interchangeable facilities. Disco well away from the main hotel. The pool, set in attractive grounds, seems large until the number of rooms is appreciated: 505 on nine floors (2 lifts). A major disadvantage in summer is that the hotel has air-conditioning only in the public rooms.

Abou Sofian★★★ in Port El Kantaoui, next door, but considerably less comfortable than the El Andalous Hotel, despite its domed foyer. Indoor and outdoor pools, direct access to northern beach, which has watersports but very little else. Food lacks inspiration. Guests on a budget would do well to order soft drinks in the night-club. 225 rooms; no air-conditioning.

OTHER RESORTS

HAMMAMET

The hotels in this resort, Moorish architecture of three or four storeys, stand next to a marvellous beach of golden sand on the

View over rooftops, Hammamet

sheltered shore of the gulf. Marvellous, that is, as long as your priority is a sun tan and not to swim in the warm sea, which is clogged by seaweed from its very edge, and has some alarming dips which can make it dangerous for small children intending to paddle. Waterskiing, windsurfing and sailing facilities are not really adequate to cope with high season demand. If you are bored with the beach, getting into Hammamet can be tiresome and expensive, as there is no public transport. Most of the hotels are three or four miles from town, those to the north entirely on their own, those to the south in a little centre of bars and restaurants, which tends to lose its appeal as the holiday progresses. Some of the hotels lay on mini-buses to Hammamet proper, where the old quarter can provide an exhausting day out, dominated, though no longer threatened, by a former Foreign Legion fort. Transfer times: from Tunis airport 1½ hours, from Monastir airport 2 hours.

THE GOOD RESORT GUIDE 39

TUNISIA

SOUSSE/PORT EL KANTAOUI

Monastir

MONASTIR
Like Hammamet and Sousse, the large hotels lead an independent existence on the edge of the town; though with less justification here, as Monastir is quiet, sophisticated, with a splendid beach (apart, that is, from the seaweed) backed by an imposing promenade, a rarity on the African shore. The bay is still dominated by the rusting old guns of the ribat, Monastir's old monastic fortress, while the medina is full of little shops whose owners plead abject poverty in the battle of wits for your money. Transfer times: only 15 minutes from Monastir airport, but from Tunis, 2½ hours.

SOUSSE FACTS

Your journey

To Monastir	Hours
From Gatwick, Heathrow	3
From Birmingham, East Midlands, Luton, Manchester	3¼

Monastir Airport is 20 minutes from Sousse, but because of local traffic, transfers to Port El Kantaoui may take twice that time.

Shopping
The siesta in the afternoon includes the shops, as most shut between 1200 and 1500 during summer, reopening until 2000 or even later. Their hours are, however, unpredictable and erratic.

40 THE GOOD RESORT GUIDE

SOUSSE/POR[T

Money matters

Banks are normally open 0800 to 1100 and 1400-1600, Monday to Friday, but during the religious festival of Ramadan, the afternoon opening times change to 1300-1430, and for brief periods banks may open 0730 to 1200 only. This is one place where asking on arrival is the only solution. What is more or less certain is that outside Tunis, banks will be closed on January 1, January 18, March 20, April 9, May 1, June 1, June 2, July 25, August 3, August 13, September 3, October 15, as well as on movable religious festivals. In Tunis, however, a few branches (usually inside big hotels) stay open seven days a week, holidays included, with hours depending on the demand.

Tunisian dinars may not be imported or exported. Tourists should expect to be asked to declare foreign currency at the airport on arrival, and again on departure. Even by keeping receipts not more than one third of the Tunisian dinars purchased on arrival may be reconverted into foreign currency. Do not count on the airport branch being open when you leave, even during normal banking hours.

Tunisian minaret tower

Weather

Averages	Jan	Feb	Mar	Apr	May	Jun	Jul	Aug	Sep	Oct	Nov	Dec
Temperature	61	62	64	70	73	80	88	90	88	79	70	62
Sun hours	7	7	7	9	11	11	12	11	9	7	7	7
Rain days	7	5	5	3	2	1	0	0	2	4	5	7
Sea temp.	59	57	59	63	66	71	75	79	79	75	65	54

In Tunisia, the daytime temperatures shown above are always at least 20 degrees higher than the temperatures at night, so even during the height of summer, warm clothing is advisable. In summer desert temperatures can exceed 100 degrees during the day. Sousse receives very little rain in summer but is substantially cooler than inland areas. The sea temperature is not warm enough for less than hardy swimmers between December and March.

Local transport

The most popular form of transport is a shared taxi, called louages. On long distances, you can book a seat in advance. Grand taxis are more comfortable and much more expensive ... rarely metered. Taxis-bébé can take only 3 passengers at a time, must use their meter, and are restricted to city and airport rides. Bus services are adequate within city centres, but to be avoided on long-distance travel unless you have unending patience.

From Sousse, a train runs to Tunis: as it is very cheap, paying extra in order to travel in the air-conditioned first class section makes the journey much more agreeable. A British driving licence is valid for Tunisia, provided that you are over 21. Check hire cars carefully before accepting them, and keep to the main roads at all costs.

TUNISIA

THE GOOD RESORT GUIDE 41

CYPRUS

CYPRUS

The only Mediterranean package tour destination literally east of Suez, Cyprus is tucked beneath Turkey, an island with an exceptional climate and sustained sunshine. The British, who colonised it, gave Cyprus independence without pacifying its warring peoples, Greek against Turk. In 1974 Turkey took the law into her own hands and invaded the northern half of the island, eventually making it an independent state. Whatever the justification, they destroyed the tourist industry, turning the most famous Cypriot resort, Famagusta, into a ghost town.

But the Greek Cypriots have come again, rebuilding their hotels in the south of the island, with equal opportunism, but fewer natural advantages. Some of the beaches consist of grey shingle and look singularly uninspiring. Some of the older hotels, too, reflect the urgency of their construction and have not stood the test of time. It follows that this is one destination where a careful choice of both resort and hotel can have a major effect on the success of your holiday.

What southern Cyprus does have in abundance, however, is a carefree spontaneity and warmth. Its people are immensely hospitable, and need only the slightest excuse

Beach near Paphos

THE GOOD RESORT GUIDE 43

CYPRUS

to stage an evening where the wine flows relentlessly and the Greek dancers are on their feet until dawn. At a Cypriot wedding feast, only a determined bride and groom make it home in time for bed.

The British influence is not simply the continued presence of military bases. English is understood if not actually spoken as frequently as Greek. The Cypriots spend pounds: though visitors should appreciate they are worth rather more than sterling. They drive on the left and sometimes overtake on the right. Virtually everything non-perishable sold in the UK is available in Cyprus — at a price.

Although the unattractive end of international food such as hamburgers and pizzas are widely available, the real value comes in eating local specialities. Meze, usually an appetizer in Greece or the Greek islands, is often a full-scale meal here comprising a dozen different dishes. Fresh fish, especially mullet, is plentiful and excellent. Kleftiko, roast lamb cooked in aromatic herbs; and aphelia, pork marinated in wine, are both great favourites. Cypriot wine is both cheap and eminently drinkable. Visitors should also try Cyprus sherry and filfar, a liqueur made from oranges that packs a powerful punch.

Excursions

The history of Cyprus stretches back almost to

Beach at Ayia Napa   Inset church of St Lazarus, Larnaca

44 THE GOOD RESORT GUIDE

CYPRUS

he beginning of the known world, to epic tales nd epic times when man was but a plaything f the gods. Somehow it no longer seems quite o improbable amid such vivid, contrasting cenery. You can almost accept that Aphrodite's ock on the southern coast was indeed where he goddess of love first emerged from the sea, er legendary birthplace. Not far away is the nore substantial city of Curium, where the oices of the orators in its ancient mphitheatre carried beyond the Roman udience and far out to sea. Roman baths, dorned with delightful mosaics, still survive earby. On the coast itself, Kolossi castle, now nly a shell, still waits for Moorish invaders; it vas built by those vigorous defenders of Malta, he Knights of St. John. Inland, the Troodos nountains shelter ancient monasteries, of which he most famous is Kykko, built in the eleventh entury. Kykko still possesses many precious kons, but most major archeological finds can e found in the Cyprus museum in Nicosia. Whether that in itself justifies a visit to the sland's divided capital may depend on the time f year, for in high season Nicosia is a weltering, unpleasant place. And for the time eing, at least, visitors can no longer cross into orthern Cypriot territory.

Kolossi Castle

south coast and is therefore convenient for excursions, the transfer time from Larnaca airport is 90 minutes.

Hotel Amathus Beach ★ ★ ★ ★ its architecture will make the purists shudder but it does have the facilities to disguise the limitations of Limassol, six miles to the west. Two outdoor pools, one with underwater music presumably audible only to underwater swimmers; a children's pool, playroom and ban on children under six at evening meals in the main restaurant. On sandy beach. 244 rooms on seven floors (3 lifts).

RESORTS AND HOTELS

LIMASSOL

he largest and longest established resort on he south coast, stretching eastwards for seven niles from the edge of the rather uninteresting own. Hotels, apartment blocks and shopping omplexes now form an almost unbroken line ven though by no means all are complete; and etween them and the beach is a fast, noisy oad which means that many of the rooms /ith a sea view may become the haunt of nsomniacs. At Dassoudi, three miles east of he centre, the local authorities have created a ne beach with groynes and changing facilities; lsewhere, a few private hotel beaches apart, a arrow, grey strip of pebbles must make some ourists wonder a little why they bothered to ome at all. A group of tiny tavernas around he old port offer perhaps the only plausible eason why visitors should stir from the nmediate vicinity of their hotel, as night life is cattered liberally throughout the resort. lthough Limassol is centrally located on the

LARNACA

A row of jolly open-air tavernas facing a palm-lined promenade noticeably lacking in maintenance is perhaps a reminder of quieter days before Larnaca found it had an international airport on its doorstep. Unfortunately the closest group of hotels to the airport, two miles west of the town in a district called Scala, have been constructed in the middle of Larnaca's poorest quarter, both socially and visually depressing. The hotels located actually in the middle of the town are no more pleasing to the eye, and it is left to the hotels lying five or more miles to the east to rescue the resort, but only after you have travelled past a long line of petrol depots and oil refineries. Once there, a long, narrow stretch of good if rather greyish sand is popular with visitors, perhaps a little too popular at the height of summer. Water sports are widely available, ranging from pedaloes and canoes to speed boats, water-skiing, windsurfing and the

THE GOOD RESORT GUIDE 45

CYPRUS

Amphitheatre at Curium Inset: Curium mosaic

more ambitious paragliding. Although a few restaurants have opened up to cater for visitors, the lack of local amenities makes frequent trips necessary into Larnaca itself. However the short transfer time is a decided asset: around 20 minutes to the airport.

Hotel Sandy Beach ★ ★ ★ ★ as its name suggests, directly by the main beach in Larnaca Bay, six miles north east of Larnaca itself. Large swimming pool, spacious sun terrace, children's pool, cheerful restaurant facing the sea, spacious and comfortable rooms. Live music most nights in summer. Lacks character. 205 rooms on seven floors.

AYIA NAPA

A rapidly developing resort, which may eventually be its undoing, some twenty-five miles east of Larnaca (transfer time: 1 hour 15 minutes). Rather distant from the main excursion routes, two beautiful beaches of gently sloping, golden sand are its main attraction, the first in Nissi Bay, about half a mile away from some of the principal hotels; the second at Mackronisson, nearly four miles from the original fishing village. The town beach, immediately to the east of Ayia Napa's tiny port, is nowhere near as pleasant but still better than most other Cyprus beaches. Water sports are plentiful for the enthusiast, including at Mackronisson, a scuba diving school. Many visitors hire bicycles to get about: some of them have brakes. Tavernas and discos come alive at night on the waterfront, which is just beginning to lose its charming, relaxed atmosphere. As the old cliché goes, you should have been here last year.

Hotel Nissi Beach ★ ★ ★ probably the best compromise between staying in Ayia Napa itself and out at Mackronisson, as the village is less than 20 minutes' walk, and the beach, in Nissi Bay, is the best in Cyprus. Swimming pool, wide range of entertainments, disco and nightclub. Bungalows are available in the grounds with convertible sofas in the lounge. 251 rooms on five floors.

PAPHOS

On the western coast, a place of great appeal, especially its tiny port where tavernas jostle one another for space on the harbour front, most of them constructed, one suspects, from stone filched long ago from the ancient ruined fortress behind. However the actual resort is Kato Paphos, about 15 minutes walk away, and even further from the actual town, which is 1½

THE GOOD RESORT GUIDE

CYPRUS

...miles distant and linked by a regular shuttle bus. That would be tolerable enough if the beaches at Paphos were agreeable but frankly they are not: they consist mainly of rocks, and the exposed sea is frequently rough. For a really good beach, you have to travel to Coral Beach, eight miles to the north. The transfer time is also a serious disadvantage, 2¾ hours from Larnaca Airport. Look for one of the occasional charter flights into Paphos Airport, less than 25 minutes away.

Cypria Maris ★★★★ two miles east of the resort centre, more than three from Paphos itself, a stylish modern hotel with a remarkable range of facilities, including a gymnasium and a billiards room. Large swimming pool, though shaped to deter serious swimmers; children's pool, playground and supervised playroom. Unfortunately the adjacent beach has many rocks and an uncomfortably steep slope. Fine if you can afford a car. 217 rooms on six floors; most have a sea view.

CYPRUS FACTS

Your journey

	Hours
From Gatwick, Heathrow, Luton	4¼
From Birmingham, East Midlands, Manchester	5

Flight times are to Larnaca Airport, 3 miles south of the town. Transfer times are given under individual resorts.

Shopping

Most shops open 0800 to 1300, and again from 1500 to 1900 in summer; in winter, the lunch break is shorter and afternoon opening times are usually 1500 to 1800, or 1600 to 1900. Wednesday and Saturday are half day closing.

Money matters

Banks are open from 0830 to 1200, Monday to Saturday, though some re-open in the afternoons in the main resorts for currency exchange only. Apart from the airport, expect all banks to be closed on January 1, January 6, January 19, March 25, Good Friday, Easter Monday, April 1, May 1, August 3, August 15, October 1, October 28, December 24, December 25, December 26.

Eurocheques, travellers' cheques and credit cards are widely accepted.

Weather

Averages	Jan	Feb	Mar	Apr	May	Jun	Jul	Aug	Sep	Oct	Nov	Dec
Temperature	61	63	66	75	84	91	99	97	91	83	73	66
Sun hours	5	6	7	8	10	12	12	12	10	8	6	5
Rain days	11	7	6	3	2	1	0	0	1	3	5	9
Sea temp.	61	62	64	66	68	77	82	82	77	72	68	64

The extremely high temperatures in July and August are sometimes reduced along the coast by a sea breeze, but even then it may be over 85 degrees, too hot for comfort. The most agreeable time to visit Cyprus is in the late Spring and Autumn. December and January, though still mild, are comparatively wet.

Local transport

Away from the main resorts, many of the roads are extremely rough; even the pot holes have pot holes. Local buses are cheap but extremely slow and unreliable. The seats are hard: take your own cushion. The best means of travel is a 'service taxi', usually a large Mercedes with room for six, which runs between major resorts and elsewhere if the driver agrees. You pay a fixed rate for your seat, whether the taxi fills up or not.

Duty-free

Cyprus sherry, brandy and wine is cheapest in supermarkets. International brands of cigarettes and spirits are better value at Larnaca airport.

THE GOOD RESORT GUIDE

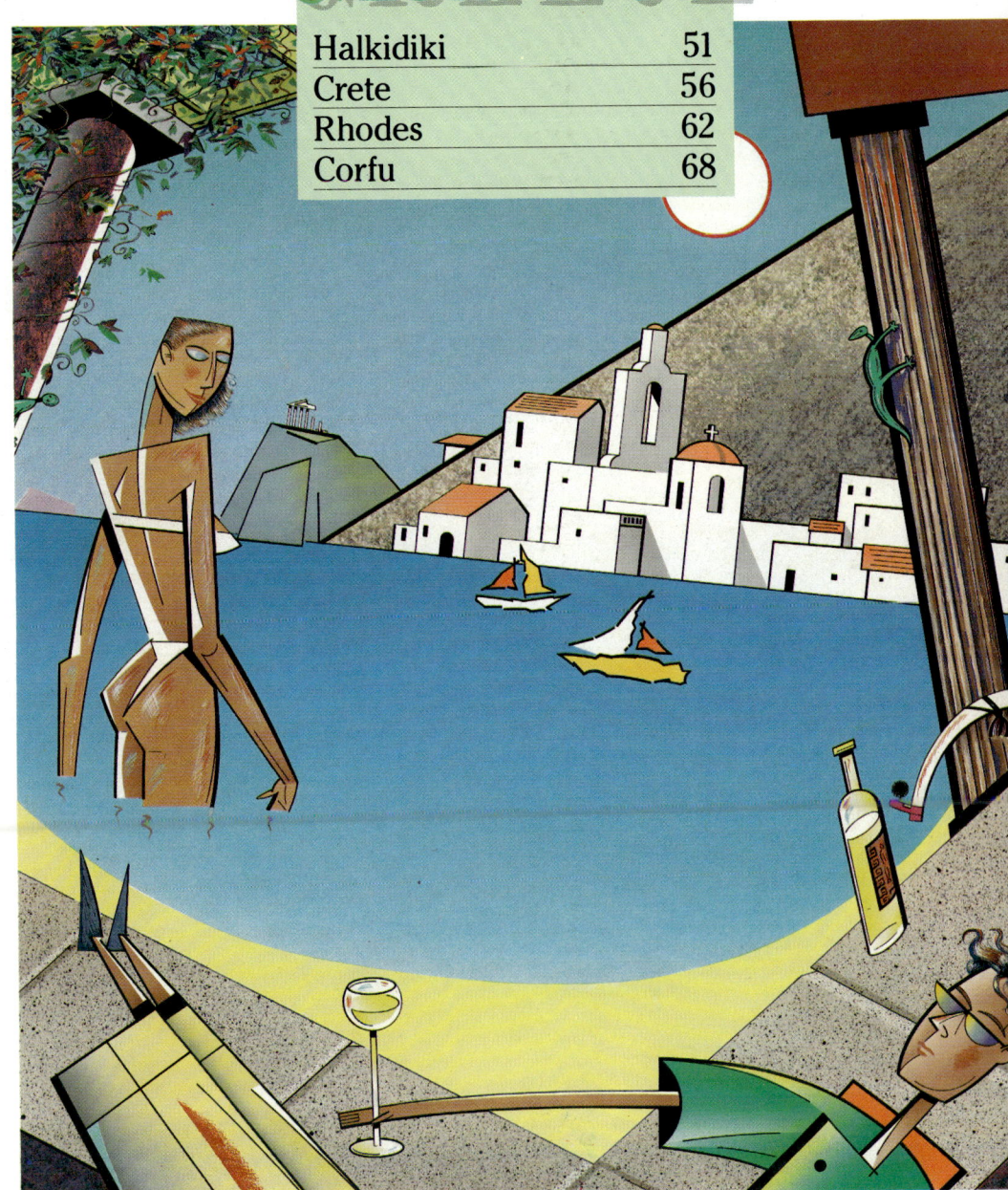

GREECE

Halkidiki	51
Crete	56
Rhodes	62
Corfu	68

48 THE GOOD RESORT GUIDE

GREECE

The islands and peninsulas of Greece have a combined coastline of more than nine thousand miles, where holidaymakers can bask in the assured summer sun and swim in the warm waters of the Aegean sea. Whenever they go, they will find a nonchalant attitude to life that is instantly contagious, where the most demanding occupation is watching the rest of the world go by. And behind the beaches, harsh mountains and scorched plains are the perfect backcloth to the epic tales of Greek history, where the heroes of the past somehow still haunt the ruins of the present. Great temples and beautiful shrines remain as tangible evidence of a civilisation that flourished more than two thousand years ago.

But few holidays can be based entirely on the pursuit of Greek antiquities, and not everyone will find Greece to their liking. Its nightlife is disorganised and lethargic. Many (though by no means all) of its hotels are a little rough at the edges, much of its food indifferent and monotonous, some of its beaches sadly disappointing. What redeems Greece is the incredibly low local prices and the genuine pleasure and enthusiasm with which they greet visitors, making it almost impossible to look upon their lack of planning and maintenance with a critical eye. However, as food on holiday is a major source of pain or pleasure, or sometimes both, for the tourist, understanding the Greek mentality can help to avoid really disastrous experiences.

First, accept the fact that only Athens and Thessaloniki (which we call Salonica) have top class restaurants run by professionals, where

Kalithea coastline

THE GOOD RESORT GUIDE 49

GREECE

the decor is merely the prelude to a superb meal in sophisticated surroundings. Restaurants that look smart elsewhere merely add to the bill without guaranteeing the quality of their dishes. Indeed, they may be deliberately attempting to cater for the tourist rather than offering genuine Greek cuisine, with disastrous results. Choose a taverna, the more rough and ready, the better. Except in really tiny islands, never eat before nine at night: restaurants in full swing earlier than that are for tourists, not Greeks, and the place to eat is where the locals eat.

Second, look at the food in the kitchen. The owner/chef will not be offended: quite the opposite. A personal inspection of the available dishes will nearly always confirm that they are at best lukewarm. Greek tavernas do all their cooking in the morning and see nothing wrong with letting the dishes stand cooling until they are eaten. Resign yourself to the inevitable: it is, after all, far too hot a climate for hot food to be vital.

Unless of course you order while in the kitchen, fresh meat or more likely fresh fish, by size and weight. Quite apart from actually promising to be hot (though do not count on it), this has the advantage of preventing the waiter from bringing you something that you did not order. This happens frequently, because a

Monastery at Mount Athos

MAINLAND GREECE

HALKIDIKI

waiter is told by the owner to try to get rid of something not being chosen. He counts on the fact that tourists will rarely complain, and even if they do, it can be put down to a misunderstanding due to different languages.

Whatever you order, do not expect it to arrive in neat little parcels from starter to sweet. 'Course' is untranslatable in Greek, because the whole idea is foreign to them. As a consequence, salads and soups and sweets (not that there really are any genuine Greek puddings) tend to arrive all together or in a hopelessly wrong order.

Finally, assume that the bill will be wrong. As the restaurant may not have a written menu, let alone prices on display, the opportunities for fiddling are enormous. When ordering, ask what each dish costs, and let the waiter see you writing it down. It may not improve the service, which you have to pay for in any case, but it will certainly enhance his mathematics.

That most famous Greek mathematician, Pythagoras, would not have thought much of Halkidiki, the three-fingered peninsula on

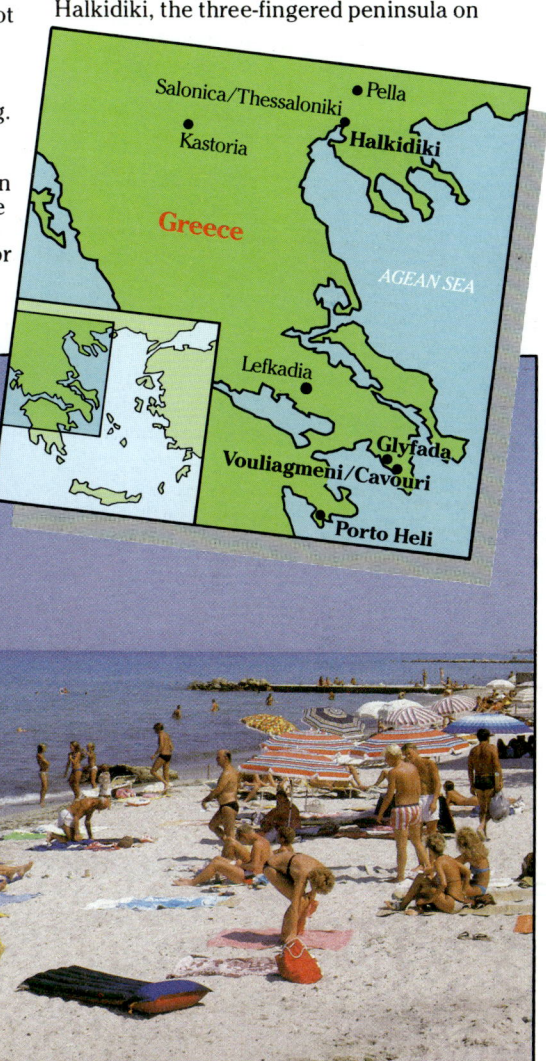

Beach at Kalithea

THE GOOD RESORT GUIDE 51

MAINLAND GREECE

Rock at Meteora   Inset: Monastery at Meteora

52 THE GOOD RESORT GUIDE

MAINLAND GREECE

northern Greece reached by way of flights to Salonica. It is simply too far north, too cold in the winter, to have attracted the fair-weather philosophers of ancient Greece. Provided that you do not expect to find a ruined acropolis around every corner, it is nevertheless an agreeable summer destination. Kassandra, the western prong of the peninsula, has many of the trappings of an organised resort, and beautiful sandy beaches. Sithonia, in the centre, is much less developed and offers many almost deserted coves. Mount Athos, the most easterly, does not really welcome tourists. And much of the peninsula is a closed monastic territory where women are not allowed, presumably for fear of placing too much temptation in the way of the monks. Many inclusive tours concentrate on Kassandra, in particular Kalithea, which has an increasing number of restaurants and souvenir shops to supplement the hotels, most of which lead directly on to sheltered sandy beaches. Kalithea's problem is that it has no recognisable centre and, apart from the occasional bar, no real night life. Visitors have to rely on their hotel for most of their entertainment. Haniotis, further along the coast, is much more lively. Its main square is packed with tavernas and bars, and in the back streets, two discos boom away into the early hours of the morning. However this is not the spot to choose for sun bathing, as in the summer the beach is narrow and crowded. The worst period is the first two weeks in August, when half the population of northern Greece seems to be jammed into this tiny peninsula; because the Greeks have holidays, too.

Excursions

In short, Halkidiki does not have any. Local trips go to Petralona Cave, rather indifferent stalagmites and stalactites, and to Thessaloniki (or Salonica), the second city of Greece, with an interesting old Turkish quarter and some sophisticated shops.

If you can arrange a package tour which includes a few nights on the road, or you are prepared in effect to pay double for the nights when you are away from your resort hotel, Thessaloniki offers several appealing coach tours. The best in terms of its startling scenery visits Meteora, an extraordinary pinnacle of rock far to the south-west, with a uniquely remote monastery on top. Pella, to the west but rather closer, is the birthplace of Alexander the Great, an excursion usually combined with Lefkadia to see the Great Macedonian Tomb. Further west, another popular trip includes the town of Kastoria on one of the Prespa Lakes, more superb scenery, quite close to the Albanian border.

HALKIDIKI HOTELS

Meliton Beach★★★★ on the central peninsula of Sithonia, part of the Porto Carras complex just outside Nea Marmaras village. It also embraces two other hotels, **Sithonia Beach**★★★ and, sandwiched between them, the small **Village Inn**★★. However guests are allowed to use any of the amenities, which include a marina, two big swimming pools, nine tennis courts, a taxing golfing course, three restaurants, two cinemas, and a casino. Holidaymakers who like individual attention should perhaps note that the complex has 998 rooms. Transfer time from Salonica airport: at least two hours, but transport is usually provided by the hotels.

Mount Athos Hotel★★ the only hotel of any consequence on the Mount Athos spur, three miles from the monastic territory on a remote but sheltered stretch of coast. Elderly guests may have problems getting up and down to the coarse sandy beach, which involves over 80 steps. A splendid boat, owned by the hotel, is available for local excursions. Rather rustic atmosphere, reinforced by the fact that much of the accommodation is in bungalows away from the main hotel. 162 rooms in all. Transfer time: 3 hours from Salonica airport, though transport is laid on by the hotel without charge.

Athos Palace★★★ not to Mount Athos but on the Kassandra peninsula, part of a huge complex which includes the adjacent **Pallini Beach**★★★. Between them they have an indoor pool, enormous outdoor pool, cinema, disco, children's playground and playroom, private jetty. Athos Palace is the more attractive, but shrewd guests use the beach in front of Pallini Beach hotel, which has a much more gentle slope and is safer for children. The best restaurant, a Greek taverna, is not usually included in package tour prices. Athos Palace has 427 rooms on ten floors (4 lifts) but the two hotels and bungalows have 1,095 rooms in all. Transfer time from Salonica airport: 1½ hours.

THE GOOD RESORT GUIDE 53

MAINLAND GREECE

Kassandra Palace ★★★ isolated hotel four miles south of Kalithea on the Kassandra peninsula, but set in agreeable wooded grounds beside a long, sandy shoreline. Large swimming pool, children's playground conveniently located next to the beach, many organised water sports. However the food is unexciting unless you pay extra to eat in the taverna. 192 rooms, all air-conditioned, on four floors (2 lifts). Transfer time from Salonica airport: 1½ hours.

Corinth Canal   Inset: old Corinth

MAINLAND GREECE

Gerakina Beach ★ ★ on the road leading to the Kassandra peninsula, which is distinguished by the presence of ugly hills of mining waste products. Fortunately these Greek slag heaps cannot be seen from the hotel, whose 30-acre sight is well screened by trees. The sandy beach is outstanding, with a swimming pool next to the sea and many organised water sports. The meal arrangements for the two hotel restaurants and the snack bar by the pool are extremely flexible, but taverna meals still cost extra and they are much the best. 503 rooms on seven floors (2 lifts) in the hotel and comfortable bungalows. Transfer time from Salonica airport: 1¼ hours.

Pella ★ ★ on Kassandra, close to Haniotis village, uninspiring architecture and mediocre shingle beach. Swimming pool, children's pool, air-conditioned disco. The taverna meals are an optional extra but most guests widely elect to walk into the village and eat out. 179 rooms, none of which incidentally has a full sea view, on six floors (2 lifts). Transfer time from Salonica airport: 1½ hours.

OTHER RESORTS

Porto Heli
In the north-east of the Peloponnese peninsula, Portokhelion, as it is more properly known, has a series of delightful beaches close to the larger hotels. However it is also ideally suited for visitors prepared for demanding excursions, which include the Corinth Canal and the city of Mycenae, where King Agamemnon once ruled and, if archaeology and mythology come together, launched the expedition (though not of course the thousand ships) to recover Helen from the Trojans. Rather closer, indeed just across the water, is the island of Spetsai, which has an exhausting night life. Porto Heli's huge disadvantage, however, is the transfer time from Athens airport, 3½ hours by coach and hydrofoil or 4½ hours all the way by coach.

Glyfada
A resort noted for its night clubs and discos, located east of Piraeus, the port of Athens. Alas, it is not only half an hour from Athens but on the flight path to the airport, and the noise is deafening. Nor is there any respite between take-offs and landings, which are frequent enough, as the main road in front of the hotels carries heavy traffic day and night. A charge is made for the principal beach, which suffers from pollution from Piraeus. Transfer time: 10 minutes from Athens Airport, but you will have to be desperate to stay here.

Vouliagmeni/Cavouri
Two miles south of Glyfada (see above), a resort inexplicably popular with the Athenians, especially for dining out. It is, however, on exactly the same flight path as Glyfada, and if the aircraft are a little higher in the sky, the noise is still extremely disagreeable. The best beach, operated by the local tourist office, charges for both entry and changing facilities. Transfer time from Athens airport: 20 minutes.

GREEK MAINLAND FACTS

Your journey

To Salonica	Hours
From Gatwick	3¼
From Birmingham	3½
From Manchester	3¾

Thessaloniki airport is ten miles south of the city.

To Athens	Hours
From Gatwick, Luton, Heathrow	3½
From Birmingham, East Midlands	3¾
From Manchester	4
From Glasgow	4¼

Hellinikon airport is nine miles south of Athens.

Shopping
There are no fixed hours for shops, and in resorts many tend to stay open as long as there are customers about, closing instead for the whole winter (as do most hotels in the Halkidiki area). In Thessaloniki and Athens, many shops open at 0800, close at 1430, avoiding the afternoon heat, then reopen from 1730 to 2030.

Money matters
Banks open 0800 to 1400 or 1430, Monday to

MAINLAND GREECE/CRETE

Friday. In summer in larger towns, banks take it in turns to reopen from 1700 to 1900 and briefly on Saturday morning for foreign exchange transactions only. In summer there are banks open in Athens from 0800 to 2000, including Saturdays and Sundays.

Visitors are allowed only 3,000 drachmas of Greek currency on both their arrival and departure, which should not be in notes above 500 drachmas.

Weather
Thessaloniki/Salonica

Averages	Jan	Feb	Mar	Apr	May	Jun	Jul	Aug	Sep	Oct	Nov	Dec
Temperature	48	54	57	68	77	84	90	90	82	70	61	52
Sun hours	4	5	5	8	9	10	12	11	8	6	4	4
Rain days	6	6	6	6	6	3	3	2	3	6	6	8
Sea temp.	55	55	57	61	65	74	77	77	74	66	61	57

Athens/Piraeus:

Averages	Jan	Feb	Mar	Apr	May	Jun	Jul	Aug	Sep	Oct	Nov	Dec
Temperature	54	54	60	66	76	84	90	90	84	74	65	58
Sun hours	4	5	6	8	9	11	12	12	9	7	5	4
Rain days	7	6	5	3	3	2	1	1	2	4	6	7
Sea temp.	57	57	55	59	64	72	77	77	75	72	64	61

The most agreeable period to visit mainland Greece, especially if you plan inland excursions, is late Spring and early Autumn. Large cities such as Athens, where the temperature regularly reaches above 90 degrees in midsummer, can be oppressively hot and crowded in the peak tourist season. Light summer breezes around Halkidiki, a pleasant relief in summer, turn to cold, northerly winds which make it a practical proposition only as a summer resort.

Local Transport
Bus services are generally unpredictable, uncomfortable, crammed with locals, but cheap and great fun. In the Halkidiki peninsula, many hotels run their own mini-buses to the nearest village. However a frequent and fairly reliable bus service operates between the Apollo coast resorts of Glyfada, Vouliagmeni and Cavouri, and Athens. Piraeus is linked to Athens by an underground railway, extremely crowded in summer, but nevertheless efficient.

CRETE

In the deep southern waters of the Aegean sea, Crete commands the crossroads of three continents, and has suffered a turbulent history as a consequence. The Venetians, the Turks and the Nazis have all seized the island by force, subduing its territory, but never its people. Cretan culture can be traced back more than four thousand years, to the time of King Minos, in an island where the paralysing summer sun and arduous terrain encourage only lethargy. It has a backbone of three formidable mountain ranges, interspersed with dangerous gorges and ravines. Scrub saturates the flatter tracts of land, dominated by olive groves, and dotted with hopeful windmills, searching for a cheap source of power. In the resorts, concrete collides with the deep-rooted traditions of the past, winning a round here, losing a round there. The Cretans are aware that their prosperity lies not simply in their brasher resorts, many with indifferent and

CRETE

Cretan windmills

...ften crowded beaches, but in their ability to ...rike a balance between those visitors who ...ant nothing more than to lie on the sand, and ...ose determined to soak up the archaeological ...easures of Europe's first civilisation. Indeed ...r those bent on both, Crete offers a unique ...ombination of sightseeing and sunshine.

AGHIOS NIKOLAOS

...he largest, and therefore the most crowded ...esort on the island is Aghios Nikolaos, called ...fter the church of St. Nicholas near the ...arbour; indeed the church and the fishing ...eet once were Aghios, in the days before ...ackage tours. The purists would argue that ...ass tourism has ruined the place, but in a ...aradoxical way, it has added to it. Twenty ...ears ago, when the sun went down the local ...opulation by and large went inside and closed ...heir doors: nowadays it is the time of the *volta*, ...e evening stroll, when the girls try to catch a ...oung man's eye (or vice-versa). Aghios has the ...erfect place for that, Lake Voulismeni, a deep ...ner harbour joined to the outer harbour by a ...arrow canal which in turn is spanned by a ...ridge; a lovely walk around sunset. A few of ...e hotels and most of the tavernas are ...ustered hereabout, though the better the

Harbour at Aghios Nikolaos

THE GOOD RESORT GUIDE 57

CRETE

Aghios Nikolaos

CRETE

view, the higher their prices. The rather shabby back streets have numerous cafes and bars, many with music and dancing. Of the discos, discriminating visitors seem to prefer Scorpio, the Studio, or Rocky's. However a colourful night life does not in itself make a resort. For beaches, Aghios leaves a lot to be desired. The municipal beach is little more than a narrow strip of shingle, around the headland from the harbour is another tiny shingle beach, and in the resort itself visitors have to make do with concrete bathing platforms put down between the rocks.

The nearest sandy beach, near the Dolphin Taverna two miles out, is small and impossibly crowded, though it does have a comprehensive selection of water activities, including canoes, pedaloes, snorkelling, water-skiing and windsurfing. But you have to travel four miles out of Aghios, to Amoudra, if you are determined to find a sandy beach free from risk of claustrophobia.

Most of the superior hotels are also outside the town, though their beaches are by no means their most attractive feature. Nor is Aghios Nikolaos particularly convenient as a centre to tour the island. It is located on the north coast in the eastern corner of Crete, a long way from many of the interesting excursions, and 43 miles from the capital, Heraklion. Potential visitors who intend to spend a lot of their holiday on excursions would perhaps be better off elsewhere. Transfer time: 1¼ hours from Heraklion airport.

Excursions

Of the four Minoan palaces on Crete, Knossos is the best: no visit to Crete would be complete without seeing it. The Minoan civilisation of 4000 years ago had flushing toilets and hot and cold running water, which is more than can be said for every guest house in modern Crete. The huge palace of King Minos at Knossos near Heraklion is evidence of that, excavated and reconstructed by Sir Arthur Evans from the turn of the century. A lot of Sir Arthur's recreations depend more on his imagination than architectural accuracy, but then visitors need to exercise their imagination to make the quantum jump forward from beautiful frescoes to the incredible legend of Theseus and the Minotaur.

There is evidence that the Minoans worshipped bulls and practised the almost suicidal sport of facing a charging, consecrated bull, grasping its horns and somersaulting to safety over its back. Legend has it that Queen Pasiphae, wife of king Minos, made love with a white bull (itself a remarkable feat) and with the help of Daedalus hid the product of her folly, the half-man, half-beast Minotaur, in a labyrinth that Daedalus devised. Theseus penetrated the labyrinth to kill the Minotaur and found his way out by using a ball of twine given to him by Ariadne, daughter of King Minos. The story has a ring of plausibility if only because when Theseus returned in triumph to Athens, he ditched Ariadne on the way home in the island of Naxos. As for Daedalus, when King Minos discovered his part in covering up the Queen's infidelity, he was imprisoned in his own labyrinth. Daedalus and his son Icarus made wings fastened to their shoulders by wax in order to escape from Crete, but Icarus flew too close to the sun, the wax melted, and he fell to his death . . . or so the story goes.

Ruins at Knossos

THE GOOD RESORT GUIDE

CRETE

AGHIOS NIKOLAOS HOTELS

Minos Beach ★★★ a hotel/bungalow complex two miles outside the town, in lovely gardens that lead direct to a sandy cove. Large swimming pool, outstanding restaurant, but very little entertainment. 112 rooms, of which 12 are in the main hotel building and the rest in bungalows.

Hermes ★★★ shares its facilities with the adjoining Coral Hotel, both of which are located on the sea front in the centre of the town. Hermes has a small rooftop swimming pool, an attractive restaurant in the open air and a pizzeria. However to reach the rocky beach opposite, guests have to pass through a tunnel under the busy, and noisy, main road. Hermes has 204 rooms on seven floors (2 lifts).

Spinalonga island

Old streets of Spinalonga

Minos Palace ★★★ isolated, on a headland two miles north of the resort, opposite a man-made and rather uninspiring beach. However the swimming pool is particularly attractive, children (otherwise not encouraged) have a pool of their own and there is plenty of evening entertainment. 160 rooms, all air-conditioned, on three floors.

Mirabello ★★★ a hotel/bungalow complex, two miles from Aghios, bisected by a busy main road. The hotel has the beach, mostly rock and shingle; the bungalows (open summer only) have the swimming pool and make a charge for sunbeds. Plenty of facilities for children, including a separate pool and meals. 128 rooms in bungalows, 174 in the main hotel on seven floors (2 lifts).

Hera Village ★★ a rather jolly bungalow complex built into the hillside three miles north of the resort, with superb views across the bay. However each level of the hotel involves steps or slopes and an awkward climb down to the shingle beach. Large swimming pool, separate pool for children, evening disco. Good connections to Aghios Nikolaos. 44 rooms, many with air-conditioning and separate sitting area.

Alfa ★ a simple hotel offering only breakfast, but close to many bars and tavernas at the southern end of the resort. Pleasant roof garden. Main entrance is by way of steep steps. 41 rooms, all with shower, on five floors.

OTHER RESORTS

ELOUNDA
Memorable scenery is the highlight of this rapidly expanding resort located 42 miles east of the capital, Heraklion, just before the road turns south towards Aghios Nikolaos. However its beaches are mediocre, shingle and cramped with man-made concrete and rock platforms in front of the main hotels. Good water sports, including sailing and scuba diving. Little boats take visitors to the island of Spinalonga, which has a Venetian fort and was once a leper colony. Transfer time from Heraklion airport: 1½ hours.

HANIA
The second largest town in Crete, sometimes called Chania, owes its architectural mix to Turkish and Venetian influence. The narrow, slightly sinister, alleyways full of fascinating little shops have echoes of the Kasbah: but the outer harbour, a favourite sunset walk, has typically Greek tavernas with tables on the quay. There is, however, no municipal beach:

60 THE GOOD RESORT GUIDE

CRETE

he nearest, a mile to the west, has some sand
ut can be extremely crowded. A better beach
es two miles further out but the transport to
nd fro is far from reliable. Transfer time:
¼ hours from Heraklion airport.

RETHYMNON

Zorba the Greek' was made here and though
he town now has many more tourists, the tiny
arbour retains its evocative Greek
tmosphere. Many architects are completely
ystified as to how some of the houses, which
ave Turkish balconies, Venetian arches and
reek cement, hang successfully together.
or once, the town beach is excellent, a long
retch of sand, which continues uninterrupted
or several miles to the east, where most of the
g hotels can be found. Transfer time from
eraklion airport: 1¼ hours.

rbour at Rethymnon   Inset: beach at Rethymnon

THE GOOD RESORT GUIDE

CRETE/RHODES

CRETE FACTS

Your journey

To Heraklion:	Hours
From Gatwick, Luton	4
From Birmingham, Bristol, East Midlands	4¼
From Manchester, Newcastle	4½
From Glasgow	4¾

Heraklion airport is two miles east of the capital.

Shopping

Shops are free to determine their own opening hours, but most open from 0800 to 1300 and 1700 to 2000. In the resorts, however, some shops take one or more half days, opening from 0800 to 1400.

Money matters

If you need a bank, go early to avoid the long summer queues. They open 0800 to 1300 or 1400, Monday to Friday. In the main towns and resorts banks also take it in turns to open again from around 1700 to 1900 for money exchange purposes, and again for a brief period on Saturday mornings. All banks close on January 1, January 6, March 25, Easter Monday, May 1, June 11, August 15, October 28, December 25, December 26.

Credit cards are widely accepted in the main resorts. Large hotels will change traveller cheques but the rate is generally poor.

Weather

Averages	Jan	Feb	Mar	Apr	May	Jun	Jul	Aug	Sep	Oct	Nov	Dec
Temperature	60	60	64	70	76	82	86	86	82	78	70	66
Sun hours	5	6	6	8	9	12	13	12	10	7	6	6
Rain days	11	10	5	3	2	1	0	0	1	4	6	11
Sea temp.	61	61	63	64	68	73	75	77	75	73	66	63

On cloudless days the midsummer temperature inland may top 100 degrees, making sightseeing extremely arduous. Rain is practically unheard of in July and August but in winter, though still mild, Crete is rather wet.

Local transport

Although by no means a central resort, Aghios Nikolaos is the main bus terminal for eastern Crete, making it a good starting-point for sightseeing on public transport.

Car rental is expensive on Crete, and many cars offered by the smaller firms in Aghios Nikolaos are in poor condition and should be checked carefully. Inland roads can be almost impassable in places.

Duty free

Spirits and cigarettes are cheaper in local supermarkets than in the duty-free shop at Heraklion airport.

RHODES

Lying 12 miles from the tip of Asia, larger than Corfu but smaller than Crete, Rhodes receives more than half a million visitors every year. They come not simply to enjoy what is generally regarded as the sunniest climate in Greece and the long lovely beaches on the eastern coast, but also to see the temples and castles that remain as a permanent reminder of Rhodes' fascinating history.

When Paris, promised by Aphrodite he would have the most beautiful of all women, fulfilled the goddess's prophecy by the much less mystical means of seducing and then stealing Queen Helen of Sparta, he set in motion a sequence of events whose ripples reached the far waters of the Aegean. For the affronted Spartan King Menelaus appealed for help to his brother, Agamemnon of Mycenae (see page 55), who gathered together the military might of the Greek states to attack

62 THE GOOD RESORT GUIDE

RHODES

GREECE

...et of the Knights, Rhodes Town

...y. Of the 1,000 ships that took part in the
...edition, eight came from Rhodes, who
...ered with everyone else the strain of a ten-
...r war. The island became easy prey for
...cessive invaders, including the Dorians, the
...sians, the Romans, the Arabs and the Turks,
...o finally seized the island from the Knights
...t. John.

Rhodes Town
AGEAN SEA
Faliraki
Kamiros
Rhodes
Lindos
Lardos Bay
MEDITERRANEAN SEA

THE GOOD RESORT GUIDE 63

RHODES

RHODES TOWN

These successive sackings or occupations are reflected in the extraordinary contrast in styles in Rhodes Town's medieval city, though inevitably the Knights of St. John, who held the island for more than 200 years, have the greatest influence. They were responsible for the Palace of the Grand Masters, and the Hospital of the Knights, the first known example of a quarantined area, desperately necessary in an era of virulent plague for an army that could not find reinforcements. Today it contains many archeological treasures. In contrast, the Street of the Knights has a strong Turkish flavour, full of little shops that never seem to close and a noisy Turkish bazaar. Rhodes, incidentally, must be one of the very few places in Greece where you can indulge in a genuine Turkish bath. Some of the best Rhodean dishes are truly Turkish, such as the spiced version of dolmades, vine leaves stuffed with mincemeat and rice; and tzatziki, a dip of yoghurt and cucumber laced with garlic. The narrow cobbled streets house the best restaurants, and the walls of the fortress come alive in a nightly son et lumiere. Forty feet

Harbour at Rhodes Town

RHODES

thick in places, they must have seemed quite impregnable to those forces of puny ships that bombarded them without success.

Beyond the medieval walls, the Turkish influence is most noticeable around Mandraki Harbour, where the locals have reduced lethargy to a refined art, watching the sun come up or down as the case may be in little Turkish coffee houses that would not be out of place in Ankara or Istanbul. Popular mythology would have us believe that the ships entering Mandraki Harbour passed between the straddled legs of the Colossus of Rhodes, the huge bronze statue numbered among the seven wonders of the ancient world. The fact is that the ground there could never have held its weight, so its exact location remains a mystery. Built around 300 B.C. by a sculptor from Lindos, it stood more than 100 ft. high and cost a fortune. Sixty years later it broke off at the knees in an earthquake and was left where it fell. When the Arabs sacked Rhodes in the seventh century, an enterprising Jewish merchant from Syria arrived with ships and camels and carried it away into oblivion.

Outside the medieval walls of Rhodes Town, pleasant avenues lined with trees run down to the headland in the north of the island, as thick with hotels as they are with foliage. Indeed the number of hotels is extraordinary when one considers the severe shortage of good beaches. West of the headland, the rocky beach can be battered by winds, welcome in extreme heat but often too strong to be comfortable. To the east, there is less wind and more sand, but this beach, too, slopes steeply and is not really suitable for small children. The other concentration of hotels is three miles out of Rhodes Town on the western coast, yet even here the beach consists of a thin ribbon of shingle.

Some of these hotels also suffer from traffic noise, as the main airport road runs close by. Transfer time to Rhodes airport: 25 minutes.

Excursions

Although car hire is far from cheap on Rhodes, the use of a car can transform your stay. For example, once past Lindos, where the coast road virtually dissolves into dust, a small sign post to Gennadion marks the beginning of a rewarding trip to the deserted sandy coves beyond Lardos Bay. Without a car, this trip would be impossible. Though not impossible, merely difficult, a trip to see the ancient ruins

Palace of the Grand Masters, Rhodes Town

of Kamiros, abandoned around the time of Christ and never rebuilt, is much easier by car. So is the trip inland to see Petaloudes, the valley of the butterflies, where hundreds of thousands can be seen in July, August and September. Indeed the interior of Rhodes offers superb scenery, but do not expect the AA patrolman to arrive if something goes wrong with the car.

RHODES TOWN HOTELS

Astir Palace ★★★★ a hotel of faded grandeur, though far from free of traffic noise, as its location is across the busy sea-front road from the western beach of the town. The gardens, however, are secluded, and guests have a choice of three swimming-pools, one indoor. The hotel has a Greek restaurant, a night-club, disco, English pub and a casino. 377 rooms on five floors (6 lifts).

Rodos Palace ★★★★★ at Ixia, some three miles from Rhodes Town, separated by the traffic from an uninspiring beach of shingle, though there is a tunnel under the street. However most guests will be content to use its enormous swimming pool covered by a spectacular translucent roof, which makes the weather outside irrelevant. The hotel also has another large outdoor pool, a children's pool, playground and multi-purpose cinema, night-

THE GOOD RESORT GUIDE

GREECE

RHODES

St Paul's Bay, Lindos

Lindos

club and disco. 587 rooms on 18 floors; some bungalows offering self-catering for families.

Metropolitan Capsis ★★ another three-mile trip out of the capital to Ixia, a hotel divided into three wings and still separated from its shingle beach by considerable traffic. The outdoor and indoor pools are a little small. Children's playground and, particularly useful, a supervised nursery. Roof garden with bar and disco. 650 rooms on eleven floors, and some self-catering apartments.

Lomeniz ★★ built at an angle to one of the best beaches, two miles from Rhodes Town. Lively taverna, disco. Swimming pool too small for the number of guests. Poor entertainments programme. 210 rooms on four floors; do not expect a proper sea view.

THE GOOD RESORT GUIDE

RHODES

Mediterranean ★★★ overlooking the eastern beach of Rhodes Town, but access is by a tunnel under a busy main road. Extremely convenient location for the sights and shops. Not, however, suitable for children. 154 bedrooms on seven floors.

OTHER RESORTS

LINDOS

Chares, architect of the ill-fated Colossus of Rhodes, came from here; the apostle Paul is reliably thought to have dined here on an overnight anchorage in A.D. 51 on his way to Syria. It is difficult to imagine a greater contrast between the simple fishing village he found and today's over-rated and over-priced concentration of tourism.

A great pity, of course, because the site is marvellous: an exquisite bay along the east coast 35 miles from the capital. Unfortunately the rows of little Lego houses hide an artificial atmosphere of bacon and egg breakfasts, noisy discos that keep visitors awake, and immense crowds during summer. Some of them may like the coarse sand beach, which provides windsurfing, waterskiing and sailing in the bay; but by two o'clock, it is like Blackpool in the sun. Transfer time: 1¼ hours.

FALIRAKI

Dull village but a resort of high quality hotels, well spaced out alongside a beach of rather grey coarse sand, which slopes gradually into the sea. Jetskis is the fashionable sport here. However with Rhodes town only 13 miles away along the northern coast, many visitors take the bus into the capital in search of night life. Transfer time from Rhodes airport: 45 minutes.

Acropolis at Lindos

Sailing at Faliraki

THE GOOD RESORT GUIDE 67

RHODES/CORFU

RHODES FACTS

Your journey	Hours
From Gatwick, Luton	4
From Birmingham, Cardiff, East Midlands	4¼
From Manchester, Newcastle	4½

Rhodes airport is nine miles south of the capital.

Shopping
Most shops open 0800 to 1330 and 1700 to 2100, longer in the major resorts.

Money matters
Banks open 0800 to 1330 or 1400, Monday to Saturday. In Rhodes Town a few banks also open from 1700 to 2000 for currency exchange purposes only, and for a few hours on Sunday morning.

Banks are closed on January 1, January 6, March 25, Good Friday, Easter Monday, May 1, June 11, August 15, October 28, December 25, December 26.

Large hotels will exchange travellers cheques but at a lower rate than the Banks.

Weather

Averages	Jan	Feb	Mar	Apr	May	Jun	Jul	Aug	Sep	Oct	Nov	Dec
Temperature	54	54	55	63	70	77	81	82	78	68	61	55
Sun hours	4	5	7	8	10	14	14	13	11	8	5	4
Rain days	15	10	8	4	4	1	0	0	1	6	8	13
Sea temp.	59	57	59	63	66	72	75	77	75	73	66	61

Rhodes has long periods of sustained sunshine between May and September, with rain almost unheard of in July and August. Temperatures away from the sea can be uncomfortably hot in midsummer. However, the island is quite cold and wet in winter.

Local transport
Buses are cheap and reliable, but getting a seat on one around 1330, when the shops close, can be chaotic, as the concept of queueing seems unknown in Rhodes. Hire cars are expensive.

Duty free
Spirits and cigarettes are cheaper in local supermarkets than in the duty-free shop at Rhodes Airport.

CORFU

Closer to western Europe than any other part of Greece, Corfu has been successively occupied by the Venetians, the French and the British, absorbing, by the very nature of things, a little of the best and the worst their conquerors had to offer. Unkind Athenians have been known to observe that the Corfiots possess the trustworthiness of Venetians, the sea legs of the French and the dress sense of the British. However such malice cannot disguise the fact that when it comes to tourism, Corfu has cleaned up in a way that the traditional Mediterranean holiday areas of Spain and Italy would never have dreamt

Corfu Town

THE GOOD RESORT GUIDE

CORFU

possible, helped by a decision of the Greek government to allow more charter flights direct to Corfu from regional British airports, instead of forcing them to change aircraft in Athens.

There are, of course, other reasons, notably the lush, green landscape and the clear warm water that make Corfu so inviting.

Paleokastritsa

THE GOOD RESORT GUIDE 69

CORFU

In summer, few can resist the invitation, so the tourists seem as numerous as the olive trees, particularly the young. They arrive on the cheapest charter, sleep on the beach or in sparse accommodation, drink a lot of rough cheap wine, and dash about the island on scooters while skimping on the insurance.

Only by renting an up-market villa or hiring a boat and mooring in deserted coves is it possible to escape the hurly-burly of high season. Touring the island by car is to risk frustration, for although Corfu is only 40 miles long and at most 18 miles wide, its road system would have driven Roman engineers to distraction. Finding any straight stretch is an achievement, and as for maintenance, it ended with British rule in the last century.

Excursions

An expedition in search of an exceptional sandy beach is the most common, almost the only, excursion on Corfu. Sorties on the eastern coast, which rather disconcertingly has most of the large hotels, are doomed to failure, as the beaches here are largely rock and pebbles. In the north and west, some of the superior beaches are attached to attractive resorts and invariably crowded, such as at Sidari and Paleokastritsa. However from Paleokastritsa motor boats take trippers north on the 40 mins. run to St. George's beach, a vast expanse of sand in a broad and sometimes windy bay, with little tavernas beckoning by the shore. Confusingly, but so very Greek, there is another St. George's beach further down the

Beach at Paleokastritsa

CORFU

west coast. Although villas and restaurants are beginning to spring up, it is still relatively unspoilt, a huge expanse of sand running into sand dunes behind the beach; its main disadvantage is the complete lack of shade. Just to the north, Glyfada, in no way to be confused with the awful resort on the Athens airport flight path (see page 55), has all the trappings of progress if not of civilisation: a tarmac road, a big hotel, restaurants, every conceivable water sport. About ten miles directly across the island from Corfu Town, it receives a huge influx of visitors on a day's outing. However the beach is superb and the water extremely shallow and ideal for small children. Only one beach beats it: Mirtiotissa, a little further north, sand, surf and scenery; alas, no longer solitude.

CORFU HOTELS

Miramare Beach ★★★★ a hotel in delightful grounds close to Moraitika village, exclusive water sports on its own beach, albeit shingle and rather narrow. Impressive restaurant and some excellent competition from local tavernas. Hotel bus to Corfu Town. 150 rooms, mainly in bungalows.

Corcyra Beach ★★★ close to the centre of Gouvia village, built amidst vast groves of olive trees, and close to a beach whose sand has been added subsequently and rather obviously by bulldozer. Vast amenities including two swimming pools, one for children, riding, squash and tennis. Disco; children's playground. 256 rooms, many in bungalows; ask for a room at the back with a sea view.

San Stefano ★★★ near, but not really at, Benitses, which is a 20 min. walk down a steep hill, and a good deal more coming back. The hillside views from the hotel, especially its restaurant, are impressive; its shingle beach, linked by shuttle bus, much less so. Swimming pool, children's pool, playground, daytime bus into Corfu Town. 292 rooms on five floors (2 lifts).

Paleokastritsa ★★ in the resort of that name. Most guests fail to pronounce it, never mind spell it, in under a fortnight, and the impact of the superb views begin to wear a little thin under the strain of the long steps to the main road and even longer flight to the beach. Cramped swimming pool and terrace; not much night life. 150 rooms on five floors.

Aphrodite ★ in the centre of Sidari, a small unpretentious hotel with bar and terrace backing on to the beach. Wide variety of water sports; good choice of food; lively disco in the evenings. 30 rooms; all have a shower but only a few have a good sea view.

Harbour Bar ★ in Kassiopi, not surprisingly, overlooks the harbour and the fishing fleet, though the beach is 10 mins. away. Evening bar-disco. No cooked meals but the owner runs the nearby Kyros Tavern where guests can eat at a discount. 20 rooms, all with shower.

RESORTS

BENITSES

Anyone coming here just for the beach would be disappointed, as it is largely shingle. However there are abundant water activities, including scuba-diving, and at night Benitses comes alive. Patronised by the youngsters who come the seven miles from Corfu Town, it has more than 40 bars, some of them plausible discos, on the coast road. The most popular is Spiros, right on the beach, though the Achillion Casino is just under two miles away. The local

Corfu fishing boats

tavernas are brilliant at bangers and mash but seem at a loss when you ask for moussaka. Transfer time from Corfu airport: 20 minutes.

THE GOOD RESORT GUIDE 71

CORFU

CANONI
On the flight path from Corfu Airport, a paradise for acquatic plane-spotters, as some of the hotels have swimming pools actually overlooking the runway. Plan to go on excursions on Mondays and Saturdays, when the flights reach their peak. This once beautiful headland 3 miles south of Corfu Town has been disfigured by monstrous high-rise hotels and apartment blocks. Not recommended. Transfer time: 10 minutes from Corfu airport.

GOUVIA
A crowded, over-congested resort six miles north of Corfu Town with a safe, if frequently crowded beach of sand and shingle. Splendid scenery of pine trees and olive groves; energetic water sports; two dynamic discos. Transfer time from Corfu airport: 35 minutes.

KASSIOPI
On the north-east coast, a little fishing village with a bustling harbour and a flourishing night life. The nearest beaches, however, are rather small and difficult to get to. Mainly self-catering accommodation. Transfer time from Corfu airport: 1 hour 15 minutes.

MORAITIKA/MESSONGHI
The village of Moraitika is distant from the beach, which has not hindered the development of tavernas and discos. The beach, a mixture of sand and shingle, is wider at the Moraitika end. Corfu Town is 13 miles to

Beach at Kassiopi   Inset: Kassiopi harbour

THE GOOD RESORT GUIDE

CORFU

the south. Transfer time to Corfu airport: 40 minutes.

PALEOKASTRITSA
On the west coast, a lovely combination of bays and beaches, with hotels and restaurants strung out along the winding approach road to the sea. The name means 'old castle', which still exists, a silent reminder of little wars gone by. The scuba diving here, in exceptionally clear water, rivals the best on the island. Transfer time from Corfu airport: 45 minutes.

SIDARI
A single street of unsophisticated but nevertheless charming hotels and restaurants, behind a beach, shingle but some sand, that slopes gently into the sea. What may suit families with young children may not be ideal for couples looking for bright lights after dark, as this northernmost resort has little night life. Transfer time from Corfu airport: 1¼ hours in summer.

Paleokastritsa bay

CORFU FACTS

Your journey

	Hours
From Gatwick, Luton, Stansted	3¼
From Bristol, Birmingham, Cardiff, East Midlands	3½
From Leeds, Manchester, Newcastle	3¾
From Belfast, Glasgow	4

Kerkyra airport is one mile from Corfu Town.

Shopping
Most shops open 0800 to 1300, and again from 1700 to 2000, though it varies from resort to resort.

Money matters
The only banks are in Corfu Town. They open 0830 to 1400, Monday to Saturday; closed Sundays. Most hotels will change travellers cheques and sterling but at a much poorer rate.

Weather

Averages	Jan	Feb	Mar	Apr	May	Jun	Jul	Aug	Sep	Oct	Nov	Dec
Temperature	50	50	54	59	66	75	81	79	73	66	59	54
Sun hours	5	6	7	7	9	10	11	12	9	6	4	3
Rain days	13	9	8	6	4	2	1	2	4	10	12	17
Sea temp.	59	59	59	61	64	70	75	78	75	70	66	64

Corfu is the wettest part of Greece, especially during the winter months. However in the summer it also rivals the driest and the hottest, and has the warmest sea. Temperatures drop sharply after dark.

Local transport
The bus service on Corfu, with a network centred on Corfu Town, is cheap and reliable except in outlying areas. In the summer a huge number of ticket inspectors are employed to discourage fare evasion.

THE GOOD RESORT GUIDE 73

YUGOSLAVIA

Dalmatian Riviera	76
Istrian Riviera	80

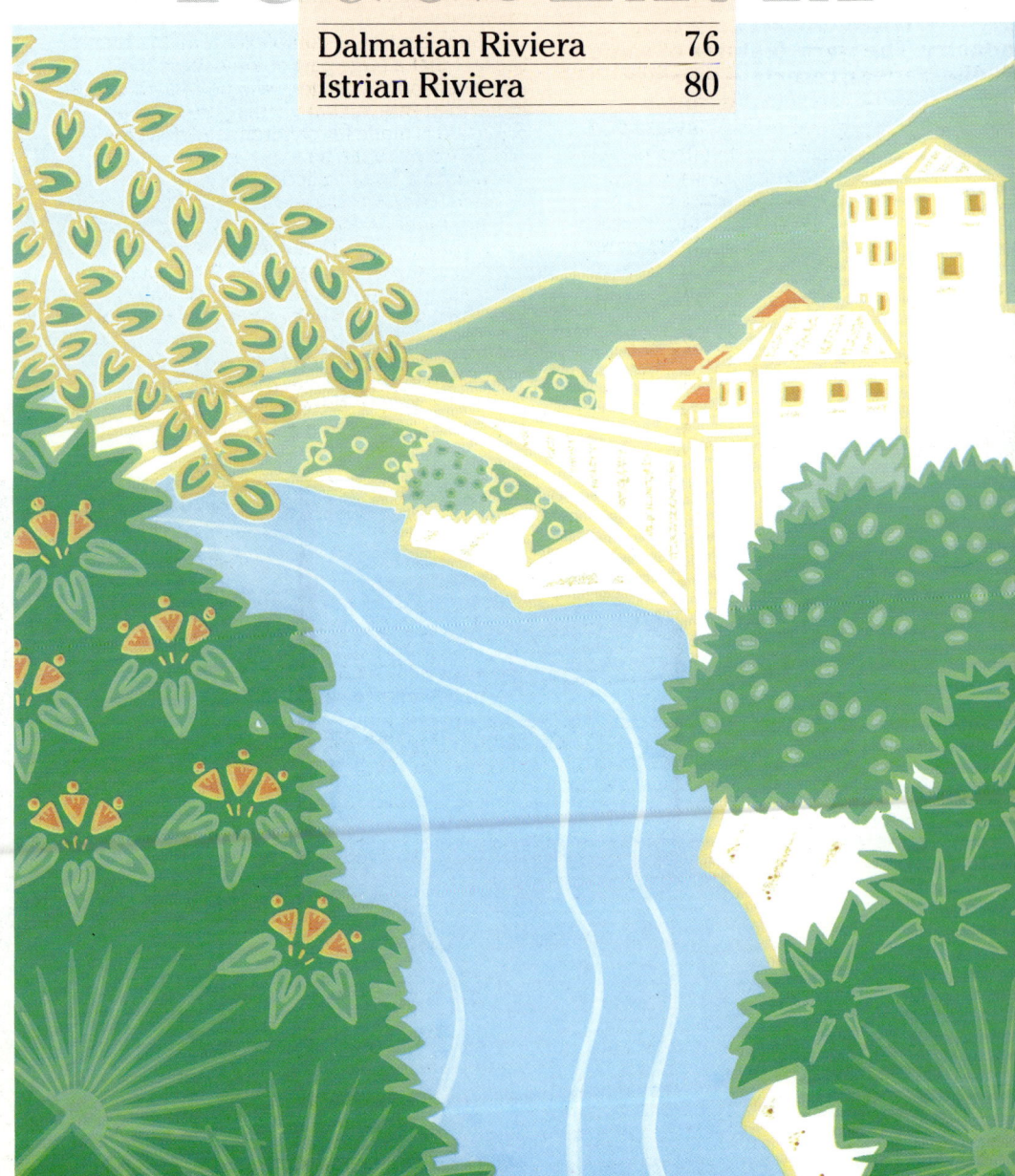

74 THE GOOD RESORT GUIDE

YUGOSLAVIA

Possibly by design, but more plausibly by accident, Yugoslavia has outflanked the full might of the package tour industry. The worst features of some Mediterranean resorts — massive, high-rise concrete development, leaving the original village swamped and stranded like some forgotten film lot; and the sea-front of stunning artificiality where visitors can take a stroll and at the same time take in a hefty dose of carbon monoxide from the continuous coastal traffic — simply do not exist here. Promenades are rare and the sea road, more often than not, is an unmade track where even the determined motorist has to crawl in low gear between groups of carefree holidaymakers. Most of the bigger hotels have been built outside towns, leaving the resort's original architecture and atmosphere more or less untouched. As they do not compete for custom, many of these hotels have formed themselves into a group, offering common water sports or night life or both. These self-contained holiday centres sometimes spread over several miles.

Such centres or complexes tend to obscure the fact that a large part of Yugoslavia has extremely poor beaches, with no sand to speak of north of Budva; that virtually no special provision is made for children; and that the sophisticated night life which is taken for granted on a Spanish holiday is almost non-existent. However the sea is warm, the scenery can be stunning, and hardly anyone spending a fortnight here returns home exhausted and in need of another holiday. While the food is generally uninspiring, the value for money is formidable. Yugoslavia's rather curious position in political limbo, belonging neither to east nor west, has left her currency struggling for survival on the foreign exchange markets; heavy inflation is almost entirely counterbalanced by an increasingly favourable exchange rate.

Budva, coastal view

THE GOOD RESORT GUIDE 75

DALMATIAN RIVIERA

DALMATIAN RIVIERA

Dalmatia is not a kingdom but a geographical expression, describing the coast of Yugoslavia running from the island of Pag, north of Split, to the bottom of Kotor Bay, below Dubrovnik. The further south you travel, the more quickly the fertile strip narrows. Everywhere it is backed by forbidding mountains that in some parts race straight into the sea, honeycombed with islands and rocky coves lapped by warm, almost tideless waters. The only true Dalmatians were pirates, who preyed on passing ships from these secure havens, until they were put down by the Venetians in the great days of the Maritime Republic.

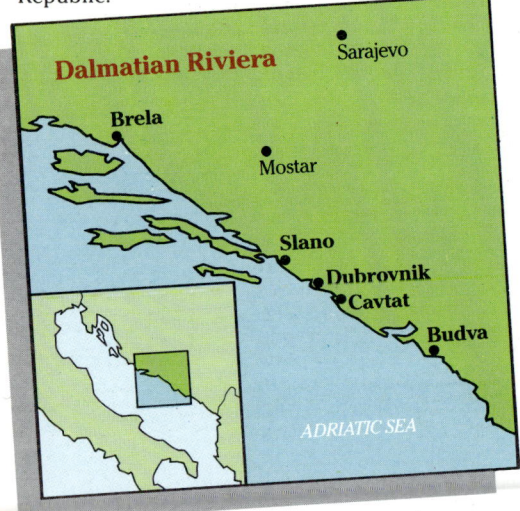

Dubrovnik

DUBROVNIK

Dubrovnik stands like a medieval colossus on a peninsula jutting out defiantly into the waters of the Adriatic. Its walls once echoed to the sound of armour and gunpowder, repulsing every army and navy before Napoleon; now they play host daily to the excited chatter of tourists from a dozen countries. The sun is barely up before visitors file in crocodile fashion on a demanding circuit of the ramparts, which becomes ever more demanding in the heat of the afternoon. Beneath them the red tiled roofs of Dubrovnik's grand houses, some of them incongruously carrying a television aerial, are a further testimony to past glories.

Wisely, Dubrovnik takes no chances with vibration and pollution. All vehicles must turn back at the Pile Gate, from where the Placa, Dubrovnik's widest and longest street, runs into Luza Square, which has more pigeons than London's Trafalgar. It is also the centre of the principal tourist attractions, which include the Sponza Palace, the Rector's Palace, the Church of St. Blaise and the Cathedral.

Much less impressive, but rather more intriguing, the claustrophobic streets north of the Palace wind sharply upwards, making the visitor glad to take refreshment in any one of a score of cafes and bars. For more serious eating, sample the fine fish restaurants of Prijeko Street, where strolling musicians serenade the tables for a bob or two, like

76 THE GOOD RESORT GUIDE

DALMATIAN RIVIERA

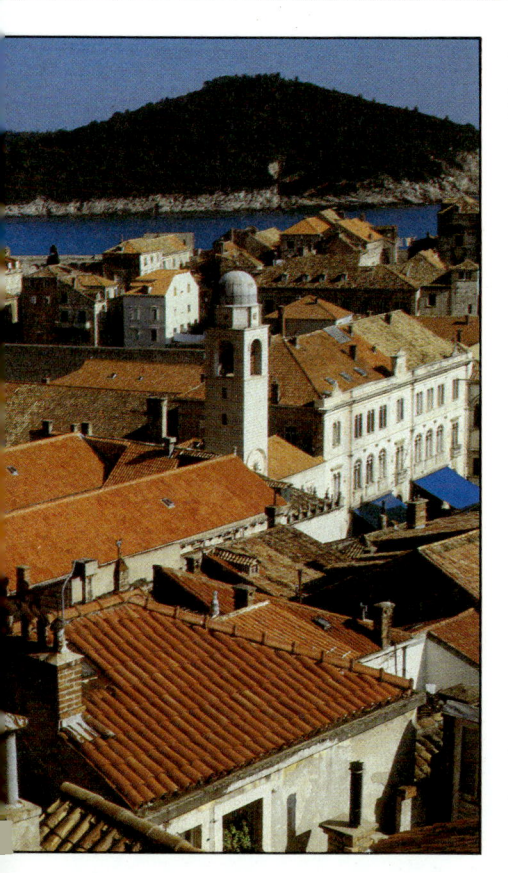

...exican mariachis. Where Pile Gate has a car ...ark and expects visitors, Ploce Gate, on the ...ther side of the city, does not, perhaps ...ecause of its proximity to a quiet residential ...rea where visitors are tolerated rather than ...ncouraged.

Ploce is also close to Dubrovnik's solitary ...each, though solitude is too much to hope for ...ere. In summer, it is hard to find a square yard ...f free space, despite the fact that you have to ...ay to go on, there is scarcely any sand, it has a ...evere slope and is frankly rather dirty. For a ...ally good beach, the only solution is to go by ...oat to one of the nearby islands. Lopud, an ...our away, has a lovely bay and coarse sandy ...eaches; Kolocep, half an hour by boat, has ...nd around the edge of the harbour; and ...okrum, a similar journey, has a unique salt ...ke in its centre, ideal for water sports.

For those who prefer to tough it out on the mainland, the Lapad Peninsula is the most promising, provided you escape from the principal, shingle beach, packed with humanity in high season.

Contrary perhaps to expectations, Dubrovnik does not have a flourishing night life. Most of the discos are improvised bars, and close early by Mediterranean standards. Only the suburb of Babin Kuk, on the northern coast of the peninsula, shows much sign of taking its nocturnal activities seriously. Transfer time: 30 minutes from Dubrovnik airport.

Excursions

The most interesting of the islands close to Dubrovnik, Mljet, is a national park with a huge pine forest and two unusual saltwater lakes in its centre. Its Benedictine Abbey has been turned into a hotel which, in case you are wondering, does serve alcohol, and an overnight stay after most of the tourists have left adds enormously to the trip.

By coach, the old bridge at Mostar, the Turkish word for 'bridgekeeper', is hugely popular, a wonderfully evocative sight spanning the Neretva River with a backcloth of mosques and mountains. Young boys still dive for tourists' coins from the top, a risky activity in the spring when the river is at its fiercest. Indeed, so fast and furious was the Neretva, that the Turkish architect responsible for its design in 1566, Harjruddin, doubted his bridge would survive. The previous bridge had collapsed, to the great fury of the Sultan, who executed its architect on the spot. Harjruddin finally was compelled to remove the wooden structure supporting the great arch, and rather than wait to face the Sultan, he went to the nearest cemetery, dug his own grave and waited for death. The bridge survived . . . and is still intact.

The longest, and most interesting trip, however, must be to Sarajevo, nowadays a large modern city whose old quarter runs alongside another river, the Miljaka. At one point it is spanned by the Princip Bridge, named after Gavrilo Princip, a revolutionary student determined to free Bosnia from the Austro-Hungarian Empire. After a series of bungles that would have been hilarious in any other context, he shot and killed the Austrian Archduke Ferdinand on June 28, 1914, setting in motion the chain of events that led, by August, to the First World War. A museum

YUGOSLAVIA

THE GOOD RESORT GUIDE 77

DALMATIAN RIVIERA

nearby depicts the momentous event and two footprints set in the paving stones mark the spot where Princip fired the most fatal bullet in modern history.

DUBROVNIK HOTELS

President★★★★ on the Lapad peninsula four miles from the city, part of the development known as Dubrava in the suburb of Babin Kuk. Interesting architecture, a series of stepped floors on an incline that runs eventually to a private beach of, unfortunately, not sand but shingle. However the huge indoor (salt water) swimming pool is considerable compensation. Plenty to do in the hotel, which has an exciting disco and live music nightly. 163 rooms: most of them have large balconies with a view of the sea. Seven floors (2 lifts).

Belvedere★★★ a mile and a half from Dubrovnik, cleverly constructed on a rocky hillside. The restaurant has a superb view of the city. Two swimming pools, the bigger one indoors, and a path down to a rocky beach with slightly over-organised water sports. Night club and disco in the hotel. 210 rooms, each air-conditioned, on 16 floors (4 lifts).

Argentina★★★ near Ploce Gate on the south side of Dubrovnik, set in charming terraced gardens leading to a man-made beach. Tends rather to rest on its laurels and assume the guests will be out a lot. However the open-air, vine-covered restaurant has a wonderful atmosphere. 155 rooms on six floors (4 lifts).

Excelsior★★★ superb position, a short stroll from the city walls and close to Ploce Beach. The better rooms overlook the sea and the hotel's private bathing platform below. Disco. 209 rooms, on nine floors (2 lifts).

Imperial★★★ elegant, 19th century mansion with a spectacular terrace set in lovely gardens on the north-western edge of the city. Its main disadvantage is the lack of a proper beach as the nearest are rocky and the hotel does not have a swimming pool. Dancing to live music all summer; Dubrovnik casino opposite, and tempting. 140 rooms on four floors (2 lifts).

OTHER RESORTS

BECICI/BUDVA

The old Budva is a ghost town, abandoned

Open air fruit and vegetable market

78 THE GOOD RESORT GUIDE

DALMATIAN RIVIERA

oon after it was wrecked by an earthquake in 1979. Guides can be found who will take you here, past the red warning signs, but be under o illusion: it is more than a little dangerous nd eerie in the extreme. The re-born Budva as no medieval walls, but some excellent eaches, though not as good as Becici, just round the bay. In Becici, guests hoping for ight life outside the hotels will be sorely isappointed. Transfer time from Dubrovnik irport: 2 hours.

BRELA

n extremely quiet and secluded resort south f Split, backed by the Biokovo mountains, vith pine trees brushing the brilliant white hingle beach. Be prepared to go to bed early. ransfer times: 1¼ hours from Split, but a ormidable 3¼ hours from Dubrovnik Airport.

CAVTAT

ively resort popular with young people, who ance till dawn along the harbour front. The each is narrow and rocky, but the water sports eem unaffected. However the whole peninsula hakes when aircraft pass by directly overhead, n their way to or from Dubrovnik Airport, hich is only five miles away. Transfer time: 5 minutes.

LANO

 quiet village in a sheltered bay 28 miles orth of Dubrovnik, where only the vigorous narket every Thursday relieves the monotony. lenty of water sports off the broad pebble each, but nothing to do after dark. There is a

Beach at Brela

bus to Dubrovnik, but it takes too long to get there. Transfer time from Dubrovnik Airport: 1½ hours.

DALMATIAN RIVIERA FACTS

Your journey
To Dubrovnik

	Hours
From Birmingham, East Midlands, Gatwick, Luton, Heathrow	2
From Manchester, Newcastle	3
From Bristol, Edinburgh, Glasgow	3¼

Dubrovnik airport is 13 miles south of the city. Flights to Split airport are usually 15 minutes horter.

Shopping

xcept for large department stores, in the outh of Yugoslavia shops have an afternoon esta, opening 0700-1200 and again from 1700 o 2000.

Mostar

YUGOSLAVIA

THE GOOD RESORT GUIDE 79

DALMATIAN/ISTRIAN RIVIERA

Money matters

In the main resort, banks open 0700 and may not close until 1900; though some shut at 1130 in the morning for an early lunch. All the banks are closed on January 1, January 2, May 1, May 2, July 4, July 22, November 29, November 30.

Only 5,000 dinars can be taken into Yugoslavia, which British banks will supply at a few days' notice; worthwhile, because the exchange rate is usually better outside the country. However, only 5,000 dinars can also be taken out of the country, and as the return exchange rate in the UK is poor, change into Yugoslav currency the minimum you need and keep currency receipts carefully. In Yugoslavia tourist offices, post offices and major department stores offer the same exchange rate as banks. Credit cards are becoming increasingly accepted in northern Yugoslavia.

Tourists are encouraged to transfer their UK travellers cheques into Dinar Cheques, which provide a ten per cent discount at many hotels, restaurants, travel agencies and shops. However, smaller establishments sometimes refuse to accept them, and they are practically worthless out Yugoslavia.

Weather

Averages	Jan	Feb	Mar	Apr	May	Jun	Jul	Aug	Sep	Oct	Nov	Dec
Temperature	54	55	57	63	70	77	84	82	77	70	63	57
Sun hours	4	5	5	6	8	10	12	11	9	7	4	3
Rain days	9	9	11	10	10	6	4	3	7	11	11	12
Sea temp.	55	53	53	55	66	70	75	75	71	68	63	58

Dubrovnik has more than 2,500 hours of sunshine annually, among the best in Europe, although the coast immediately to the north is slightly sunnier. Cloud and rain increase significantly in the spring and autumn.

Local transport

Cars are not allowed to enter Dubrovnik, but in spite of that, there is no rail connection. Ferries to all parts of the Adriatic leave from the port of Cruz, slightly over a mile from the old city, just past the bus station.

Duty-free

The duty-free shops at Dubrovnik airport accept only hard western currency.

ISTRIAN RIVIERA

Istria is a little corner of European history, a kind of perpetual garrison town across the centuries, a focal point of commerce and conflict.

POREC

Porec, the principal resort, has symmetrical streets whose paving stones were laid by slaves under the command of Roman soldiers. The modern garrison is only slightly less regimented, anything up to 35,000 tourists in any given summer week, including almost 800

80 THE GOOD RESORT GUIDE

ISTRIAN RIVIERA

Plava Laguna   Inset: Porec, old town

at the Delfin Hotel near Zelena Laguna, the Green Lagoon, an artificial pleasure complex just outside the town. The Delfin has its own way of keeping visitors fit: the lift does not go to the fourth, fifth and sixth floors. The nearby beach is pebble, typical of this stretch of shoreline, where the alternative is one of many concrete bathing platforms. At nearby Kurversada is the largest naturalist camp in Europe, so it can confidently be said that this rocky coast grazes the parts that other beaches rarely reach. The Zelena Zaguna sports centre is equally huge, providing facilities for cycling, golf, riding and tennis; or, for the less energetic, bowls and fishing.

Plava Laguna, the Blue Lagoon, a little closer to Porec, is perhaps superior for sailing or power-boating. The wooded scenery may also be superior, but definitely not the beaches. For night life, try the Zelena Laguna international club, but do not expect to be up all hours. Like many Yugoslav night clubs, it will probably close up at 12.30am, and faster than the landlord at a country pub. The authorities may approve of bare bottoms on the beach but not of late night revelry.

THE GOOD RESORT GUIDE 81

YUGOSLAVIA

ISTRIAN RIVIERA

YUGOSLAVIA

The transport system, too, operates an unofficial curfew, as the bus service from either of the two big complexes, which runs frequently during the day, stops soon after dark. Taxis are difficult to find, even at the airport near Pula, once the largest port in the Austro-Hungarian Empire. Transfer time: 1¼ hours.

Excursions
Pula, said to have been founded by the deserters from a crew sent in pursuit of Jason and the Argonauts, had its heyday in Roman times. Huge battles were staged in the arena, which is the sixth largest surviving Roman amphitheatre and one of the best preserved. Visitors to Piran, just north of the resort of Portoroz, can scarcely believe their eyes if they arrive by sea: the harbour is a superb imitation of Venice. The Venetian influence is also apparent at Rovinj, another seaside town well worth a visit (see resorts).

North-east of Trieste, a favourite diversion for some Italian pasta, the limestone Postojna Caves are one of the great natural marvels of Europe. They extend some 13 miles, of which three miles are open to the public, the first by underground railway, the second and third on foot. They are cold and damp, but astonishingly beautiful. Much further south, 50 miles inland from Senj, the fulcrum of one of the most dangerous coastal roads in Europe, more caves wind in and out of the Plitvice Lakes, 16 in all linked by a succession of cascading waterfalls; the biggest lake even has a ferry, but a lot of walking is unavoidable.

POREC HOTELS

Parentium★★★ in the Green Lagoon complex, built on a small peninsula with splendid views. Pebble beach and a small harbour close by, both good for water sports. Swimming pool, disco, and, under the main hotel, a casino. 320 rooms on seven floors.

Pical★★★ about half an hour's walk from Porec, for those who miss the last bus. However the hotel is largely self-contained, set on a headland close to a series of bathing platforms. Three swimming pools, including one for children, who also have a playground and a nursery. Considering the category, guests may be surprised to find that they have to pay to go in the disco. 250 rooms on six floors; unusually

Roman amphitheatre at Pula

for Yugoslavia, each room has a bath.

Galijot★★ built on a wooded headland in the Blue Lagoon complex, distinctive, rather grand, Spanish architecture. Exceptional location, with water on three sides and a rocky beach directly below. Swimming pool and extensive water sports facilities. Frequent bus service takes 40 miniutes to reach Porec. 71 rooms on three floors.

Materada★★ isolated hotel north of Porec, overlooking its own pebble beach. Large salt-water swimming pool, not served by the lifts (nor is the restaurant). Particularly suitable for

82 THE GOOD RESORT GUIDE

ISTRIAN RIVIERA

Lake Bled

1 hour from Ljubljana airport.

MEDULIN
Disappointing beach, grey, rocky and curiously crowded in summer, but an apparently infinite variety of water sports including an awe-inspiring water slide. Six miles south of Pula, the village night life takes place around a charming square. Transfer time from Pula airport: 30 minutes.

OPATIJA
Yugosalvia's answer to the French Riviera, a gracious and sophisticated resort in the north-east corner of the Istrian peninsula. It may not quite live up to the time before the First World War when the lovely ladies of the Viennese Court committed adultery by the sea, but it tries hard after dark with some lively night clubs and a casino. Admission charge for (artificial) sandy beaches, except where they are owned by the hotels and reserved for guests. Noisy main road just behind. Transfer times: 2 hours from Pula, 1¼ hours from Krk airport.

children, who are provided with their own pool and special meals. Live music during the summer.

OTHER RESORTS

BLED
A spectacular lake location 30 miles north-west of Ljubljana, Bled is entirely surrounded by the Slovenian mountains. Above the lake, a historic castle stands perched on a cliff; on the lake itself, a tiny island with an even smaller shrine. The high quality of the hotels is unfortunately marred by the daily arrival of dozens of organised tours. Little night life. Transfer time:

YUGOSLAVIA

THE GOOD RESORT GUIDE 83

ISTRIAN RIVIERA

Rovinj, waterfront

Rovinj

PORTOROZ
Unlike most Yugoslav resorts, this sophisticated town near the northern point of the peninsula has an impressive promenade overlooked by the best hotels. The image, unfortunately, is rather marred by an artificial beach where transported sand sits unconvincingly on top of a series of rocks. The central lido is far better for swimming. Many visitors from Italy and West Germany come here. Transfer time: 2 hours from Pula airport.

ROVINJ
Elegant Venetian houses, reminders of the great days of the Maritime Republic, dominate the narrow streets leading to a hilltop cathedral in this west coast resort. Unfortunately most of the hotels are a long way from the harbour and its lively quayside bars. Apart from hotel swimming pools, rock bathing only. A good centre for visiting the islands by way of the many ferries. Transfer time from Pula airport: 1 hour.

ISTRIAN RIVIERA FACTS

Your journey

To Pula	Hours
From Gatwick, Heathrow, Luton, Stansted	2¼
From Cardiff, Birmingham, Bristol, East Midlands, Exeter, Leeds, Manchester	2½
From Edinburgh, Glasgow, Liverpool, Newcastle, Teeside	2¾
From Belfast	3

Pula airport is four miles east of the town, but some slightly shorter flights go into Rijeka airport on the island of Krk, which is connected to the mainland by a causeway.

84 THE GOOD RESORT GUIDE

ISTRIAN RIVIERA

Shopping

In the Istrian peninsula, many shops advertise 'Non-stop', which does not mean that they stay open 24 hours, but at least for most of the day, usually from 0900 to 2000. The smaller the resort, the more likely you are to find shops open earlier, from 0800, and closing from 1200 to 1500 or even later.

Many goods whose availability is taken for granted in the UK, including recognised brands of camera film, sanitary supplies, razor blades, and real coffee are unobtainable; local substitutes are not recommended.

Money matters
(See also Dalmatian Riviera Facts)

Banks open 0800 to 1300 from Monday to Friday, except in the main resorts, where banks frequently stay open from 0700 until 1900 and also open on Saturday mornings. Most banks are closed on January 1, January 2, May 1, May 2, May 25, July 4, July 22, November 29, November 30.

The rate of exchange in travel agencies and hotels is identical to that in banks.

Opatya, coastal view

Weather

Averages	Jan	Feb	Mar	Apr	May	Jun	Jul	Aug	Sep	Oct	Nov	Dec
Temperature	47	47	52	59	66	73	77	79	73	64	55	50
Sun hours	6	6	6	7	8	9	11	10	8	6	6	6
Rain days	10	8	9	8	5	7	4	4	6	10	11	12
Sea temp.	52	48	50	55	63	70	73	75	73	66	61	55

The Adriatic coast has dry hot summers relieved by sea breezes, with a water temperature of more than 70 degrees between June and September. After September, however, the sea becomes much colder and the weather deteriorates rapidly into cloud and rain.

Local transport

Bus services are run by local communities and are cheap and reliable. However they can be crowded in summer, so try to buy a ticket in advance and reserve a seat. There is an extra charge for luggage carried in the hold.

Car hire is expensive, unless arranged in advance as part of a package tour. Petrol coupons are essential for tourists and are available from tourist offices and motoring organisations on production of a non-Yugoslavian passport.

YUGOSLAVIA

THE GOOD RESORT GUIDE 85

ITALY

Neapolitan Riviera	88
Adriatic Riviera	92
Venetian Riviera	97
Sardinia	99
Sicily	103

86 THE GOOD RESORT GUIDE

ITALY

It is perhaps presumptuous of the British to believe that Italian resorts cater for anyone other than Italians. Mainly because of the weakness of their currency abroad, most Italians take holidays at home, three out of every four somewhere at the seaside. Their tourist industry is built around small, family run hotels that welcome back the same customers every year; tiny, tireless trattorias that think nothing of providing 200 meals a day; and beaches where frenetic, sustained activity is the norm, where children run systematically riot with the blessings of their parents, where the concept of lying quietly in the sun is practically unheard of. Only in a few famous resorts on the Neapolitan and Adriatic coasts are the preferences of foreign tourists seriously taken into account, where the sheer weight of non-Italian visitors has finally won the day.

Except, that is, when it comes to bathing for free. Although the south of France is notable for its beach charges, the French are but amateurs compared with the Italians, who have turned the concept of squeezing the last lira out of visitors to a prodigiously fine art. Put simply, with the splendid exception of Lido di Jesolo (see page 97), virtually every worth-while beach around Italy's coast has been handed over (by whom, you may well ask?) to concessionaires, that is, individual businessmen who are supposed to keep the beach clear of rubbish and provide facilities — which they do, at a price, though only during the summer when it is financially worthwhile. In return, they are allowed to charge for umbrellas, deck-chairs, lilos, even little tables, and extra for using a changing cabin, renting a locker, taking a shower or using the loo. Unlike the south of France, where the major hotels often have a controlling interest in the beach across the road, and can therefore offer the facility to guests free of charge or at a reduced rate, Italian hotels invariably have no control over the concession and little influence on its prices. As a result, families can find themselves paying almost as much in hire charges for beach facilities as it would cost to buy them outright, adding a good ten per cent to the overall cost of their holiday.

If that were not bad enough, pollution has

Positano, coastal view

ITALY/NEAPOLITAN RIVIERA

now become a serious problem in the areas close to major ports, including Genoa and La Spezia, not far from the Italian Riviera; Naples and Salerno, in the Neapolitan Riviera; Taranto on the heel of Italy and Palermo in Sicily; Ancona and Venice on the Adriatic coast. This is not to suggest of course that the contamination extends for many miles beyond the port, only that resorts and beaches close to harbours and shipping lanes may be unpleasant for swimming.

Neapolitan Riviera

SORRENTO

Fortunately the Sorrento peninsula is far enough from Naples to escape this problem, although visitors who have done their homework appreciate that there are far better places for a beach holiday, and that the great attraction of Sorrento is the scenery. A series of volcanic eruptions over the centuries have ensured that the beaches here are covered in grey, lava-based deposits. As much of the coast consists of rocks running sheer into the sea, almost all the beaches are at best narrow strips of unattractive sand. As Sorrento is built on top of the cliffs, many of the leading hotels have tried to extend these bathing areas by constructing landing stages on the shore below. From here you can sail, go windsurfing or waterskiing, provided, that is, you wait patiently for the lift which is the only means of transport from the top. Swimming is discouraged by the presence of clinging and

Sorrento

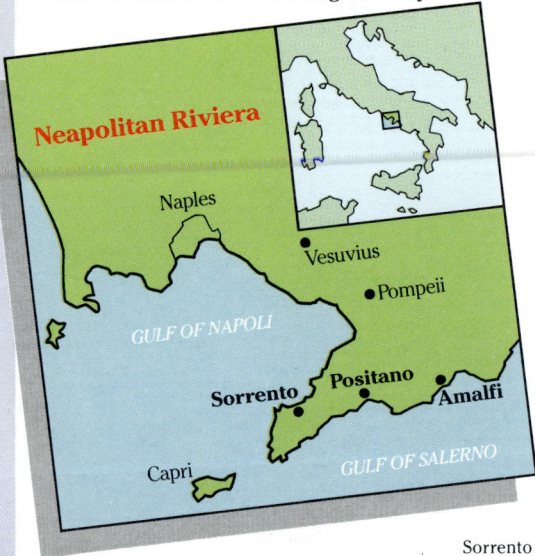

88 THE GOOD RESORT GUIDE

NEAPOLITAN RIVIERA

clammy wet seaweed, and in some parts is positively dangerous because of hidden underwater rocks. The one beach near Sorrento without these problems, Marina Grande, is overwhelmingly crowded and has occasional deposits of tar from the adjacent moorings of the local fishing fleet.

Sorrento itself is all on one level, at the end of a peninsula from where the views of Vesuvius and the Bay of Naples are stunning, especially at sunrise or sunset. Before darkness falls, visitor and resident alike will be out and about absorbing both the scenery and the slightly frenetic air of a town where almost everyone is in some way connected with the holiday business. Many come in their cars, stopping every few metres for a chat with the occupants of another vehicle, until the tiny streets are clogged with traffic. An hour or two later, the sound of hooting horns gives way to music in Sorrento's bars, never as exhuberant as in the bigger Spanish resorts, but popular with the international clientele.

Eating out is more unpredictable. Some restaurants now seem more at home with bangers and mash than with tagliatelle, though if you have supper in or around the Piazza Tasso, the proprietor will be serving traditional Italian fare, and be proud of it. One local speciality is Pizza Napoletana, a pizza with mushroom, tomato, cheese and anchovies. Another is mozzarella in carrozza, a local cream cheese fried and served as a kind of toasted sandwich. The sweets are tremendous, ranging from a dozen varieties of ice cream to sfogliatelle, a pastry cake with chocolate, jam and cream; and struffoli, a sort of doughnut fried in batter and dipped in honey. No one dares to count the calories.

Excursions

Boat trips abound from Sorrento harbour, especially to the neighbouring islands of Ischia and Capri. Ischia is the less crowded, Capri, despite the sheer number of visitors, has the greater cudos. However only by staying overnight can you appreciate its real charm.

The coast road from Sorrento to Amalfi, one of the selected resorts, is reminiscent of a corkscrew. The retaining walls have crumbled away in places, providing a superior, and even more alarming view of the rugged coastline below. Although the road was hewn out of solid rock, its was planned long before the problem arose of two luxury coaches meeting on a hairpin bend.

The only roads inside nearby Pompeii are ancient cobbles, with huge stepping stones above the mud and deep ruts for the passing chariots. When life stopped here abruptly in AD79, almost perfectly preserved under

NEAPOLITAN RIVIERA

ITALY

volcanic mud, its legacy was a corner of the Roman world, suspended completely in time. The volcano that removed Pompeii from the face of the earth, Vesuvius, still smoulders gently, like some slumbering giant. The walk around the rim of the crater is not for any tourist with the least suspicion of vertigo.

Coaches go further afield, to Naples and Rome. Naples is a city of huge contrasts: affluent restaurants and wretched slums; great scenery and even greater scandals. Rome, a really long day trip, is worthwhile only for people who know that they are unlikely to be back and for whom a glimpse of the Coliseum and the Forum is better than nothing. However, if Rome was not built in a day, logic suggests that visitors should also set a more realistic deadline.

Mt Vesuvius

Capri, harbour at Marina Grande

SORRENTO HOTELS

Ambasciatori ★ ★ ★ well back from the centre and the traffic noise, a hotel that prides itself on its service. The gardens and open air swimming pool are particularly attractive. Excellent service but an unsympathetic atmosphere for children. 103 rooms.

Bristol ★ ★ ★ its main lounge would not be out of place in a picture gallery, and the hotel is quiet and relaxed. The view from the seventh floor restaurant of the bay of Naples is truly spectacular. Swimming pool on the roof, disco in the basement. 130 rooms, many large enough for families.

Excelsior Vittoria ★ ★ ★ the best location in the resort, convenient for the shops, access to the beach below by private lift. A Grand Hotel in the grand manner, huge public rooms and an abundance of marble. Exceptional restaurant, stunning swimming pool. 192 rooms on 5 floors (2 lifts).

Palace ★ ★ ★ Believe it or not, six swimming pools on different levels, forming a continuous cascade from top to bottom. Thereafter the sense of style seems missing, for example, the sun terrace is huge, but visitors have to pay extra for a sun lounger. Many shops inside the hotel. 404 rooms on 7 floors (5 lifts).

Minerva ★ ★ you have to take a lift even to reach reception, as the hotel is high above a busy street 20 minutes from the centre. However the hotel, owned and run by an old Sorrento family, has great charm and character, full of unexpected nooks and crannies. Many visitors still feel that they are guests in a private house rather than a hotel. 63 rooms.

OTHER RESORTS

AMALFI

A masterpiece of pre-Renaissance Italy; a maritime republic that rivalled Venice; like

NEAPOLITAN RIVIERA

Pompeii, the victim of a cataclysmic disaster: Amalfi was all these things but remains an irresistible magnet for the discriminating tourist. Some of the narrow streets of the town are still lined with superb houses whose owners stroll, anonymously, in their secluded courtyards. The cathedral, complete with its charming Cloisters of Paradise, survived the tidal wave of the eleventh century, thanks mainly to Turkish workmanship on the huge doors of silver and bronze. The tide is modest today, but not as modest as the beach, swamped only by lunchtime visitors. Considering the strenuous efforts the shops and restaurants make to entice in the tourist during the day, remarkably little is directed to persuading the holidaymaker to part with his money in the evenings, when midnight is a kind of unofficial curfew. Transfer time: 2 hours.

POSITANO

Not a resort for the lazy or the lame, as many of its streets are built on a hillside, with steep slopes and multiple steps in evidence. True, a shuttle bus does go up and down for most of the day, but queues are common in midsummer, leaving the tourist to struggle on foot. The minuscule beach of greyish sand is something of an anti-climax to the overwhelming beauty of the setting. Transfer time: 2¼ hours.

NEAPOLITAN RIVIERA FACTS

Your journey

Flying times	Hours
From Birmingham, Luton, Gatwick	2¾
From Manchester	3
From Glasgow	3¼

Capodochino airport is four miles north of Naples. Transfer time from Sorrento is 1¾ hours.

Shopping
Shops are open 0830 or 0900 to 1300 and 1600 to 1930 or 2000 Monday to Saturday.

Money Matters
Banks are open 0830 to 1300 or 1320 Monday to Friday; closed weekends. All banks are closed January 1, Easter Monday, April 25, May 1, August 15, September 19, November 1, December 8, December 25, December 26.

Hotels will exchange travellers cheques and sterling banknotes outside banking hours, but at a poorer rate. Credit cards are still not widely accepted, and even those displaying a card sign will attempt to persuade customers to pay in cash in exchange for a discount.

Weather

Averages	Jan	Feb	Mar	Apr	May	Jun	Jul	Aug	Sep	Oct	Nov	Dec
Temperature	57	59	63	66	70	77	83	82	78	72	63	61
Sun hours	4	4	6	7	9	9	11	9	8	6	4	3
Rain days	8	7	7	5	4	1	0	1	3	6	9	9
Sea temp.	58	58	59	60	64	70	73	75	71	66	63	58

The west coast of Italy receives more rain than the east. The Neapolitan Riviera has mild but rather wet winters; but the sea moderates the fierce summer temperatures experienced inland.

Local transport
If you take a taxi in the Neapolitan Riviera area, more often than not, the meter will not be working. This will only become apparent after you have started the journey, so assume the worst and negotiate a rate before you start.

THE GOOD RESORT GUIDE

ADRIATIC/VENETIAN RIVIERAS

ADRIATIC RIVIERA

The Adriatic Riviera is sandwiched between the major ports of Trieste and Ancona, ranging from Lido di Jesolo in the north to Pesaro in the south. Its superb sandy beaches, sustained summer sunshine, and growing entertainment have turned this coast into high density tourism, invigorating if that is to your taste, overwhelming if not. For unlike Spain, few Italian seaside hotels offer a refuge from the crowds with spacious public rooms and vast gardens. An Italian resort hotel provides a comfortable bed and a palatable meal, but little else. Very few of them have swimming pools: if you want to swim, says the management, go in the sea. If you want a drink, find a bar. If you want night life, look for a night club. Guests who hang around the hotel are sometimes made to feel positively unwelcome, however keen they are to spend their money.

92 THE GOOD RESORT GUIDE

ADRIATIC/VENETIAN RIVIERAS

RIMINI

This bizarre attitude, as viewed by the British, has not impeded Rimini's progress: on the contrary, its hotels have multiplied at an amazing rate, and the older, slightly down-at-heel establishments have been the subject of sweeping refurbishment. Of course Rimini will never have the cudos of a truly up-market resort, but in an area where pollution is of growing concern, it has invested heavily to keep its beaches and waters scrupulously clean. The sewage plant at Rimini, though scarcely a tourist attraction in itself, is in fact one of the most modern on the Continent. The beach, ten miles in length, consisting of rather languid looking sand, is regularly swept and kept free from rubbish.

A cynic might observe that the obsession with cleanliness is motivated by financial considerations, as a charge is made for sitting on the beach, which British visitors unused to such customs sometimes vociferously resent. Attempts to circumnavigate the beach attendant by bringing one's own umbrella or deckchair are invariably doomed to failure. Nor, unless a hotel provides unambiguous vouchers, does the fact that they have territorial rights over a particular section of beach absolve its guests from paying to go on it: the concessionaire, in applying his self-made rules, makes a UK traffic warden seem like a charitable institution. However, if you object to paying on principle, remember that the five metres between the high tide mark and the sea are public property, and the operator must allow access; so if you are brave enough, you can walk through his patch and plonk yourself right in front.

Beyond a certain distance along the coast, of course, even the Italian entrepreneurial spirit fails to assert itself, and the beach becomes free by default. As the road also swings away from the coast, hotels also begin to have direct access from their terrace or gardens to the shore. However, public transport disappears with the road and the beach restaurants vanish with the concessionaires. In the centre, where the facilities are the best, the beach entry charges are at their highest and the main road at its busiest. As there are very few crossing-points, and standing on one in an effort to stop Italian traffic is tantamount to suicide, the journey between hotel and beach is extremely precarious. Certainly children cannot be left to cross roads on their own: in fact the safest place for them is a kind of acquatic adventure playground, Fiabilandia, with water chutes and fearsome-looking dragon ships; they could spend the whole fortnight there if you can afford it. On the beach itself, as a change from the unsteerable pedaloes, look for a mosconi. It is not, as one might suspect, an Italian cornetto but a miniature catamaran with oars, difficult to capsize. Little else, however, is uniquely Italian. Rimini has more than its fair share of British watering holes and international discos; some of the trattorias barely admit to serving pasta. At the last count, 30 night clubs were competing for business, all largely indistinguishable and undistinguished, with the notable exception of the smart Embassy Club.

Excursions

All roads should lead to Venice, but unfortunately many lead to a colossal traffic

Beach at Rimini

ITALY

THE GOOD RESORT GUIDE 93

ADRIATIC/VENETIAN RIVIERAS

Venice

jam, so huge, in fact, that at the height of summer the Italian police have been known to close the filter roads from the motorways leading to the city. If you must go by car, go extremely early, before dawn and look for a space in the Piazzale Roma at the Autorimessa Communale, favoured by the locals. Failing that, if you think the price too exorbitant or are wary of leaving your car in an unsupervised car park, there is another solution. Just before you reach the Piazzale Roma, a filter road to the right leads to the Isola de Tronchetto. From here a car ferry runs to the Lido, nothing to do with Lido de Jesolo, but the real and original Lido, the island directly opposite Venice itself. Services go every hour until late at night, the journey takes 30 minutes, and the view of Venice is superb. Once on the Lido, parking is relatively easy, and you can take a fast motor launch into Venice and return for a spot of sun-bathing if the crowds become too much. As the best way to arrive in Venice is undoubtedly by sea, and many of the Italian Adriatic resorts,

including Rimini, run regular services, many tourists will consider this option. The principal objections are the price and the length of the journey, which usually involves at least one overnight on the boat or in Venice itself. You can save money by using the train, as the railway runs to Rimini, Cattolica and Pesaro, and the Stazione Santa Lucia in Venice is a short stroll from the Grand Canal.

To really appreciate Venice, go early to St Mark's Square, the Basilica San Marco and the Doge's Palace and avoid organised tours. Work on the principle that apart from admission fee everything has a cheaper alternative. For example, never use water taxis. On the big ferries, or vaporetti, always pay in advance as buying a ticket on board costs more; and so do the routes marked 'diretto' which miss out a lo of landing-stages. If you want to eat at the side of the Grand Canal, the pizzeria on the hidden side of the Rialto Bridge is a fraction of the price of the luxury restaurants nearby. If you want Venetian glassware, take a ferry to the

94 THE GOOD RESORT GUIDE

ADRIATIC/VENETIAN RIVIERAS

...land of Murano in the Lagoon, and buy direct ...om one of the factories. If you want to say you ...ve been in a gondola, take the gondola ...rries, called traghetti, that cross the Grand ...anal in several places for a fraction of the ...ice. However visitors who are really short of ...oney should note that the authorities have ...eclared war on impecunious students and no ...nger allow sleeping bags alongside the Grand ...anal. Rimini and its neighbouring resorts are ...so in striking distance of Florence, simply the ...eatest art centre in the world, if you are ...epared for an extremely long and quite ...hausting day. Less tiring, and comparatively ...ss interesting, Ravenna, once the capital of ...e Roman Empire, has a wonderful collection ... mosaics. Just inland from Rimini, the ...dependent state of San Marino, a walled town ... the mountains, has a certain novelty value ...d an apparently limitless issue of postage ...amps.

IMINI HOTELS

...rand ★★★ eighteenth century palazzo ...erlooking Rimini harbour, with own sandy ...ach (for which guests must still pay extra) ...ross the road, swimming pool and night club. ...ninspiring annexe with 50 rooms. 185 in main ...tel, on five floors.

De France ★★ in the southern part of Rimini, known as Rivazzurra, a hotel that backs directly on to the beach. Unfortunately the traffic noise at the front is considerable and the swimming pool gives the impression of being in the middle of a Grand Prix. Air-conditioned dining room, where breakfast is the best meal. 65 rooms on five floors.

Eurhotel ★★ very close to the beach in the Rivazzurra district, though the view below the sixth floor is obstructed by other buildings. Swimming pool and sun terrace. Facilities for children include early meals and copious snacks. 60 rooms on nine floors.

Fabius ★★ under five minutes from the beach at Rivazzurra in a good, and surprisingly quiet location, though the hotel makes up for it at night with some lively bars. The terrace beside the swimming pool is extremely small. 54 rooms on six floors.

OTHER RESORTS

CATTOLICA
South of Rimini, between Riccione and Pesaro, a lively resort extremely popular with young holidaymakers. After dark, most of the streets are closed to vehicular traffic, and restaurants, discos and dancers spread joyously into the

Ravenna mosaic

ITALY

THE GOOD RESORT GUIDE 95

ADRIATIC/VENETI

ITALY

space. Only mopeds and bicycles are allowed through. Many vivacious night clubs, especially in the district immediately behind the beach. At the north-east end, the promenade disappears, and several hotels open directly on to the sand. Transfer time from Rimini airport: 30 minutes.

Riccione

RICCIONE
The racetrack separating most of the hotels from the beach continues south into Riccione, but this disadvantage apart, Riccione is a more sophisticated resort with a large shopping centre, a wide variety of restaurants and a flourishing night life. The sand beach is unfortunately just as crowded, but visitors are also offered golf, roller-skating, tennis and the acquascivolo water chute, a liquid bobsleigh run. Transfer time from Rimini airport: 20 minutes.

PESARO
Another crowded beach despite its width, but at least many of the hotels open directly on to the sand. Flourishing water sports, especially windsurfing and sailing. Behind the beach, an old quarter of tiny squares and sinister passageways, and a hugely popular disco called 'Why Not?', which presumably came after Pesaro's most famous visitor, the wicked Lucretia Borgia, the lady who made food-taste a booming if precarious profession. Transfer time from Rimini airport: 45 minutes.

ADRIATIC RIVIERA FACTS

Your journey

To Rimini	Hours
From Bristol, Birmingham, East Midlands, Gatwick, Luton	2½
From Manchester	3
From Glasgow	3¼

Transfer time from Rimini Airport: 15 minutes.

Shopping
Shops tend to stay open very late in the resorts. In the morning they open 1000 until 1300, then 1600 to 2200.

Money matters
Banks open 0830 to 1330, Monday to Friday; closed weekends. All banks are closed January 1, Good Friday, Easter Monday, April 25, May August 15, November 1, December 8, December 25, December 26.

Hotels will change sterling and sterling travellers cheques, but at an inferior rate. Credit cards are not widely accepted.

Weather

Averages	Jan	Feb	Mar	Apr	May	Jun	Jul	Aug	Sep	Oct	Nov	Dec
Temperature	52	55	59	66	73	82	86	86	79	70	61	55
Sun hours	3	4	4	5	8	9	10	8	6	4	2	3
Rain days	8	5	8	8	7	7	4	5	6	8	11	9
Sea temp.	52	48	50	55	63	70	73	75	73	66	61	55

Although temperatures remain high, northern Italy has a short summer season and no guarantee of sunshine; the winters are cold and wet.

Local transport
A frequent trolley bus service operates between Rimini and Riccione. Elsewhere buses are cheap but crowded; in many resorts tickets can be bought in advance from local shops and restaurants.

96 THE GOOD RESORT GUIDE

ADRIATIC/VENETIAN RIVIERAS

VENETIAN RIVIERA
LIDO DI JESOLO

If on the Adriatic Rimini is the king of the south, Lido di Jesolo is indisputedly cock of the north. It, too, has about ten miles of glorious sandy beaches but there the resemblance ends. Where Rimini is a real town, with an old (if largely uninteresting) quarter, Lido di Jesolo is rather like an abandoned film lot, stretching back barely three streets from the sea. Where Rimini is plagued with sea-front traffic, Lido di Jesolo has relatively little traffic and many hotels right on the beach. Where Rimini charges as much as it dare to use the beach facilities, in Lido di Jesolo the cost is absorbed imperceptibly in the price of the holiday. But where Rimini is justly proud of its clean sea, at Lido di Jesolo the water can look rather grubby.

Lido di Jesolo is not however identical from one end to the other. The least attractive area lies to the south, where the cheaper hotels and restaurants cluster around the beach. In the centre, largely car-free, the beach is almost entirely parcelled up between the smarter hotels, with a wide variety of water sports available from water-skiing to pedaloes. To the north-east, the resort gradually loses momentum: the hotels take on a rather languid air, self-catering villages come and go like little oases; and the beach becomes so wide that it is difficult to make out the shoreline.

However, such details apart, Lido di Jesolo (say it 'Iesolo') is another potential point of confusion. The Lido, on which all other Lidos have modelled themselves, is the island in the lagoon opposite Venice (see excursions). The beaches here are expensive. Lido di Jesolo is nowhere near Venice, but eleven miles away on a congested road, a good hour's drive. However Jesolo's beaches are free. Transfer time from Venice airport: 45 minutes.

each at Lido di Jesolo

THE GOOD RESORT GUIDE 97

Grand Canal, Venice

LIDO DI JESOLO HOTELS

Ambasciatori Palace★★★ Quiet, some would say dull, hotel but extremely well situated for Jesolo's night life. Pleasant swimming pool and gardens lead directly on to the beach. Separate children's pool. 85 rooms on six floors.

Cesare Augustus★★★ central, sedate, right by the beach. Two swimming pools, one for children. Restaurant would benefit from more sit-down meals. 120 rooms on six floors (2 lifts).

Quisisana/Monaco★★★ a glass-fronted lift that might have escaped from Charlie's Chocolate Factory, for those who have read their Raoul Dahl, is the main concession of these twin hotels to modernisation. They also share a swimming pool, which leads straight on to the sand. Together they have 118 rooms on five floors (3 lifts).

VENETIAN RIVIERA FACTS

Your journey

To Venice	Hours
From Stansted	2
From Gatwick, Heathrow	2¼
From Bristol, Cardiff, Manchester	2½
From Glasgow	3

Transfer time from Marco Polo Airport: 45 minutes

Shopping
Shops in Venice are allowed to open when they wish. Elsewhere, shops open 0800 or 0900 to 1300 and 1700 to 2000.

Money matters
Most banks open 0830-1330 and 1445-1545.
Credit cards are widely accepted in Venice comparatively less in Lido di Jesolo.

Weather

Averages	Jan	Feb	Mar	Apr	May	Jun	Jul	Aug	Sep	Oct	Nov	Dec
Temperature	43	46	54	63	70	77	81	81	75	66	52	46
Sun hours	3	4	4	6	8	9	10	10	7	6	4	3
Rain days	6	6	7	9	8	8	7	7	5	7	9	8
Sea temp.	46	45	46	52	60	68	74	73	70	62	56	51

Sunshine is never assured on this part of the Adriatic coast. The sunniest months, July and August, are also the most unsuitable for visiting Venice because of the high temperatures.

ITALY

THE GOOD RESORT GUIDE

SARDINIA

SARDINIA

Remote but ruggedly beautiful, Sardinia has escaped the worst ravages of the package tour industry. More than 100 miles west of the Italian mainland, the island is huge, almost 150 miles in length, in parts 75 miles in width; and yet it has the casual undemanding air of a tiny Greek island tucked away in some forgotten area of the Aegean. There are no concrete skyscrapers here: most of its hotels are small, family-run, priding themselves on their personal touch; some nestling in quiet bays close to beaches of rich golden sand. Spectacular mountains run straight into the dazzling emerald and turquoise sea, clear enough to glimpse huge shoals of fish in the depths below. Olive groves, pine trees and wild flowers add vivid splashes of colour to the dark granite scenery. For holidaymakers seeking an atmosphere of genteel tranquility, Sardinia reigns supreme.

Paradise Coast, Sardinia

SARDINIA

RESORTS AND HOTELS

ALGHERO

A fishing port on the north-west coast, Sardinia's largest resort, with an old walled city whose cobbled streets once echoed to the sound of Spanish soldiers. In the fourteenth century Alghero was seized by the Spanish kingdom of Aragon: the street names still appear in Spanish and the local inhabitants talk to one another in Catalan rather than Italian.

The bustling streets are reminiscent of Barcelona's 'ramblas', scattered with open-air cafes where you can watch the world go by.

The best beach of vivid white sand begins nearly a mile north of the harbour and stretches almost to the village of Fertilia, close to Alghero airport, but fortunately not on its flight path. However apart from the occasional hotel, the streets behind this beach are drab and ugly. Windsurfing and sailing are available, but there are very few facilities for children.

Beyond Fertilia, another half dozen hotels

Fishing boats in Alghero harbour

SARDINIA

attributed to Alghero are a long way from the resort, some as much as ten miles out, in the bay of Porto Conte. The superior hotels are largely to be found immediately south of Alghero, a long way from a good beach, although some have a path to a rocky beach below with a tiny stretch of sand. Nearest airport: Alghero. Transfer time: 15-30 minutes, depending on hotel location.

Hotel Calabona★★ 1 mile south of the town, overlooking its own rock beach which, like the swimming pool, can become rather crowded in high season as guests from the Continental Hotel are free to make use of them. The Calabona likes children, who have their own playground. Shuttle bus to the old city every hour. 113 rooms, all air-conditioned in summer.

Hotel Carlos V★★★★ south of Alghero, just over a mile from the centre, a modern but well-designed hotel overlooking the sea but separated by a road from a small rocky beach. Large saltwater pool and sun terrace. Particularly generous breakfasts. 110 rooms, air conditioned in summer, on three floors (3 lifts).

Hotel El Faro★★★★★ if you are prepared to travel ten miles to Alghero for shopping or even a drink (you will be lucky to find a single ethnic bar within walking distance of the hotel), and do not mind bathing and swimming from a rocky headland alongside a retired lighthouse, then the El Faro, at Porto Conte, is ideal. Excellent food, outstanding service, 92 extremely comfortable rooms, all air-conditioned, on three floors (1 lift).

BAIA SARDINIA

A tiny resort in a delightful curved bay in the north-west of the island consisting almost entirely of hotels and self-catering villas, but with an extremely lively night life, the best in Sardinia. The beach of fine white sand offers particularly safe swimming. Nearest airport: Olbia. Transfer time: 45 minutes.

Hotel Bisaccia★★★ beautifully designed hotel overlooking the beach below where deckchairs and umbrellas are provided free for hotel guests. Huge swimming pool next to the beach. Many of the rooms, which have simple furnishings, overlook the bay. Annexe across the road is better equipped but lacks the atmosphere of the main hotel.

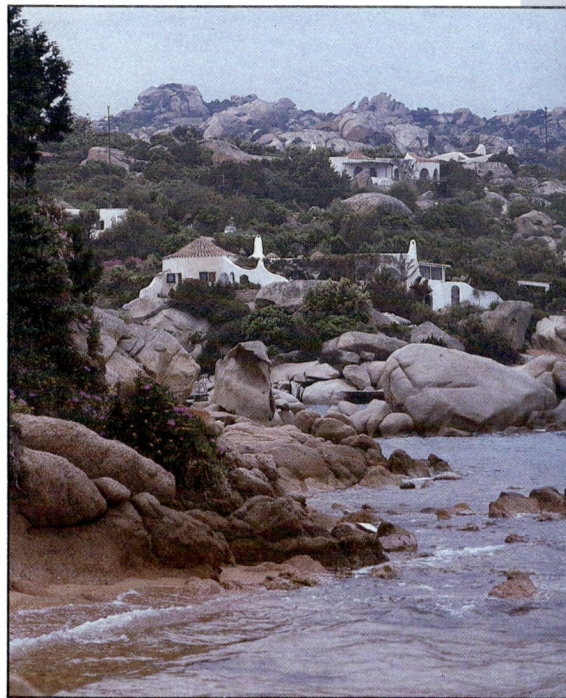

Porto Raffael

PORTO CERVO

The Costa Smeralda on the north-east tip of the island is a millionaire's playground with a distinct shortage of millionaires, developed by the Agha Khan with an emphasis on privacy and seclusion. The beaches are beautiful but short on amenities, and the atmosphere and architecture singularly contrived at Porto Cervo itself, a yachting resort packed with fair weather sailors. Nearest airport: Olbia. Transfer time: 45 minutes.

Hotel Pitrizza★★★★★ in an isolated cove leading through some exquisite gardens to a beach of coarse sand. You eat in grand style in the main hotel building, and live in one of the half dozen villas in the grounds, each of which has 3 or 4 bedrooms. The air-conditioning is needed more to keep away the mosquitoes than to keep down the temperature. 28 rooms. Children sharing with their parents receive a much-needed discount. Closed October-April.

THE GOOD RESORT GUIDE

SARDINIA

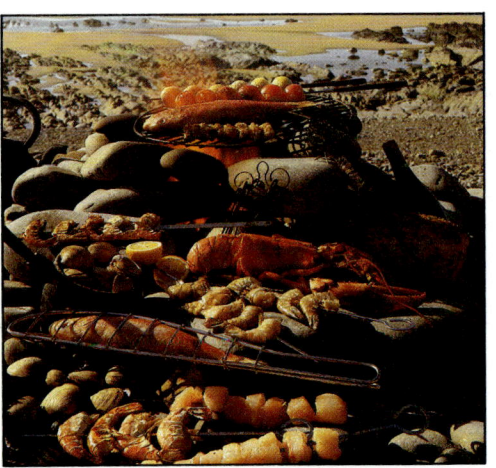

Seafood barbecue

SANTA MARGHERITA DI PULA

A resort that does not really exist, except as a collection of hotels strung out along the southern coast, about 20 miles from Sardinia's capital, Cagliari. Many of the hotels have private beaches of fine white sand, extremely safe and ideal for children. For anyone not content with a beach holiday, however, a hire car is really essential. Nearest airport: Cagliari. Transfer time: 50 minutes.

Hotel Is Morus ★★★ charming hotel in landscaped gardens with a large swimming pool and attractive arched veranda. Direct access to a small sandy beach, which offers water-skiing, wind-surfing and power-boating. Children's playground. Luxurious, attentive service, extremely relaxed atmosphere. 85 rooms on two floors in the hotel or in detached cottages, ideal for families.
Closed November-March.

Excursions

The old part of Cagliari, constructed on the side of an extremely steep hill overlooking the port, has many attractive narrow streets winding their way towards the cathedral. For shopping, however, try the department stores on the busy road opposite the harbour.

South of Cagliari, and just north of Santa Margherita, is the ruined Phoenician town of Nora, evocative and peaceful, but preserved just enough for visitors to re-construct, in the mind's eye, the bustling life of the ancient city. The coastline setting is truly beautiful, exquisitely so at sunset.

North of Cagliari, the even older prehistoric site of Su Nuraxi, near Barumini, contains a remarkably well-preserved fortress with splendid views from the ruins over the surrounding countryside. From here it is an easy drive to the remote mountain area known as the Barbagia, around the Monti del Gennargentu, where tiny villages exist almost oblivious to the outside world. In the far north, the coastal town of Castelsardo is an interesting excursion, with its claustrophobic winding streets leading up to a medieval castle.

SARDINIA FACTS

Your journey

	Hours
From Gatwick	2¼
From Birmingham	2½
From Manchester	2¾

Gatwick has flights to Alghero, Cagliari and Olbia Airports; Birmingham and Manchester only to Alghero. A flight to an airport not convenient for your resort can result in extremely long transfer times: the domestic flight time alone between Olbia and Cagliari is 35 minutes. Alghero and Olbia do not have duty-free facilities.

The shortest crossing by ferry is from Civitavecchia, just north of Rome, to Olbia, which takes six hours. Advance reservations are essential in summer.

Shopping

Shops are generally open 0830 to 1300 and 1600 to 1920 Monday to Saturday in the larger towns.

Money matters

Banks are open 0830 to 1300 Monday to Friday
All banks are closed on January 1, Easter Monday, April 25, May 1, June 29, August 15, November 1, December 8, December 25, December 26.

Hotels will exchange travellers' cheques and sterling banknotes outside banking hours, but at a much poorer rate. Although credit cards are becoming increasingly accepted, many shops will offer a discount for cash.

SARDINIA/SICILY

Weather

Averages	Jan	Feb	Mar	Apr	May	Jun	Jul	Aug	Sep	Oct	Nov	Dec
Temperature	57	59	63	66	73	81	86	86	81	73	66	61
Sun hours	4	4	6	7	9	9	11	10	8	6	4	3
Rain days	8	7	7	5	4	1	0	1	3	6	9	9
Sea temp.	57	57	59	59	62	70	76	77	76	72	66	60

Sunshine is almost guaranteed in June, July and August, which can be oppressively hot away from the coast. November and December are, by comparison, conspicuously wet. The north of the island is affected by a cold north wind (the French 'mistral' becoming the Italian 'meastrale') in some winter months; the south receives the 'sirocco', a sultry wind from the Sahara.

Local transport

Hire cars should be examined carefully before acceptance. Do not expect them to have seat belts.

SICILY

Once the crossroads of the Ancient World, just three miles from Italy and under 100 from Africa, Sicily was both battlefield and playground for the armies of Carthage, Greece, and Rome; the Normans came along later, too. The great city of Syracuse took on, and defeated, the Athenians, and at the height of its power was the richest state in the

Syracuse, Caves of Dionysius

THE GOOD RESORT GUIDE 103

SICILY

ITALY

Mediterranean and probably the most beautiful. The result is a spectacular collection of ruins and remains to provide a diversion from the seaside. Which is probably just as well, because Sicily's beaches are singularly uninspired, and even the best are a long way from the popular resorts. However the scenery in the north and east is superb, where the skyline is dominated by the active volcano of Mount Etna, forever smouldering ominously.

TAORMINA

Taormina is that rare resort that transcends the problems of mass tourism. Its incredible setting, perched on a plateau 750 feet above the sea, with dramatic views of Mount Etna to

Taormina, Greek theatre

104 THE GOOD RESORT GUIDE

SICILY

the south, makes its commercial atmosphere somehow acceptable. The village was abandoned to the tourist long ago, with hotels, restaurants, bars and souvenir shops jostling for position on the hill. Only the main street, the Corso Umberto, has by some accident found itself on the level; elsewhere visitors are forever clambering up and down steps or slopes. Frequently they pile up in some flat corner in an effort to regain their balance, like a row of skittles in a bowling alley, making the village seem congested even when it is not. The only real breathing space can be found at the Greek amphitheatre on the hill in the centre, ruined but magnificent.

Taormina's hotels are divided between two areas, the village centre and the sea front, called Taormina Mare, at the bottom of a series of hairpin bends. The two are linked by an erratic and seasonable cable car, and an even more unpredictable bus service. Visitors who resent the price of taxis (unmetered) should appreciate that the alternative steps are exhausting and in damp weather positively dangerous.

Most of the beaches are pebble and rock, except where Taormina Mare merges with Mazzaro, whose beaches are predominantly sand. However very few of them are immune to the noise of coastal traffic which largely seems to scorn the expensive toll motorway to the rear of the town, and for good measure, the railway line runs along in between for much of the way, too.

Excursions

If you have a taste for volcanoes, the rugged Aeolian islands to the north can offer two, Stromboli, still active, and Vulcan, closer but merely smouldering. Or you can live dangerously on Sicily itself and climb Mount Etna, still very much alive and kicking. However, would-be visitors should know that following the destruction of the upper route of the cable-car, burned through by leaping torrents of fire during the 1983 eruption, the only way to the top, from Lingualossa on the northern side, involves an extremely bumpy land rover ride, then a short walk. This excursion is only for people with a good head for heights, and not for small children; warm clothing is essential, as the mountain reaches 11,000 feet. Indeed it is still growing: every eruption spills lava on to the upper slopes.

For something rather less precarious, visit

Mount Etna

the Valley of the Temples at Agrigento on the south coast, a long day trip from Taormina, but well worth the effort to see so beautiful a setting. You can wander among the pillars of what is believed to be the largest Greek temple ever constructed, the Olympian Temple of Zeus, and see the Temple of Concord, which owes its remarkable state of preservation to the early Christians, who subsequently used it as a church.

Syracuse, to the east, was the home of many famous figures from ancient history. Its tyrannical ruler, Dionysius, was the one who entertained Damocles under the threat of a razor-sharp sword, suspended precariously above his head. Archimedes ran naked through the streets of Syracuse shouting 'Eureka!' ('I've cracked it!') after discovering that his considerable volume could be precisely measured by the amount his bath water dropped when he got out. The Neapolis district has many Greek and Roman remains, including a superb Greek theatre.

Medieval architecture has also survived, particularly at Erice in the north-east, a medieval town with marvellous views, perched on a rock above Trapani. The Cathedral, originally a watch-tower, possesses a magnificent Gothic portal. Cefalu (see resorts) has a Norman cathedral, the product of a Norman conquest in the 11th century, showing that the Norman knights went to Sicily as well as Hastings. The mosaics and Arab carvings provide a striking contrast in styles.

ITALY

THE GOOD RESORT GUIDE 105

SICILY

Every summer the knights ride out in miniature at the traditional puppet theatres operating in many towns. Beautifully dressed figures in tiny armour slug it out on stage, Christians against Saracens, with monsters and magicians thrown in for good measure. Punch and Judy will never seem quite the same again.

Mazzaro beach

TAORMINA HOTELS

Belvedere ★★ central, close to a public park, with a garden terrace overlooking the woods. The best rooms have a wonderful view of Mount Etna and the sea, but take care, as some other rooms are drab and noisy. Swimming pool. Bed and breakfast only. 42 rooms (1 lift). Closed Christmas and New Year.

Mazzaro Sea Palace ★★★★ in the best position in Taormina Mare, where the railway line disappears, along with its noise, into a tunnel. Built right next to the sea, overlooking a beach of slightly off-putting grey sand, with a seawater swimming pool alongside. Epic terrace lunch. Discounts for children and special meals. Cable car to town centre nearby. 81 rooms. Closed November-March.

Paradiso ★★ close to the shops and the public park, a charming hotel with a reputation for good service. The restaurant, on the fourth floor, is outstanding, but the absence of a swimming pool may prove a disadvantage in high summer. 33 rooms: those at the back have the best view. Closed November to Mid-December.

San Domenico Palace ★★★★ central, on a promontory overlooking the bay, a former 14th century convent with grand and exquisitely furnished public rooms. Impeccable service. The garden leading from the original cloisters is truly a masterpiece, with Mount Etna as its backcloth. Swimming pool, snack bar, and an irritatingly erratic restaurant. 108 rather small rooms, all air-conditioned.

Sant' Andrea ★★★ a converted house just off the main road in Taormina Mare, leading directly to its own private shingle beach. Attractive sun terrace but no swimming pool. Agreeable restaurant. 48 rooms.
Transfer time to Taormina: 2 hours from Catania.

OTHER RESORTS

CEFALU

A fishing village situated midway along the northern coast, with an old quarter tucked in below an enormous outcrop of rock known locally, if unsurprisingly, as 'La Rocca'. A single piazza leans, Pisa-like, beneath the great Norman cathedral, so bring a book to wedge under your cafe table. The sloping streets down to the port are honeycombed with dingy, rather sinister alleyways. Cefalu's hotels can be found mainly to the west on an attractive sandy beach; the beach to the east of town is much less pleasant. But even this is superb in comparison with the beaches out of town, most of which are ruined or rendered inaccessible by the coastal railway line, which also runs

Temple at Agrigento

106 THE GOOD RESORT GUIDE

SICILY

uncomfortably close to several Cefalu hotels. Transfer time: 1¾ hours from Palermo, 2½ hours from Catania.

GIARDINI/NAXOS

Two miles south-west of Taormina, a noisy resort flanked by the main road and railway line on which trains run quite late at night. In the central village of Giardini the sandy beach, too, is noisy, mainly young Italian families. Part of it is taken up by a Lido for which an admission fee is payable. Where Giardini gives way to Naxos, the beach consists of black rocks; further out still, in the most recently developed area, it improves to tiny pebbles. Giardini, with a good selection of bars, has a gentle night life. Transfer time: 1¼ hours from Catania or Palermo.

SICILY FACTS

Your journey

	Hours
From Gatwick, Luton	3

Fontanarossa Airport, which has a duty-free shop, lies 5 miles due south of Catania; Punta Raisi Airport, located 20 miles west of Palermo, does not.

Car ferries to Palermo operate from as far north as Genoa, taking 22 hours; from Livorno, 18 hours; or Naples, 9 hours. Naples also has services to Catania, 14 hours, or Syracuse, five hours longer. Ferry services are extremely crowded in summer and advance booking is essential.

Shopping
Most shops open from 0830 to 1300, then again from 1600 to 1900. However in July and August, the afternoon siesta may be extended to 1700.

Money matters
Banks are open from 0830 to 1330, Monday to Friday.

All banks are closed on January 1, Easter Monday, April 25, May 1, June 29, August 15, November 1, December 8, December 25 and December 26.

Bureau de change, known as cambio, usually give a slightly better rate than the banks; they are also open on Saturday mornings. Credit cards are still not widely accepted outside large towns.

Weather

Averages	Jan	Feb	Mar	Apr	May	Jun	Jul	Aug	Sep	Oct	Nov	Dec
Temperature	57	59	63	66	73	82	88	88	82	73	66	60
Sun hours	4	5	6	7	8	10	10	9	8	6	6	4
Rain days	9	5	6	4	3	2	1	1	3	7	7	8
Sea temp.	57	57	57	59	63	70	76	79	76	72	67	61

Wet weather is extremely rare between May and September, but quite frequent between October and January. The temperature in Sicily can become particularly oppressive in July and August away from the cooling breezes of the coast. In August there is great risk from the sirocco, a humid wind blowing from Africa, which causes overcast weather and can last three or four days. In winter, despite mild weather on the coast, freezing temperatures in the mountains are common — good for skiing.

Local transport
Sicily is an extremely crowded island, so its roads and railways are correspondingly congested. Traffic conditions in major towns, especially Palermo and Messina, are quite chaotic. Hire cars should be examined carefully before accepting them. Taxis are becoming increasingly expensive, and drivers think nothing of adding surcharges to the meter for fuel(!), luggage, night time, weekends, holidays, airports, in fact, just for being there. Negotiate in advance.

ITALY

THE GOOD RESORT GUIDE   **107**

MALTA

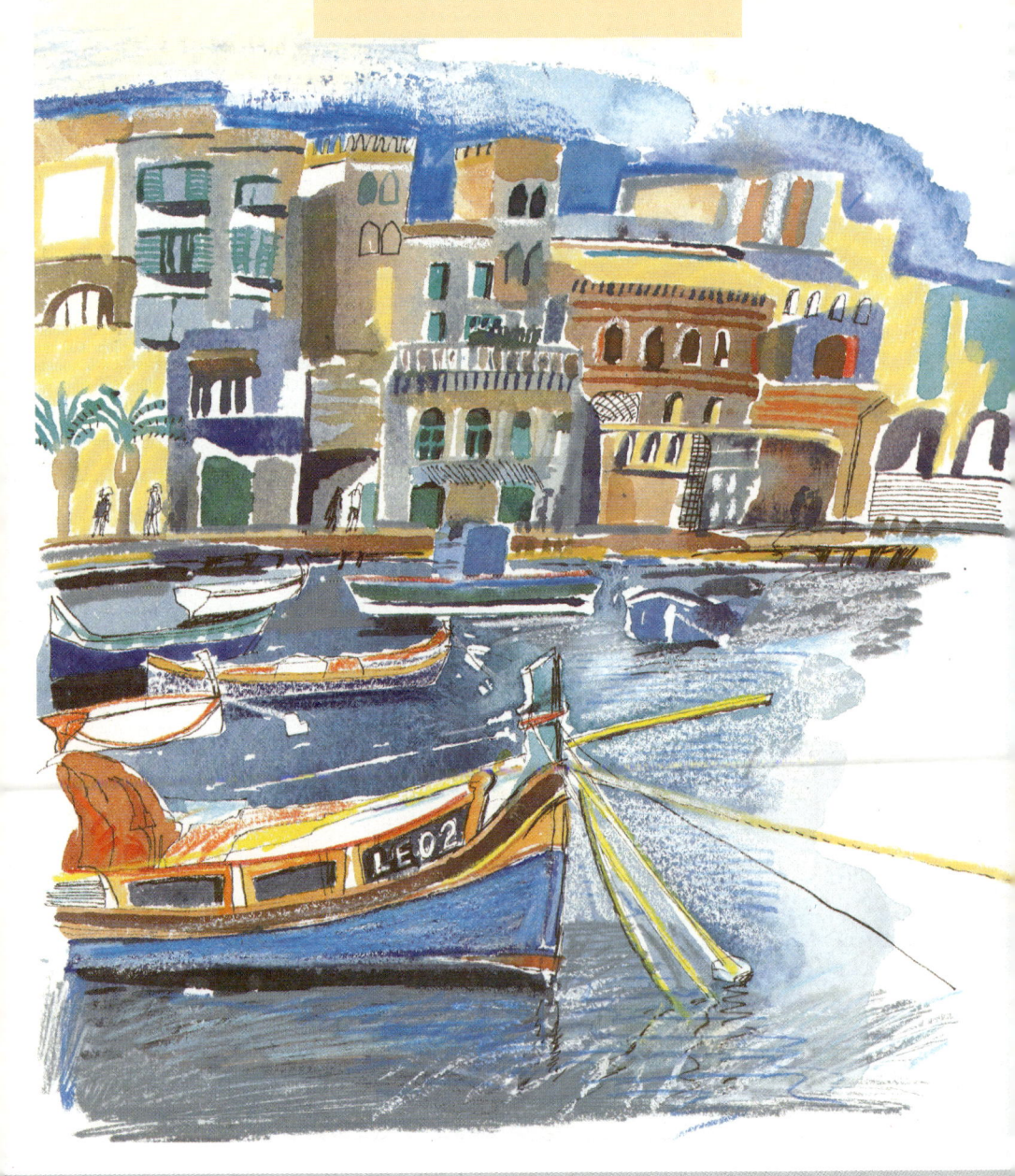

108 THE GOOD RESORT GUIDE

MALTA

A tiny island at the crossroads of the ancient world, Malta has always been vulnerable to outside influence; but her people have brilliantly absorbed the best and beaten back the worst, notably in two great sieges, four centuries apart, the Turks and the Luftwaffe. Her only invaders today are tourists, attracted by the phenomenal summer climate, with temperatures in the mid-eighties and rain about as frequent as Halley's Comet.

A former British colony, Malta still retains its corner shop atmosphere (the currency is pounds, though alas, not pounds sterling) and its fluency in English. In theory at least, vehicles drive on the left, although on an island measuring only 17 miles by nine, the opportunities for speed are limited. Which is perhaps just as well, because while basic hire car tariffs are cheap, insurance is expensive, a reflection of the fact that the traditional Maltese reputation for friendliness evaporates when they are behind the wheel. Not only the standard of driving leaves much to be desired:

Grand Harbour, Valletta

THE GOOD RESORT GUIDE 109

MALTA

many of the roads have precarious pot-holes, contradictory signposts and a complete absence of lighting at night.

The lack of rain can lead to a shortage of water, despite the construction of new storage facilities. Except in the very best hotels, the water may occasionally be turned off for certain periods in the summer months. Although it is perfectly safe to drink, it has an odd, rather brackish taste; most visitors keep to bottled water throughout their stay.

Malta also has a severe shortage of good beaches. The best are Golden Bay and the adjacent Ghajn Tuffieha Bay on the north-west coast; Mellieha Bay, by the north-east peninsula; and Ramla Bay on the nearby island of Gozo (as distinct from the resort of the same name on the northern coast of Malta itself). Elsewhere bathing is largely restricted to rocks and hotel pools.

However the sea is ideal for every kind of water sport. Many hotels offer tuition in scuba diving, wind surfing, water-skiing and sailing. Snorkelling is also popular because of the exceptionally clear water. Deep sea fishing off the Maltese coast is widely available during the summer months.

In many respects, Malta offers exceptionally good value for money, especially its local wine, beer, take-away restaurants and food shops, making a self-catering holiday extremely cheap. Cooking is often a mixture of British and Italian styles and by no means their best. Maltese specialities include timpana, a macaroni pie with meat, cheese, eggs and tomatoes; bragioli, beef olives; lampuki, a tasty local white fish; and rabbit. Local lager and wines are an acquired taste. Beware menus that look cheap but do not include service charges.

Golden Bay beach

110 THE GOOD RESORT GUIDE

MALTA

The grading of Maltese hotels is unintentionally deceptive, as their categories are different and in any case do not reflect the standard available on the same grade for example, in parts of Spain. The best hotels are, however, very good indeed. Recommended hotels below have been given grades which conform with other Mediterranean countries.

Valletta

Blue Grotto, Gozo

Excursions

Valletta, Malta's capital, sits on a promontory jutting out between two harbours. Built by the Knights of St. John after they had repelled the Turks in the great Siege, its massive fortifications survive to this day. You can see the Palace of the Grand Masters of the Knights, and St. John's Cathedral, full of elaborate carvings. But most visitors are content to wander along the narrow streets, a kind of orderly spider's web, and look for bargains in leather and lace.

The former capital, Mdina, inland and in the western half of the island, is little more than a ghost town. Perched above the surrounding countryside, there is a fine view from its walls. When the tourists go home, only a few splendid 17th century houses remain occupied, in the main by the remnants of Malta's aristocracy. And not far from these eerie, silent streets and tiny squares lie the catacombs, the refuge of the oppressed Christians in the days of the Romans.

Day cruises around Malta's coast are a particularly popular excursion. Many have as their climax a visit to the Blue Grotto, neither as popular nor as stunning as its namesake on Capri, but decidedly worth a visit. For visitors who want to see the grotto in smaller numbers, boats can be hired just outside Zurrieq on the nearby southern coast.

North of Malta lies Gozo, both a resort (see next page) and an excursion. On Gozo's west coast three superb natural sights attract a constant stream of tourists in the summer. They

THE GOOD RESORT GUIDE

MALTA

come to see Fungus Rock, a tiny peninsula where the Knights of St. John gathered herbs and developed their considerable skills in medicine; Azure Window, a breathtaking rock formation shaped like a bridge across the vigorous waters below; and the so-called Inland Sea, a salt lake entirely surrounded by forbidding cliffs but connected to the open sea by a narrow tunnel.

RESORTS AND HOTELS

SLIEMA
The largest resort on the island, located on a headland immediately to the north of Valletta harbour. An attractive promenade unfortunately does little to disguise the absence of sandy beaches on the north-west side (where lidos and hotel pools have been hewn out of the solid, smooth rocky shore) and of any beaches at all on the harbour side, where the water is decidedly dirty. Sliema does, however, have a vigorous night life with dozens of bars and several discos, of which Il Fortizza is perhaps the best. Valetta lies just three miles away. Transfer time from Luqa airport: 25 minutes.

Hotel Fortina ★★★ despite its central position alongside the sea road, the lack of through traffic makes it relatively quiet. The road separates the hotel from its pool and sun terraces above the rocks, but the view is uniformly superb. Plenty of entertainment during the summer. Restaurant with full waiter service. 98 rooms on six floors (3 lifts), including some family rooms.

ST. JULIAN'S BAY
A mile to the north-west of Sliema and the centre for night-life on the island, St. Julian's was once a quiet little fishing harbour. It now has a startling concentration of brightly lit restaurants, discos and night clubs, though in the main they are reasonably priced. The beaches, however, at best consist of tiny patches of sand on which seaweed collects incessantly. Transfer time: 25 minutes.

Hotel Dragonara Palace ★★★★ a self-contained holiday complex on an isolated headland, which visitors need never leave if they feel so inclined, as it has a vast range of water sports and evening entertainment. The principal pool is huge but the nearest beach is predictably rocky. Live music every night.

St Julian's Bay

THE GOOD RESORT GUIDE

MALTA

extensive a la carte menus. 200 rooms on four floors (2 lifts).

ST. PAUL'S BAY
On the north-east coast, ten miles from Valletta, three resorts in one, St. Paul's, Bugibba and Qawra. St. Paul's is the largest and liveliest, with many bustling bars and throbbing discos, but in the longer term Bugibba seems certain to become a major centre of the Maltese self-catering industry. For the moment, however, expect a mixture of finished and unfinished buildings, made and unmade roads. Quawra is ideal for visitors who like a night life within easy reach but prefer to stay in a quiet, residential area. Transfer time: 40 minutes.

Hotel Concorde ★★ five minutes' walk from the sea front promenade at Bugibba, a small modern hotel, one of the few in the resort with an adequate swimming pool and sun terrace. Attractive restaurant, waiter service. Live music in the evenings. 42 rooms on five floors, but only a glimpse of the sea.

MARSASKALA
Once a sleepy fishing village seven miles south-east of Valletta in an isolated corner of the island, Marsaskala has been changed, and not really for the better, by the construction of a luxury hotel (see below) on its outskirts. The harbour area now has several restaurants and bars, some of them masquerading as discos, whose main source of business is the hotel clientele. Transfer time: 35 minutes.

Hotel Jerma Palace ★★★★ stunning Moorish architecture, standing on a rocky headland overlooking the creek that leads towards Marsaskala village. A huge seawater pool with extensive sun terrace; freshwater indoor pool; children's pool, separate meals, cots and babysitters. Small marina with extensive water sports. 350 rooms, all air-conditioned, on five floors (6 lifts). Courtesy bus to Valletta but a hire car is really necessary.

GOLDEN BAY
On the west coast, certainly the best beach on the island, beautiful golden sand (hence its name) and another smaller sandy cove next door. Water sports, including water skiing and scuba diving, are widely available, and there are facilities for horse-riding. It does, however, have a number of disadvantages. The apparently

St Paul's Bay

safe bathing is subject to occasional dangerous currents and warnings should be taken seriously. As the beach is so attractive, at weekends it is packed with Maltese day trippers. Night life is almost entirely restricted to the Golden Sands hotel (see below). Golden Bay is 14 miles from the airport, so transfer time is around 50 minutes.

Hotel Golden Sands ★★ overlooking Golden Bay (see above) but with the considerable handicap of 140 steps leading down to a private corner of the beach (there is a lift, which always seems to be at the bottom when you are at the top). Large seawater pool, children's pool, early suppers, high chairs, cots, baby sitters. Not much to do. 322 rooms on 5 floors, sea view supplement.

COMINO
Only a handful of people, other than seasonal hotel staff, live on this tiny island between Malta and Gozo (see below) which is best known for its Blue Lagoon excursion. The island, under two miles in any direction, consists of barren rock and some small sandy beaches. Its ferry service, which is extremely limited, takes 15 minutes from Gozo and 25

THE GOOD RESORT GUIDE 113

MALTA

M'Garr Harbour, Gozo

minutes from Cirkewwa, near Malta's Paradise Bay, which in turn is 45 minutes by coach from the airport.
Hotel Comino★★★★ totally isolated, splendid sea views, large swimming pool, children's pool, two small sandy beaches. Integrated with the adjacent Club Nautico on Santa Maria Beach which has self-catering apartments and facilities for many water sports. Quiet, relaxing. Hotel has free private ferry to Malta. 162 rooms, including many for families, on two floors (no lifts).

MALTA

GOZO

The arrival of a helicopter service linking Gozo with Malta airport is an ominous sign that the island's tranquility may be coming to an end. Gozo, with its fascinating natural beauty (see excursions), is much greener and more rural than Malta. The capital, Victoria, seems reminiscent of a quiet English market town, distinguished only by a walled fortress to which the local inhabitants used to retreat whenever pirates landed on the island, which was a distressingly regular occurrence in earlier times. Marsalforn is the principal resort, a fishing village in the north west. The best beach, Ramla Bay, which has sailing, scuba diving and windsurfing facilities, lies close by. Transfer time:
45 minutes by coach, 30 minutes by ferry; or 20 minutes by helicopter.

Hotel Ta' Cenc ★★★★ on a clifftop near the village of Sannat in the south of the island, a hotel-bungalow complex with terraces and patios elegantly set into the landscape. Lovely fresh water swimming pool whose panoramic sea views dissuade most holiday makers from making the long slog to the beach. 50 rooms including 10 suites and several family units. Disco. Car hire more or less essential.

MALTA FACTS

Your journey

	Hours
From Gatwick, Luton, Heathrow	3¼
From East Midlands	3½
From Manchester	3¾
From Glasgow	4

Luqa airport is four miles south of Valletta, which is 20 minutes away. Transfer times are given under each resort area.

Shopping

Most shops open from 0900-1330 and again from 1600-1900, Monday to Saturday. The St. James' Market in Valletta, which is exceptionally interesting, opens from 0800-1230 on Sundays.

Money matters

Banks are open 0830-1230, Monday to Friday; 0830 to 1200, Saturday.
Banks are closed on January 1, Good Friday, Easter Saturday, Easter Monday, May 1, August 15, December 13, December 25. It is possible to bargain on the rate of exchange offered by many shops and even some restaurants, and frequently to improve on the official exchange rate. Credit cards are widely accepted.

Weather

Averages	Jan	Feb	Mar	Apr	May	Jun	Jul	Aug	Sep	Oct	Nov	Dec
Temperature	55	54	58	60	64	74	78	78	75	68	66	57
Sun hours	6	6	7	9	11	11	12	11	9	8	6	5
Rain days	12	8	5	2	2	0	0	1	3	6	9	13
Sea temp.	59	59	59	59	64	69	75	79	75	71	66	63

Malta has more than 3,000 hours of sunshine each year and is one of the sunniest parts of Europe. The hottest months are July and August, with temperatures reaching 90 degrees, and rain is almost unheard of during the summer. In the spring a hot, dusty wind sometimes blows from the Sahara. December and January are particularly wet and cloudy.

Local transport

Taxis are metered, and relatively inexpensive. However local buses, crowded and swelteringly hot in summer, are astonishingly cheap. They run to all parts of the island on (almost literally) a hit and miss basis. A bus timetable is Malta's rarest commodity.

THE GOOD RESORT GUIDE

FRANCE

MEDITERRANEAN FRANCE

Spectacular scenery, warm seas, sparkling resorts and sophisticated night life sum up the south of France, an irresistible magnet for many Continental holidaymakers every summer. So why does it feature so sparingly in British brochures, indeed, scarcely at all among the major operators? The principal explanation lies in the unbending opposition of French aviation to charter flights, especially charters on the massive scale that might otherwise be possible from the UK, given that the Riviera is less than two hours flying time from the south of England. Inclusive tours using scheduled flights are inevitably more expensive, in an area where already no presentable hotel can ever be described as cheap. Put simply, for the moment

St Tropez

THE GOOD RESORT GUIDE 117

MEDITERRANEAN FRANCE

St Tropez harbour

at least, for anyone practising sensible economies in their choice of holiday destination, the Riviera has priced itself out of the British air package tour market. At the height of summer, it is also incredibly crowded: the slight shift in French holidays has simply meant that the last two weeks of July are as impossible as August. However, for those families who think nothing of a car journey from one end of France to the other, even better assisted by motorail, a Riviera holiday still represents good value for money.

The Cote d'Azur, strictly speaking the coastline from Menton to Cannes, is the area within easiest reach of Nice airport and correspondingly expensive. Further west, the towns are more casual yet just as chic, and the hotels possess much more individual charm. None more so that at two neighbouring and contrasting resorts, Port Grimaud and St. Tropez.

ST. TROPEZ

You can tell that you have almost arrived at St. Tropez by the traffic jam a few kilometres away. Indeed cars seize up, both metaphorically and literally, at a huge roundabout marking the midpoint between Cannes and Toulon, where a hypermarket has been built in the middle, a bizarre refuge from the risks of the road. When the motorist finally arrives at St. Tropez, if he is lucky, he will be shoehorned into the one and only car park. Owning a car in St. Tropez is a liability, not an asset, as its cobbled streets are quite unsuitable for traffic.

One upmanship here is to have a boat, not just any boat, but a colossal floating gin palace moored in the harbour directly opposite the gawping tourists in the row of quayside cafés. If envy could sink them, these luxury yachts would disappear without trace — as indeed

MEDITERRANEAN FRANCE

many of them did under the French socialist regime, which clamped down on company entertainment. The change of government has heralded a revival, though not quite the ostentatious luxury that characterised St. Tropez in its heyday of the sixties and seventies.

But the charm of St. Tropez is much more durable. It has inspired artists since Paul Signac moved to what was then an obscure fishing village before the turn of the century. His work, and that of many others who followed, is part of an exceptional collection of paintings in the Annonciade Museum, housed in an old chapel on the edge of the port.

For somewhere allegedly past its peak, however, St. Tropez retains a vigorous lifestyle that many other resorts can only envy. It remains a genuine fishing village, where the day's catch is sold soon after dawn on a harbour front splashed with grease and strewn with tackle, from old tubs still doing duty in the bay. Its boutiques sell next summer's fashions at twice next year's prices. Its open air restaurants are still places to see and be seen.

Whether the place would ever have attained its jet-set image without Brigitte Bardot, no one can be sure. Her fame became St. Tropez's fortune; her house on its hilly peninsula a constant battle between her wish for privacy and the lenses of prying photographers. Although of doubtful legality, many of the roads and footpaths running across this wooded hillside have been barred to the general public and are patrolled by a security firm that would look more in keeping with a Hollywood gangster movie. But then as some of the people they are protecting are summer refugees from Hollywood, perhaps they never notice.

St. Tropez also has beaches, but only one of them, the quaintly named Bouillabaisse (presumably after the fish stew), is within walking distance of the centre. For the others, you have to get your car out of the park, fight your way through the traffic, and out on another road around the back of the town. However Tahiti plage and plage de Pampelonne, together making up more than three miles of superb sand, are well worth the effort. The beach restaurants cost the proverbial arm and a leg, extravagance matched only by the unimaginably expensive bikinis which for most of the day are taken off in any case.

When the sun goes down St Tropez begins to look more and more like a misplaced Greek Island, lacking only the bouzouki music to perfect the atmosphere. Its night clubs and discos never turn out until dawn, when the really smart set goes home by boat, safe from the vigorous French breathalizer. More often than not they set sail for Port Grimaud, which in daylight hours is roughly half an hour's ride by ancient ferry across the bay.

Port Grimaud

PORT GRIMAUD

Grimaud was, and is, a village perched high in the hills to discourage unwelcome visitors, from which it is safe to conclude that it never had much use for a port. On the nearby coast, what has become known as Port Grimaud is entirely artificial, a Provencal village marina constructed on a series of man-made canals, linked by little hump-backed bridges and clusters of houses around a large lagoon. It could have been a hideous miscalculation but is actually charming, the more so because unlike St. Tropez, Port Grimaud has successfully declared war on the motorist. A few privileged residents apart, they are kept firmly outside in a huge car park, protected by a barrier and security check that would do credit to the East German border.

The only sensible way to get about is by boat; a tiny one with an outboard motor is ample if you have no intention of wandering outside the breakwater. Anchoring outside candlelit waterside restaurants, or dropping in

THE GOOD RESORT GUIDE   119

MEDITERRANEAN FRANCE

Port Grimaud

on the only square for a game of boule or an evening aperitif, soon becomes a way of life. Although there are some agreeable hotels, the majority of visitors rent one of the narrow houses on the canals, each with its little lawn and precious mooring point.

Port Grimaud does have a lovely sandy beach, with a gentle slope into the sea, extremely safe for children. Apart from occasional summer weekends, it is never crowded. The only transport link is the ferry to the harbour entrance from St. Tropez; casual cars are not allowed into even the western end of the marina complex and reaching the beach from outside requires a formidably long walk. A few houses back directly on to the sands, particularly suitable for families with small children. Transfer times: from Nice airport, expect to take 1 hour 15 minutes to Port Grimaud, at least 1½ hours to St. Tropez, longer in high season. From Marseille airport, expect a transfer time of two hours in the summer to either Port Grimaud or St. Tropez. As taxis are formidably expensive, a hire car is recommended.

Excursions

As St. Tropez and Port Grimaud are off the regular foreign tourist track, there are virtually no organised excursions to any other part of the Riviera; local buses are sparse, and the railway does not run along this part of the coast. Boats of all sizes and description can be hired in Port Grimaud, provided that you have a certificate to prove your competence as a sailor; cars rather more easily in St. Tropez,

MEDITERRANEAN FRANCE

though do not expect either form of transport to be cheap.

St. Maxime, along the coast to the north-east, is certainly worth a visit. It has a lovely promenade, some exceptional fish restaurants, a fascinating food market and even a casino. The best beach along this stretch of coast is at the next town, St. Raphael, which has a lively night life but little else of interest. It does however mark the beginning of the Esterel Massif, a wild stretch of rugged coastline that continues almost to Cannes. The dilemma for the motorist is the huge weight of summer traffic, which certainly mars the scenery and makes the journey tedious in the extreme. Many tourists give up the unequal struggle and head north from St. Maxime to pick up the motorway, dropping back to the coast for selective visits.

The advantage of the motorway is that Monte Carlo, part of the independent skyscraper principality of Monaco, can be visited comfortably in a day, comfortably, that is, apart from the thousands of other tourists bent on the same objective. Parts of the Royal Palace, somehow not quite the same without Princess Grace, are open to visitors, together with an exquisite tropical garden on the rock above the harbour. What everyone wants to see, however, is Monte Carlo casino. Contrary to popular opinion, it is open to the general public wearing less than evening dress —

St Raphael beach

indeed the inside is rather disappointing, the sumptuous decor rather overshadowed by row upon row of scruffy slot machines. The serious gambling still takes place in discreet private rooms, but you have to convince the management of your substantial financial standing to be allowed even a glimpse.

Hotel de Paris, Monte Carlo

THE GOOD RESORT GUIDE 121

MEDITERRANEAN FRANCE

Monte Carlo Casino

MEDITERRANEAN FRANCE

Monte Carlo is almost at the easternmost point of the Cote d'Azur. Either side of the principality are prime examples of perched villages, built in high, isolated positions for better defence and advance warning of attack. Eze, to the west is part fishing village, part fortress, narrow lanes and an impossibly steep route to the castle 1,500 feet above, hewn out of the rock like some precarious high altitude camp in the Himalayas. Roquebrune, to the east, is even more picturesque. Its castle, built to keep out the Saracens, is an architectural masterpiece, with walls four feet thick. The old streets of the village, a succession of narrow archways and sudden steps, recreate the atmosphere of medieval France.

West of Port Grimaud and St. Tropez, beyond more interesting perched villages called Gassin and Ramatuelle, the scenery of the Corniche des Maures is rugged and dramatic. Pine-tree forests resist the pull of gravity and cling to the steepest slopes, so that they seem to be almost dropping into the turquoise blue sea below. Just beyond the Corniche, a narrow peninsula road leads to the fascinating hill village of Giens. Its harbour is full of little ferries running between the exotic islands of Hyeres, Port-Cros, Porquerolles, and Levant. All are worth a visit, though Porquerolles has the best beaches and Levant is famous for its nudist colony.

PORT GRIMAUD/ ST. TROPEZ HOTELS

Byblos ★★★★★ in St. Tropez, an elegant group of Provence style buildings ranged round a central square. The hotel is extremely luxurious, with a fine swimming pool, immaculate decor and service, plus of course prices to match. Several splendid suites are available with sea views. The Byblos restaurant, les Arcades, is renowned in its own right, superb food in a superb setting provided that money is no object. 40 rooms and 19 suites.

Residence de la Pinede ★★★ overlooking the plage de la Bouillabaisse at the back of St. Tropez, with a small swimming pool and its own private section of the beach, from where many water sports are available. The 35 rooms and 5 apartments are exceptionally spacious, even for a hotel of this category.

Le Mas de Chastelas ★★★ two miles inland, off the road to Gassin, a converted Provence farmhouse, family run, in the midst of vineyards and orchards. Relaxed atmosphere, delightful heated swimming pool, jacuzzi, children's playground. No choice of meals but they are always delicious. 21 rooms and 10 suites, most of them extremely comfortable with lovely bathrooms attached. Closed October to March.

La Ponche ★★ in among the action, tucked away behind St. Tropez's shopping centre with pleasing views over the bay. Restaurant and terrace are particularly pleasant for evening meals. Public rooms are little more than corridors but the bedrooms are agreeably decorated and relatively spacious. 23 bedrooms. Closed October to March.

Le Giraglia ★★★ Port Grimaud's best hotel, located at the edge of the marina complex, about ten minutes' walk from the centre. The hotel is right on the beach, though not the best stretch west of the harbour, with a swimming pool and sun terrace. Restaurant overlooking the sea. The hotel has its own parking: vital in this resort. The 48 rooms vary a good deal in size and quality. Closed November and early December.

OTHER RESORTS

Nice
A famous yet remarkably relaxed resort with the considerable advantage of a car-free old quarter, full of open-air restaurants and cafes. Most of the hotels overlook the sea and are both grand and expensive. If you can make it across the busy sea-front road, the legendary Promenade des Anglais overlooks the pebble beaches, full of neat little rows of lilos and umbrellas. Unfortunately you have to pay for the privilege of using them, and the beach restaurants, which serve surprisingly good food, are far from cheap. Transfer time from Nice Airport: 15 minutes.

Cannes
Night and day life centres around and along the Croisette, the sea front promenade where French motorists are forever pretending to be out in front in the European Grand Prix, and where the hotels, still the wrong side of the

THE GOOD RESORT GUIDE

MEDITERRANEAN FRANCE

Menton, harbour and town   Inset: Nice

MEDITERRANEAN

raffic, are breathtakingly extravagant and correspondingly luxurious. The beaches, however, are superior to Nice, and not just those which are private; the public beaches at the eastern end of the Croisette are quite acceptable if you can do without the amenities. An amusement park for the children is conveniently close by. Transfer time from Nice airport: 1 hour.

Cannes

Menton

The last place in France before Italy, with strong claims to be the warmest spot on the Riviera, sheltered from the north wind by the mountain range to the rear. The season here is correspondingly long, the beaches, artificially constructed of long, inviting sand, full well into autumn. Flower festivals and carnivals are common but the nightlife seems less sophisticated than in the more renowned resorts, though the network of narrow streets in the old town has some splendid restaurants. Transfer time from Nice airport: 1¼ hours.

RIVIERA FACTS

Your journey

	Hours
From Heathrow to Nice	1¾
From Heathrow to Marseille	2

Nice Cote d'Azur airport is 4 miles west of the city. Marignane airport is 17 miles north-west of Marseille.

Money matters

Banking hours vary from place to place but most are open 0900-1230 and 1430-1630, Monday to Friday; some open Tuesday to Saturday, especially in market towns, when Saturday opening times are likely to be 0900-1400 without a lunch break.

French franc travellers cheques are preferable to sterling, as both hotels and banks in France give a rather unfavourable rate of exchange for sterling cheques; but beware both banks and hotels trying to charge a commission on franc cheques, which they are not supposed to do.

In high season, hotels are likely to ask for a desposit on rooms booked in advance to make certain that you will turn up.

Credit cards are widely recognised, except at many petrol stations. If you offer to pay for goods in cash, prices can be correspondingly negotiable.

Shopping

Shops, other than food shops, open 0900-1300, 1430-1830, Monday to Saturday, occasionally with early closing on either Monday, Tuesday or Wednesday. Food shops usually open 0800-1230 and 1430-1900 from Tuesday to Friday, 0800-1300 Saturday, 0830-1230 Sunday, often not at all on Mondays.

Weather

Averages	Jan	Feb	Mar	Apr	May	Jun	Jul	Aug	Sep	Oct	Nov	Dec
Temperature	55	55	59	63	68	75	81	81	77	70	63	55
Sun hours	5	6	6	8	9	10	12	10	9	6	5	4
Rain days	6	7	7	7	5	4	2	3	5	8	9	8
Sea temp.	55	54	55	57	61	68	72	73	70	66	61	57

Although mild from mid-April to November, sustained sunshine is reasonably assured only in July and early August. Thunderstorms and unsettled weather are common throughout Autumn. The sea is significantly warm only in mid-summer.

THE GOOD RESORT GUIDE 125

SPAIN

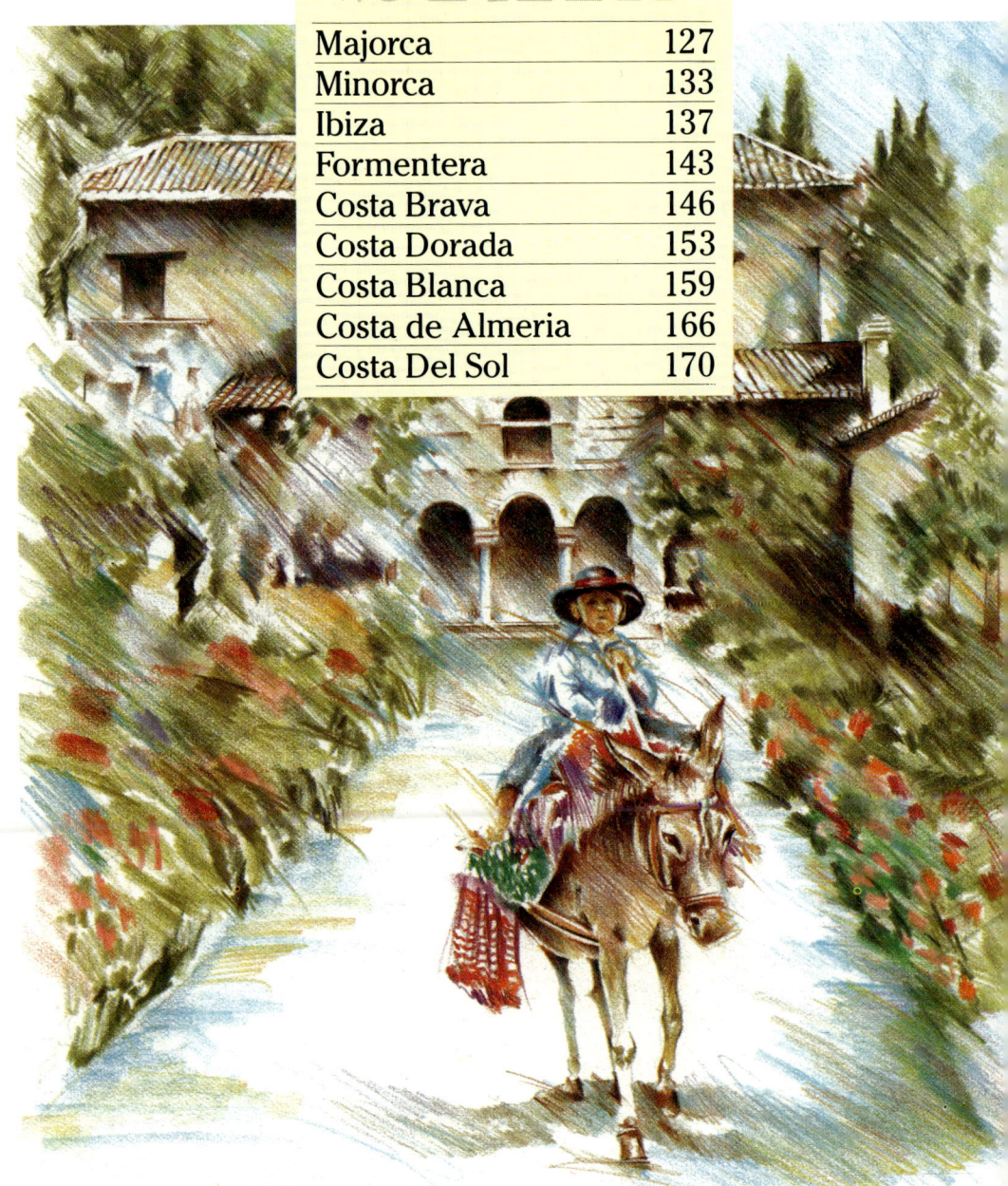

Majorca	127
Minorca	133
Ibiza	137
Formentera	143
Costa Brava	146
Costa Dorada	153
Costa Blanca	159
Costa de Almeria	166
Costa Del Sol	170

MAJORCA

MAJORCA

The largest and most beautiful of the Balearics, a group of Mediterranean islands belonging to Spain, Majorca receives more than three million tourists each year. Scarcely a single airport in the United Kingdom possessing passport and customs facilities does not have a flight (which takes a little over two hours) to the island some time during the summer. At the bottom end of the market, this mass tourism is reflected in some spectacularly over-developed resorts and indifferent hotels. But its 250 miles of coastline also play host to some pretty seaside towns, secluded rocky coves, enchanting villages and vivid mountain peaks. By hiring a car for at least part of his stay, the discriminating holidaymaker can have the best of both worlds: a resort with an outstanding beach, outstanding weather on the south coast in summer, a comfortable hotel, and night life till dawn; and a chance to explore and discover some wonderful scenery in out-of-the-way places. Majorca is indeed unique: an island where no category of tourist need return home disappointed.

Puerto de Soller

THE GOOD RESORT GUIDE 127

SPAIN

MAJORCA

MAGALUF/PALMA NOVA

Twenty years ago not so much as a fishing village stood in the spot now occupied by the huge twin resorts of Magaluf and Palma Nova, which are not only artificial, but carbon copies of one another. In each case the tree-lined hills behind them seem virtually blotted out by towering hotels and apartment blocks, lacking any kind of architectural distinction.

Only the presence of a promontory called Terranova makes it possible to distinguish one from the other, although in fact Magaluf, slightly further away from the capital, Palma, has the wider beaches. Palma Nova's shoreline is distinctly cramped at the end nearest Palma. However in high season this becomes wholly academic when the tourists in Palma proper, without a beach in front of their hotel, arrive on the shuttle bus to fill up every spare inch of space. For those at home in the water, the Bay of Palma does offer room to move, whether you fancy parasailing or pedaloes, windsurfing or waterskiing, sailing or being taken far out to sea where shoals of tropical fish swim beneath your glass-bottomed boat. Nor is there any shortage of land-based activities, including golf, a fine 18-hole course near Poniente, tennis and riding. Many families devote a day to Marineland, on the main road between Palma Nova and Portals Nous, which has a supervised playground for the children, an aquarium, and a zoo.

When the sun sets behind the promenade with its gently waving palms, attention switches to the hill streets back from the beach, where every imaginable hostelry catering for the none too distinctive tastes of British, German, Dutch and Scandinavian visitors begins to come alive. The noise can be shattering, especially if you stand equidistant from three or four of them on some street corner. For more sophisticated sound, try the Atlantis or Bananas discos, but they do not really get going much before midnight. Some night clubs will be still in their stride after dawn, although not as many as in Benidorm or at San Antonio in Ibiza. For the dedicated gambler, the casino near Magaluf shuts at 4a.m., though the quality entertainment and the restaurant close a good deal before that.

Palma, 15 minutes by bus or 40 minutes by boat, a lovely evening excursion, has a rich

Magaluf old town

Magalu

128 THE GOOD RESORT GUIDE

MAJORCA

variety of night life, though not in the centre. The El Terreno district beside the sea, with its steep streets and gleaming white houses, is a good starting point: you will gravitate with the crowd to the Plaza Gomila, all neon and noise, with enough bars, discos and restaurants to last you a year if you decided not to go home. Rather less salubrious is the Barrio de San Antonio, hardly Amsterdam or Hamburg, but a red light district just the same.

Rather safer for people with a team spirit is the medieval banquet at Comte Mal, or a candlelit dinner and show at Es Fogueró. Both, however, require a coach trip, and there are superior night spots in El Jonquet, the district behind the Paseo Maritimo, which has a wild, bohemian air.

If you plan to eat out, look for a restaurant with Majorcans in evidence, as all too many eating places offer bland international compromises which neither the chef nor the waiters provide with much enthusiasm. A good sign may be the presence on the menu of both lechona, roast suckling-pig, the island's speciality; and frito Mallorquin, a fry-up of liver, kidneys, leeks and potatoes, much more appetising than it sounds. Two points to watch: in Majorca, restaurants stop serving much earlier than on the mainland, usually around 10p.m. The number of forks outside a restaurant says little about the quality of the food, and a great deal about the lavishness of the decor. It has even been seriously suggested that the origin of the British expression to 'fork out' could be found in the conspicuously poor value of some up-market Palma restaurants.

Excursions

Majorca has so many caves, that it is a wonder it does not collapse like an overgrown honeycomb. The Caves of Drach, on the eastern coast, in a different class to Cheddar and Wookey Hole, are said to attract the most visitors of any cave in the world. That may be difficult to establish, but Drach is definitely worth the 165-mile round trip from Palma. Located some 75 feet above sea level, they consist of four enormous limestone chambers, with such clever lighting that one half expects Marlon Brando to emerge with the baby Superman in an underground Krypton. Some of the most effective stalagmites and stalactites could easily be mistaken for organ pipes, especially around midday, when live classical music is played while the tourists float around

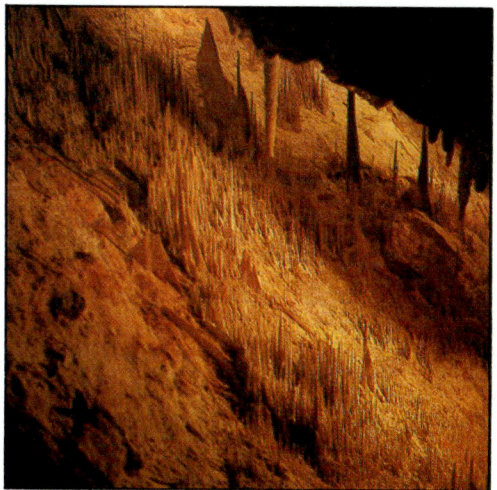

Caves of Drach

the huge Martel lake. Presumably the musicians are on undertime.

By now, however, the crowds are disconcertingly large, so visitors who arrive by hire car are advised to come early, or to devote the peak lunchtime period to seeing other caves nearby. The Hams Caves, less than 2 miles away, follow the bed of an underground river, and are much smaller. However one chamber contains stalagmites shaped like hooks ('hams' in Spanish), a freak of nature where intermittent air currents have bent the dripping stone in mid-petrification.

Further north, the Caves of Arta, much, much larger, have been shaped by the sea, which splashes disconsolately more than a hundred feet below the enormous entrance. It is so vast that Jules Verne is popularly supposed to have had it in mind as the way into another world when he wrote *Journey to the Centre of the Earth*.

The north of the island has other attractions. In the north-west, eight miles of successive and unprotected hair-pin bends await the would-be visitor to Sa Calobra, the sheltered cove at the bottom.

To the north-east, the Romans established a settlement at Alcudia, where a tiny amphitheatre marks the centre of what was once a prosperous little town. Not much of the Roman walls remain, as the Moors reclaimed the rubble for fresh fortifications many centuries later.

THE GOOD RESORT GUIDE 129

MAJORCA

Much closer to the main resorts, only 12 miles from Palma, the Valldemossa Monastery stands in an exquisite setting, row after row of olive trees. Built by Carthusian monks who fell foul of the government, it was rented out in 1838 to the great composer, Frederic Chopin, and his French mistress, the writer George Sand. As they lived in a damp cell during a particularly wet winter, their ardour was somewhat inconvenienced, which may have benefited posterity as Chopin created some of his masterpieces during their stay. The lovers were not, however, flush with funds and fled the island at the first hint of spring, abandoning many of their possessions to deceive their creditors.

Palma itself, a large, but uninspiring city, is overlooked by a massive gothic cathedral, whose huge stained glass window may well be the largest single piece in existence. However the best opportunity to appreciate the city is by horse and carriage, trotting from the cathedral to the grand gateways of the old city by way of the waterfront.

Valldemossa monastery

Palma Cathedral

MAGALUF HOTELS

Atlantic★★★ central, near the Terranova promontory, but seems to escape the worst of the night-time noise. Swimming pool, none too large, leads from a shaded rear terrace directly on to the beach. Breakfast is the best meal of the day; not much to do at night; children tolerated rather than welcomed. 80 rooms on 5 floors, 35 with a view of the sea.

Antillas Sol★★★ on a tiny headland at the western end overlooking the sea, with direct access to the beach, sharing many facilities with its sister hotel Barbados Sol. Between them, they have two swimming pools, one of which can be covered in. Antillas Sol has the edge for children, offering a supervised nursery, separate meals, separate pool, and baby-sitters, so really determined parents need hardly see their offspring before the flight home. 332 rooms on 10 floors (3 lifts).

Barbados Sol★★★ behind its sister hotel, the Antillas Sol, which hogs the views and blocks the way to the beach. That makes the Barbados's shared outdoor pool more important, and its bizarre shape goes back to the period when hotels actually designed pools to deter swimming on the basis that it interfered with drinking. Disco. Particularly good restaurant. 428 rooms on 11 floors (3 lifts).

Coral Playa Sol★★★ on the Terranova headland, built into the cliff, with a lift down to its own private beach. The choice of three swimming pools, one for children, would be more impressive if the terraces were not shaded by other nearby hotels. Steep walk to the centre. 185 rooms.

PALMA NOVA HOTELS

Hawaii★★ superb views, as one might expect from a hotel built on the Terranova headland. The swimming pool and the round

130 THE GOOD RESORT GUIDE

MAJORCA

children's pool are set in a grand terrace at the water's edge, with awkward steps down to a tiny beach. Large programme of evening entertainment. 212 rooms.

Playa Palma Nova ★★ probably the best position in the resort, though next to a narrow stretch of beach. Not much to do in the evenings, but the night life is not far away. Uninspired restaurant. 53 rooms on 3 floors.

OTHER RESORTS

C'AN PICAFORT
Facing the broad Alcudia Bay, an unappealing resort blemished by ugly concrete towers but rescued by a superb, six-mile sandy beach that slips gently into the sea. At the western end, several hotels have direct access to the sea on a path strewn with seaweed. However hotels at the eastern end, towards the harbour, lead on to a much rockier and narrow section of beach, not really suitable for families, so check before you book. Discos provide the only significant nightlife, and enthusiasts for water sports would do better elsewhere. Transfer time from Palma Airport; 1½ hours.

CALA MAYOR
Difficult to distinguish in geography or appearance from C'as Catala and San Augustin, two adjoining and equally featureless suburbs of Palma, whose traffic makes a point of ignoring the by-pass and running through Cala Mayor. Crowded beach, though the waterskiing is excellent; golf course nearby. Palma is easily accessible and the transfer time from the airport a plus point: only 20 minutes.

CALA MILLOR
A splendid beach, long, sandy with a gentle slope; but just behind are the highrise hotels, most of them, admittedly, separated from the seashore only by a pedestrian zone. The activities available include golf, tennis, riding, sailing and windsurfing. Transfer time: 1½ hours.

EL ARENAL
In any other major resort, the presence of aircraft landing or taking off from Palma Airport would be cause for complaint. However most people who stay here never notice, either because they are sleeping off the consequences of the previous nights revelry, or because the discos drown the sound of the engines. For disco dancing, El Arenal is tremendous, and teenagers rave about it. The long, sandy beach has a rich variety of water sports. However slightly older and squarer visitors may care to note that a busy main road separates all of Arenal's hotels from the sea. Most of them are high-rise boxes, but the quality, curiously, improves as you go further back. Transfer time: 15 minutes.

PAGUERA
South-west of Palma, a resort that lacks really good beaches; what there are, seem crowded and rather grubby, with one exception, at the wooded, eastern end near the Beverly Playa hotel, popular with the large number of German tourists. The attractive promenade cannot disguise the fact that most of the hotels are on the wrong side of an extremely busy through road. Transfer time: 45 minutes.

Beach at El Arenal

THE GOOD RESORT GUIDE 131

MAJORCA

PUERTO DE SOLLER
Day trippers from Palma, who take the ancient train to Soller then transfer to an equally decrepit tram, suffocate this lovely resort on the main north-west coast. However at night the atmosphere is transformed and can be quite enchanting. Beach enthusiasts should note that there is not much sand to spare. The coach from Palma Airport takes 1½ hours.

PUERTO DE ALCUDIA
You will search in vain among the brochures for the rather conspicuous power station beside the resort, though by keeping to the smaller of the two harbours, you can pretend it is not there. In fact many of the hotels are so far away from the centre, cocooned on their own stretch of the superb beach, that they can barely claim to be part of the resort. Transfer time 1½ hours.

PUERTO DE POLLENSA
Another quiet resort, in the extreme north of the island, whose peace is shattered at lunchtime by the coachloads of sightseers from Palma and all points south. The view is lovely, a delightful bay with a backcloth of rugged mountains, and the beach provides waterskiing, windsurfing and, from the nearby harbour, quite demanding sailing. In the evenings, however, it is so quiet that you almost wish the trippers had not departed. Almost. Transfer time: 1¼ hours.

Puerto de Soller

132 THE GOOD RESORT GUIDE

MAJORCA/MINORCA

MAJORCA FACTS

Your journey

Flight time to Palma	Hours
From Bristol, Cardiff, Exeter, Gatwick, Heathrow, Luton, Stansted	2¼
From Birmingham, East Midlands, Manchester, Norwich, Southend	2½
From Leeds, Newcastle, Teesside	2¾
From Belfast, Edinburgh, Glasgow	3
From Aberdeen	3¼

Transfer time to Magaluf or Palma Nova: 30 to 45 minutes from Palma airport.

Shopping

Most shops are open from 0900 to 1330 and from 1630 or 1700 to 2000. Many items can be bought tax free (a saving of ten per cent) by completing a form which enables the shop to recover the duty and send it by cheque to your home address.

Money matters

Banks are open from 0900 to 1300 (a few until 1400) Monday to Saturday, closed Sunday.

Most banks are closed on public holidays, which include January 1, January 5, January 6, March 19, Thursday, Friday and Monday of Easter weekend, May 1, July 25, August 15, October 12, December 8, December 24, December 25, December 31. Most hotels, and many travel agencies, exchange travellers cheques and sterling although the rate, particularly at travel agencies, is not as favourable as at the banks. Credit cards are widely accepted. Many shops, particularly in Palma, readily take sterling but shrewd holidaymakers insist on paying in pesetas.

Weather

Averages	Jan	Feb	Mar	Apr	May	Jun	Jul	Aug	Sep	Oct	Nov	Dec
Temperature	57	59	62	66	72	79	84	84	77	74	64	59
Sun hours	5	6	6	8	9	11	11	10	8	6	5	4
Rain days	6	5	5	4	3	2	1	2	4	7	7	7
Sea temp.	56	57	57	61	67	71	76	80	73	68	65	61

Magaluf and Palma Nova receive less than 16 inches of rain in a whole year. However, the northern part of Majorca, with the resorts of Alcudia, Formentera and Pollensa, receives over 32 inches.

Local Transport

Taxis are supposed to have signs displaying official prices, but frequently do not. The cost of hiring a car throughout Spain has gone down following a reduction in 1987, of VAT. The two rail routes, one to Arta, the other to Soller, offer splendid scenery, but are not a means of fast transport. Buses on Majorca are frequent and cheap but run late at night only between the major resorts close to Palma.

MINORCA

For every ten holidaymakers flying to Majorca, Minorca receives only one, making it the least crowded and relaxed of the three major Balearic islands. Lying north-east of Majorca, the island is actually larger than Ibiza, 28 miles long and 12 miles across at its widest point, but it lacks entirely the other islands' dynamic night life and large, unsophisticated resorts.

Even with a car, many of Minorca's finest attractions will elude all but the most determined visitor, for the roads do not run to the best and therefore most secluded beaches. In the north of the island, where the green forests merge with a turquoise sea, little sandy coves sit beckoning amidst the rugged coastline.

SPAIN

THE GOOD RESORT GUIDE 133

MINORCA

CALA SANTA GALDANA

However for a package tour, the discriminating visitor may well select a resort on the southern coast, Cala Santa Galdana, a broad, windless bay with a marvellous beach of white sand, sloping gently into the water, reassuringly secure for children. Boats are available for hire, so you can picnic in the enchanting and almost deserted coves of Mitjana and Macarella, just around the headland. The more energetic holidaymaker may prefer to take out a proper sailing boat, or go waterskiing, or windsurfing or even scuba diving. A local club, subsidised by the main hotels, 'Aquasport Menorca', offers particularly good lessons for everyone from complete novices to absolute experts. The

Cala de Santa Galdana

MINORCA

SPAIN

Mahon, capital of Minorca

night life is also dominated by the hotels, although the village of Santa Galdana has a Spanish wine bar and a British pub (with British beer) called the Green Dragon. Some beer is actually more expensive than gintonica, gin and tonic of course, because gin is a local product, made at a factory just outside Mahon, the island's capital. The recipe is courtesy of the British Navy, a legacy of British occupation on and off during the 18th century.

Excursions

Apart from offering a tour of the gin distillery, complete with samples, Mahon has also given its name to Mahon-sauce … or mayonnaise. Apparently the Duc de Richelieu arrived with his entourage unexpectedly at a local inn, and the only meat the inn-keeper had to offer was decidedly past its prime. In order to disguise its appalling taste, he added a sauce of his own invention which so delighted the Duke, that he took the recipe back home and introduced it to some of the noble families of Europe. History does not record meanwhile what misadventure befell the Duke's stomach on that innovative night. Mahon also boasts a superb deep water harbour, once a bone of contention between the British and French fleets. Its shops, predominantly in the old quarter on top of the hill, are cheaper than the main resorts, particularly if you want leather or jewellery, a local speciality. The other large town, Ciudadela, 30 miles away on the west coast, has a 3-day festival in July incorporating a jousting tournament. There are some interesting shops under the shaded arcades of the main square, and in the maze of narrow streets behind, two unexpectedly good discos, the centre of the island's night life. If that seems too far to travel, visit the Caves of Xoroi south-west of Santa Galdana. There is not much sign of the troglodytes, but then perhaps they cannot afford the admission to the nightly disco. If you have a car, the best place to eat is in the far north, at Fornells, a village with a legendary line of fish restaurants overlooking the sea. For the best view, climb Monte Toro or 'bull mountain', the highest point right in the centre of the island.

CALA SANTA GALDANA HOTELS

Audax★★★★ splendid views of the bay, but quite a climb down to the beach, by way of a footbridge and rather narrow steps. The swimming pool is small and long shadows spoil the sun terrace. Disco. 250 rooms on 7 foors (4 lifts).

THE GOOD RESORT GUIDE 135

MINORCA

Los Gavilanes Sol ★★★ cleverly integrated with the cliffs above the bay, but the sandy beach below is tough going if you use the steps. The hotel has four lifts but at peak times it can take a long time to go up or down. Special entertainment for children. 357 rooms.

Cala (Santa) Galdana ★★ no problems with lifts or long flights of steps, but still 400 yards from the sea. Which makes the size of the swimming pool, and the adjoining sun terrace more important: and both are quite small. However the paddling pool is supervised during the peak season. An ingenious credits system allows guests to choose between the air-conditioned restaurant and the 'Benamar' restaurant in the village, or you can eat out, at a price, on the hotel's private boat. 204 rooms in hotel, plus 70 villas and bungalows available.

OTHER RESORTS

ARENA D'EN CASTELL
Another potential brochure confusion, with El Arenal on Majorca (see page 131). Arena d'en Castell could not be more of a contrast as it is quiet and isolated, although the architect who designed the modern hotels evidently had an off day. However the beach, at the back of a deep bay, is superb. With Mahon, 13 miles away, the nearest night life, there is not much to do in the evenings. Transfer time: 40 minutes.

CALA'N PORTER
The resort has many lively bars and excellent restaurants, including the Caves of Xoroi (see page 135). However its attractive, sandy beach is some distance away, at the bottom of a steep road. Transfer time: 25 minutes.

SANTO TOMAS
A resort with no recognisable centre, south-east of Cala Santa Galdana. Hotels, restaurants and bars are all scattered haphazardly above the sandy beach. Transfer time: 45 minutes.

VILLA CARLOS
Two miles south-east of Mahon, on the edge of the river estuary, but no real beaches. Coach excursions stop for lunch at the restaurants surrounding the tiny harbour, which tends to ruin the atmosphere. Transfer time: 20 minutes.

Cala'n Porter   Inset: Ciudadel

MINORCA/IBIZA

MINORCA FACTS

Your journey

Flight times to Minorca	Hours
From Bristol, Cardiff, Gatwick, Heathrow, Luton, Stansted	2¼
From Birmingham, East Midlands, Manchester	2½
From Glasgow, Newcastle	2¾

Minorca airport is three miles south-west of Mahon. Transfer time to Cala Santa Galdana: 45 minutes.

Shopping
Shops open from 0830 to 1300 and 1630 to 2000 in the main towns (see also excursions, page 135). In resorts and hotels they can be expected to stay open all day.

Money matters
Banks open from 0830 to 1330, Monday to Saturday; closed Sunday. Most banks are closed on January 1, January 6, Good Friday, May 1, July 25, August 15, October 12, December 8, December 25.

Ciudadela and Mahon have banks with full facilities, but elsewhere there are very few exchange bureau. The exchange rate given by hotels is generally poor. Do not assume that credit cards will be accepted, even in the main resorts.

Weather

Averages	Jan	Feb	Mar	Apr	May	Jun	Jul	Aug	Sep	Oct	Nov	Dec
Temperature	57	59	62	64	70	77	83	83	79	72	64	59
Sun hours	5	6	6	7	9	10	12	10	7	5	5	4
Rain days	7	6	6	5	4	3	2	2	4	8	8	8
Sea temp.	56	57	57	61	66	70	75	78	73	68	65	60

Minorca has an annual rainfall of 22 inches, rather more than Majorca, which together with comparatively low temperatures between December and March, makes it an unattractive prospect for a mid-winter holiday.

Local transport
Car hire is essential to see the island thoroughly. Cala Santa Galdana and Santa Tomas have particularly poor local transport, but the island bus service is unreliable.

IBIZA

Closer both to the Spanish mainland and the North African coast than the other Balearic Islands, Ibiza and its tiny neighbour Formentera have a character and a culture of their own. Indeed, they were always a separate entity to sailors, who called them the 'pine islands', because of the pine-clad hillsides sheltering the countless inlets around a rugged and dramatic coastline. Although Ibiza retains memories of its past in the old walled quarter of the capital, it is the sustained sunshine and the sandy shores that have established its reputation as a major holiday

SPAIN

IBIZA

Beach at Cala Bassa

destination. Unlike Majorca, many of Ibiza's best beaches are to be found outside its main resorts, no longer undeveloped in terms of tanning equipment, water sports and bars, but still nevertheless in beautiful settings. The atmosphere is one of complete informality, the accent on youth, the passing population totally cosmopolitan. As for the employees of the service industries sustained by the influx of summer visitors, they have reached a new level of refinement in the art of procrastination which, coupled with their infectious charm, outwits all attempts to find a cure.

They do have some excuse. At the lower end of the package tour market, there is a small minority who seem to believe that going abroad is a licence to abandon most forms of civilised behaviour, and some do find their way to Ibiza's biggest resort, San Antonio Abad. They are unforgivably rude to hotel and restaurant staff, vandalise their accommodation, and sometimes drink themselves insensible. Small wonder the local people do not want to do much for them in return. However the hotels selected for Ibiza are among the least likely to experience this problem.

SAN ANTONIO ABAD

San Antonio Abad, literally 'Abbot St Anthony', was once, like so many Spanish resorts, a tiny fishing village whose houses were easily outnumbered by the pine trees at the back of the bay. However it had been prosperous in much earlier times: the Romans called it *portus magnus* or 'great port', and the harbour is still packed with small boats. However their trade today is people not produce, because — however implausible it may seem — San Antonio has the worst local beach of any major resort in the Mediterranean. Where the sea laps gently in front of some of the larger hotels, the narrow streak of sand is seriously polluted and strewn with clinging seaweed — so it is both

THE GOOD RESORT GUIDE

IBIZA

unpleasant and hazardous to health. You have to travel three miles to Porto de Torrente for the nearest proper town beach, and even here the sand gives way to painful shingle right by the water.

So the answer to the question, who pays the ferrymen, is that the holidaymakers do — at least twice a day when, morning and evening, they are carried back and forth between San Antonio proper and the three sandy beaches, Cala Bassa, Cala Conta and Cala Tarida, all on the southern headland. True, these remote beaches are plentifully supplied with water activities, including fishing, sailing and, particularly at Cala Bassa, waterskiing. If you have never tried it, the waterskiing instruction is particularly encouraging here. For the more lethargic, there are trips on a glass-bottomed boat which offers glimpses of spectacular marine life. However, these beaches become, in effect, major excursions, with a considerable part of the day devoted to arriving and departing. While most of the tourists do not seem to object, families with small children sometimes feel the strain of not having easy access to their hotel. A few apartments and hotels have been developed close to these distant beaches, but then the same problem presents itself in reverse: visiting San Antonio proper to go shopping or for entertainment also involves a double ferry trip.

The activities available in San Antonio include riding, tennis, mini-golf and a full-scale course 15 miles out, at the Club Roca Lisa.

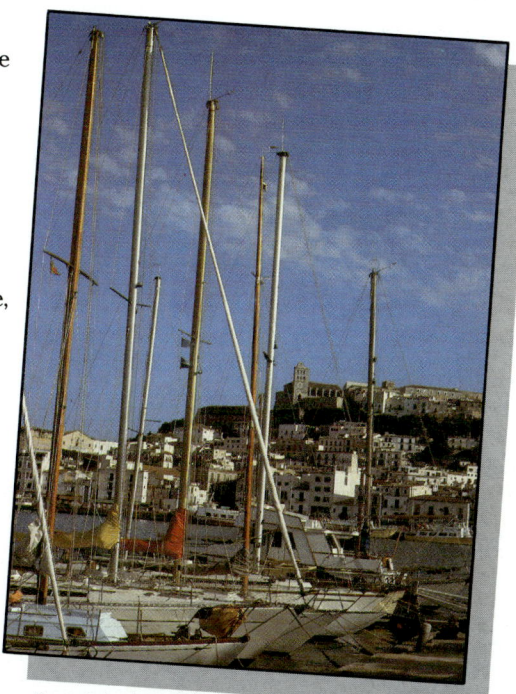

Boats in harbour, Ibiza

However for those who like nothing better than to while away their time with a glass of real ale in their hand, Ibiza is ideal. San Antonio has half a dozen allegedly British pubs serving beer which tastes much the same as it does back home, with the added incentive of course that licensing hours and drinking-up time are simply not part of the Spanish vocabulary.

The Spaniards, incidentally, do have bars that specialise in beer but for every 'cerveceria' they sell, they also encourage you to try one of the dozens of liqueurs on their shelves, especially the odder varieties made from the least expected fruit. For someone who has sworn never to touch a drop of the hard stuff again, the Balearic Islands' speciality is horchata, non-alcoholic and usually served in a long glass with lots of ice. It is made from almonds and milk, sweetened with honey, and tastes delicious.

When they go out to dinner, the Spaniards like to finish with a brandy; if they cannot afford the more expensive blends, they pour a cheap glassful into their coffee. For anyone looking for a cheap dish to eat, squid is plentiful and never expensive, though not

Ibiza Town at night

THE GOOD RESORT GUIDE 139

SPAIN

IBIZA

everyone likes the taste. Fish is the base of one of the most popular local dishes, zarzuela, but it is transformed by the addition of a hot, spicy sauce. Sofrit payes, a stew with meat and potatoes, also involves extensive use of spices and makes a vindaloo curry seem mild in comparison.

Most hotels have given up offering an alternative to the night life in the resort, as almost everyone goes there anyway, even from three or four miles away. In San Antonio, many of the streets become traffic-free precincts after dark, when markets spring up like magic on the pavement, with traders spreading out their wares on rugs and street artists prepared to dig up a paving stone complete with chalk picture if you offer them enough money.

As the hours slip by, the music, a mixture of multi-track stereo and little live groups, doubles its decibels until the whole town seems to be gently vibrating. A lot of the action takes place on the waterfront in fashionable bars like the Cafe de Mar; of the night-clubs, Sa Tanca is popular and far from ridiculously priced. There are discos by the dozen, but the Star Club still reigns supreme; some of the minority groups take refuge in Es Paradis, a few doors away. Many night-clubs and discos are not allowed by law to open before 10p.m., and an increasing number charge for admission. The usual system is 'con consuncion', which means your first drink (except champagne) is free when you get inside. Of course, your first drink is unlikely to be your last. A great many beds remain

Old Ibiza Town

THE GOOD RESORT GUIDE

IBIZA

nslept in by the time the first cautious rays of the sun signal the oncoming dawn.

Excursions

A so-called pirates cruise is a fancy description for a day out to the nearby island of Formentera (see page 143). There are however all-day cruises around Ibiza itself, and any number of boats (with or without crew) for hire where you choose the itinerary — at a price. The complete round trip is 106 miles, which is not realistic in a single day. On land, Ibiza Town on the east coast offers sight-seeing and shopping. Climb the streets of the old town towards the ancient citadel, and see the formidably strong walls that defied the Barbary pirates. Then walk down the fishermen's quarter of La Pena, a maze of little alleys and cul-de-sacs, where you can be hopelessly lost and still hear the buzz of main street pedestrians somewhere beyond the tiny houses. La Marina, the district closest to the quayside, has the most fashionable restaurants but you have to arrive early to be sure of getting in. Four miles north is Ku, a fashionable complex of bars with a restaurant and spectacular disco. The lighting and special effects are quite prodigious.

Open air restaurants in Ibiza

SAN ANTONIO ABAD HOTELS

Nautilus Fiesta★★★ on the eastern end of the San Antonio bay, one of the very few hotels with direct access to an acceptable beach, good clean sand. Unfortunately it is too small to cope with the number of visitors, and the same might be said for the hotel swimming pool in high season. Although the atmosphere is relaxed and the service excellent, the hotel does not go out of its way to cater for children. 156 rooms, all air-conditioned, on seven floors (2 lifts).

Arenal★★ the public rooms often seem to have guests in swim-suits paddling through, as the artificial beach is on one side, the swimming pool on the other. There are no special facilities for children and virtually no evening entertainment, but the harbour and resort centre are a matter of minutes away. 131 rooms on three floors.

Pinet Playa★★ could not be better placed for transport to the superior beaches, as the ferries leave from the hotel's own landing stage. Buses going to the town centre, which is 1½ miles away, also stop outside the front door. The road, unfortunately, is noisy. The hotel's own small sandy beach would be much more easily accessible if there was a lift from the terrace. Splendid swimming pool, children welcomed and provided with substantial facilities. 290 rooms on 6 floors (2 lifts).

OTHER RESORTS

ES CANA

On the north-east coast, a lively little village with an excellent sandy beach. The hotels are nicely spaced along the shoreline, each with a fine view of pine tree forests running almost to the shore. Unfortunately this potentially idyllic scene is shattered almost every lunchtime by the arrival of day-trippers from elsewhere. Good for business perhaps, but no resident want a rugby scrum in every bar or restaurant, which occurs particularly on days when the hippy market is operating on the road outside the village. Transfer time: 45 minutes.

PLAYA D'EN BOSSA

Strong claims to have the best beach of any

THE GOOD RESORT GUIDE

IBIZA

Portinatx Inset: Es Cana

resort on the island, which sounds too good to be true. It is. Unfortunately both the beach, three miles south of Ibiza Town, and the best hotels are right on the flight path from the nearby airport. There may not be a flight every 30 seconds such as at Heathrow, but in summer they still come in thick and fast, especially at weekends, so the level of disturbance is considerable. One advantage of course, a transfer time of under 15 minutes.

PORTINATX

Film buffs may recognise part of the location as the backcloth to 'South Pacific', part of which was made here on the grounds of economy, and for a long time no-one was any the wiser. The resort is much more built up now, of course, but still a pleasant place for a holiday, particularly for families. Transfer time: 1¼ hours.

PUERTO SAN MIGUEL

Rather easier to reach than Portinatx because of a superior road from Ibiza Town, a resort that lies in a beautiful bay. It is noted for its warm water and its facilities for water sports, including waterskiing and windsurfing. Day trippers from Ibiza Town in high season tend to spoil what is otherwise a quiet, relaxed resort. Transfer time: 50 minutes.

142 THE GOOD RESORT GUIDE

IBIZA/FORMENTERA

IBIZA FACTS

Your journey

Flight time to Ibiza	Hours
From Gatwick, Heathrow, Luton	2¼
From Bristol, Birmingham, Cardiff, East Midlands	2½
From Leeds, Manchester	2¾
From Edinburgh, Glasgow, Newcastle	3

Transfer time to San Antonio Abad is 45 minutes.

Shopping

Most shops open 0900 to 1300 and 1600 to 2000, except in the smaller resorts, where lunchtime closing is unusual.

Money matters

Banks open 0830 to 1500 Monday to Friday, 0830 to 1400 Saturday; closed Sunday. All banks are shut on January 1, January 6, Good Friday, May 1, July 25, August 5, August 15, October 12, December 8 and December 25.

Outside the main towns, banks are few and far between: travellers cheques can be cashed at most large hotels but the rate is generally poor.

Weather

Averages	Jan	Feb	Mar	Apr	May	Jun	Jul	Aug	Sep	Oct	Nov	Dec
Temperature	58	58	62	66	73	80	84	86	81	74	65	61
Sun hours	5	6	7	7	10	10	11	11	8	6	5	5
Rain days	8	6	8	6	5	3	1	3	5	9	9	9
Sea temp.	56	57	57	61	67	71	76	80	73	68	65	61

Ibiza is the opposite to Majorca, receiving more rainfall in the south and west of the island. However it is still less than 16 inches annually, and wet days consist of occasional showers rather than a continuous downpour. The temperature is extremely hot in high season, and still mild in mid-winter.

Local transport

Travel in the day time for economy, for buses are frequent and cheap, but almost all the services stop soon after 9p.m. Taxis, also modestly priced during the day-time, suddenly acquire huge surcharges after that magic hour. In the summer months, be resigned to the fact that finding a taxi may be difficult and that buses will be absolutely packed and suffocatingly uncomfortable.

FORMENTERA

The smallest and most southerly of the Balearic islands, Formentera lies 11 miles from Ibiza, whose ferry is the only regular means of contact with the outside world. Its flat bleak landscape, punctuated only by windmills and fields of wheat, is redeemed by mile upon mile of superb sandy beaches. Only ten miles long and slimming in the centre to a mere mile wide, Formentera has but one area of organised activities, Es Pujols in the north-west, with two discotheques, two bars, Ca Nostra and La Barca, that stay open after midnight (though only just), and a cinema. The emphasis, however, is on self-catering in this area. Most of the hotels are clustered around the western end of the Playa de Mitjorn, a narrow strip of beach on the southern coast. It is marred, however, by underwater rocks close to the shore, so children, especially, need to beware. Except in best hotels, there is not an inexhaustible supply of water, which is drawn from wells and tastes rather salty. However the primitive nature of the island is part of its fascination, and few people complain,

THE GOOD RESORT GUIDE 143

SPAIN

FORMENTERA

Windsurfing at Formentera

particulary as the local red wine is cheap and drinkable, far better than any other produced in the Balearics.

Water sports are offered in abundance. If you have a proficiency certificate (for example, signed by a sailing club in the UK), you can go off in a sailing boat unsupervised; or join the island's scuba diving school (for which, again, a licence and a medical certificate are necessary). Local conditions ensure that windsurfing rivals the best the Mediterranean has to offer.

Formentera is now offered as a two-centre holiday with, for example, San Antonio on Ibiza. But if one appeals to you it seems almost inconceivable that you will truly enjoy the other.

FORMENTERA HOTELS

Formentera Playa★★★ situated in splendid isolation on the south beach of the Playa de Mitjorn, this hotel is ideal for families who like to go to bed early after a hard day on the beach. The hotel is one minute from the sea. Children's playground. Es Pujols, with its discos, is 2½ miles away. 211 rooms on 5 floors (2 lifts).

La Mola★★★★★ a luxurious 'club' complex consisting of two separate hotel buildings and a series of bungalows adjacent to the Playa Mitjorn, with two swimming pools, sailing and diving schools (see above), tennis and volleyball. However if it is important to you to be really close to the beach, make sure you are booked in the building known as 'Hotel 1'. Three restaurants, including a poolside grill, and a disco. 262 rooms (4 lifts).

Beach at Formentera

144 THE GOOD RESORT GUIDE

FORMENTERA

FORMENTERA FACTS

Away from it all holidays involve some inconvenience, and it must be said bluntly that the journey to Formentera is no exception. As the island has no airport, and little prospect of one, travel is always by way of Ibiza (for journey times from the UK see page 143) and on package tours the choice of flight may also be much more restricted. At Ibiza airport, collecting baggage and clearing customs can take up to an hour at peak times. Once under way, the holidaymaker has a 15 minute coach transfer to the port in Ibiza Town, then a wait for the ferry of, say, 15 minutes on average, the ferry ride itself of 1 hour to the little port of La Sabina, then a 20 minute transfer if you are staying at one of the hotels in the south of the island. Your journey can therefore take the best part of three hours not counting, say a 2½ hour flight from the UK.

Weather

Averages	Jan	Feb	Mar	Apr	May	Jun	Jul	Aug	Sep	Oct	Nov	Dec
Temperature	57	58	61	65	72	78	82	84	80	73	63	60
Sun hours	5	6	7	7	10	10	11	11	8	6	5	5
Rain days	8	6	8	6	5	3	1	3	5	8	9	9
Sea temp.	56	57	57	62	68	72	77	80	74	68	66	62

Formentera is fractionally cooler than Ibiza but the sea temperature is a degree or two higher for much of the year.

Local transport

Forget the idea of a night out in Ibiza Town, unless you book a room, as the last ferry goes at 8p.m., even in summer. On Formentera itself, the bus service can charitably be described as erratic. The few taxis charge what they please, and if you want one after midnight, it would almost be cheaper to buy a car. What cars, mopeds and scooters there are for hire often seem to be mechanically suspect. The island has only one petrol station, and supplies have been known to run out during periods of peak demand. Bicycles are the best bet, but do check the brakes.

COSTA BRAVA

Costa Brava — map showing Estartit, Pals, Calella De Palafrugell, Palamos, San Feliu, Tossa De Mar, Lloret De Mar, Blanes, Malgrat, Pineda, Barcelona, Mediterranean Sea

COSTA BRAVA

The Costa Brava has been a mecca for holidaymakers since the package tour was in its infancy. It offers indefatigable night life, outstanding beaches, and some of the best coastal scenery to be found anywhere in the Mediterranean. Costa Brava means 'wild' or 'rugged' as indeed it is in parts, with stark cliffs above tiny rocky bays, where the pine trees crowd down to the sea. Gerona airport receives charters from every part of the United Kingdom, and coaches roll down the French

Costa Brava

146 THE GOOD RESORT GUIDE

COSTA BRAVA

motorways to cross into this north-eastern corner of Spanish seaside. From the French border to Blanes the Costa Brava stretches for 125 miles, ranging from tiny fishing villages to huge holiday resorts, of which the biggest and best-known is Lloret de Mar.

LLORET DE MAR

Although some of the beaches are particularly attractive, the sand is not. Indeed along much of this coast, including Lloret, the sand is far outnumbered by tiny pebbles, which are less comfortable to walk on, and rather less agreeable for sun bathing. The main Lloret beach also slopes steeply into the sea, making it precarious for toddlers and off-putting for inexperienced swimmers, who find themselves instantly out of their depth. It has more to offer for experienced sea-goers, including waterskiing, windsurfing, sailing and parasailing. You can watch other people hard at work enjoying themselves from the Paseo Verdaguer promenade, lined with palm trees and exotic flowers, the place to see and be seen as the sun slowly sets.

If the density of exposed flesh becomes too much, the Fanals Beach, a mile to the south, has marginally more space, perhaps because many visitors to Lloret are unaware of its existence. It has similar acquatic activities on offer to the main Lloret beach, plus snorkelling on a nearby headland. Further south still, Santa Cristina cove, bordered by pine trees lapped by the sea, offers a relaxed atmosphere if not exactly seclusion.

Back in Lloret itself, go-karts, indoor bowls and skittles supplement the familiar offerings of riding and tennis. At the rear of the town is a casino and a bull-ring, largely stage-managed for the tourist. To get there on foot, however, demands a steep walk uphill, which is also a disadvantage of hotels in this part of the resort.

At night, Lloret really comes to life, with British pubs serving (almost) British beer, little bars throbbing gently to the sound of the Spanish guitar, and discotheques or night clubs with an extremely effective sound system that stay open until daybreak. The best are associated with hotels, such as Gloria or Oasis, with discos in the basement; Casino Royal, wall to wall mirrors, and among the night-clubs, Guitart, Marisc and Niza. At the sophisticated Gran Palace club, the flamenco show can be truly superb.

With such a large number of British visitors, Lloret caters relentlessly for British tastes: bacon, egg and sausage seem available 24 hours a day. Wimpy and McDonalds have set up business in competition with dozens of snack bars and pizzerias whose fare is advertised by blaring music without and electronic games within. However the traditional Spanish restaurants do offer well cooked fresh fish and grilled meats, usually presented with a fine range of salads and vegetables. The local speciality is 'habas a la Catalana', delicious home-produced beans mixed with ham. Local Catalan wines are among the best in Spain and represent extremely good value.

Church at Lloret de Mar

In the daytime, Lloret looks rather less attractive, mainly because the planners have abandoned any pretence of preserving the past. Apart from the 16th century church with its multiple minarets, worth a visit to see the dome of exquisite mosaic, the old quarter has been spoilt by modern shop development along its narrow streets. However at least the town council has been much more strict about high-rise development, which is far less apparent in Lloret than in many other resorts on Spain's Mediterranean coast.

Excursions
The Costa Brava coast can be visited by coach or by boat: the Cruceros line offers regular

SPAIN

THE GOOD RESORT GUIDE 147

COSTA BRAVA

ladies of Catalan society flutter in and out of cafés in their finery, like peahens on parade. Near the waterfront, the ladies are less interested in style and more in matters of the flesh.

If you can give the shops a miss, or intend to visit the city twice, Saturday or Sunday afternoon is an ideal choice. The traffic is light, the fountains flow and are floodlit after dark. So, too, on alternate weekends is Nou Camp, Barcelona's stadium, where Terry Venables and Gary Lineker sustain a tiny English presence in European football.

High above Barcelona, Montjuich, a hillside park offers entertainment for the whole family, including a children's funfair and some impressive museums. To reach it, find the cable car station near the harbour, and take in some superb city views.

Even higher, outside Barcelona to the north-west, lies the working Benedictine monastery of Montserrat. Finding the church choir in full voice seems a pleasing chance on

Monastery at Montserrat

small ferries to Tossa de Mar, San Feliu, Palamos, Blanes, Malgrat, Calella and Pineda, while Costa Brava coastline drives are a full day coach excursion. Shorter trips include Ampurias, extensive Greek and Roman remains with, on hot days, an opportunity to bathe off lovely nearby beaches; and Pals, a picturesque medieval village set, no doubt for security, on top of a hill.

However most people are tempted by the prospect of a full day in Spain's second city, Barcelona, where the relics of its medieval glory blend neatly with its modern department stores. For the history, find the Barrio Gotico, a quarter of sinuous narrow lanes, ripe for ambush and the assassin's knife, dominated by gothic buildings and cool courtyards screened from the savage sun. But a couple of blocks away the mood becomes modern, especially in La Rambla or more accurately Les Rambles, five interconnecting streets that together become Barcelona's most famous boulevard. Everything is for sale here from fine clothes to flowers and cage-birds. Nor are all the birds irretrievably caged. Away from the port, the

La Rambla, Barcelona

148 THE GOOD RESORT GUIDE

COSTA BRAVA

one's first visit, until you realise that they scarcely have time off for lunch. Even without them, the restaurants are packed and the souvenir shops manned by overworked monks who must have little time left for more devout duties. Still, it is all enormous fun, with the climax to the visit a trip on an ominously creaking cable car to the top of the mountain. Try to choose a clear day, when with binoculars you can just make out the islands of Majorca and Minorca to the east and the snow-covered peaks of the Pyrenees to the north.

The Pyrenees enclose the independent principality of Andorra, an anachronism of the past tucked away between Spain and France, who exact some nominal dues in exchange for their protection. In Andorra itself, dues are a novelty, as almost everthing is tax-free, which has led to the main street in the capital, Andorra La Vella, becoming a kind of Aladdin's cave of duty-free alcohol, cameras, hi-fi and cigarettes. That apart, however, there is little to see and almost nothing to do in its mere 187 square miles outside the skiing season. Most of the excursions involve an overnight stop.

LLORET DE MAR HOTELS

Monterrey ★★★ set in pleasant gardens to the rear of the town, spacious public rooms, with a strong claim to be the best hotel in Lloret. The beach is 15 minutes walk, the centre not much less, but many guests are happy to settle for the large swimming pool with its generous barbecue at lunchtime. There is a wide choice of food in the restaurant, too. Children's pool and playground. 228 rooms, not quite all with air-conditioning, on 9 floors (3 lifts).

Rigat Park ★★★ on a small headland leading directly on to Fanals Beach, a sophisticated hotel with traditional Spanish architecture, rather too sophisticated for most children. Of the three restaurants, one, out-of-doors, is particularly attractive. The centre of Lloret is about 1 mile away. 99 rooms on 5 floors.

SPAIN

Barcelona Cathedral

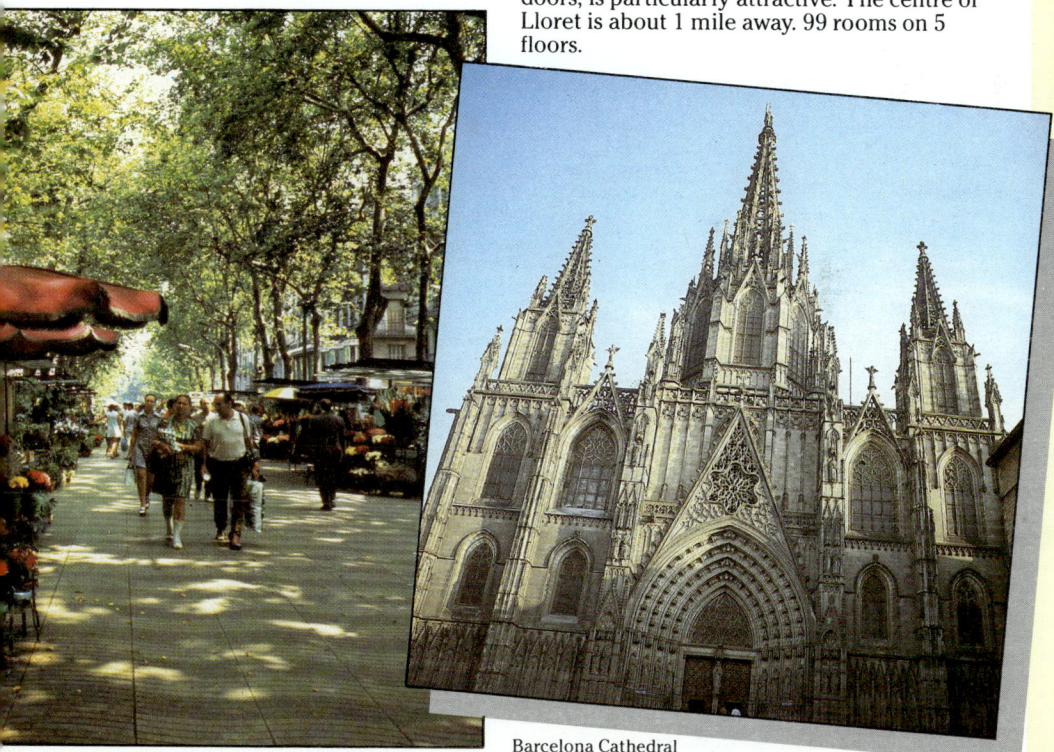

THE GOOD RESORT GUIDE

SPAIN

COSTA BRAVA

Calella de Palafruge[ll]

Calella de Palafrugell

Don Quijote★★★ a few minutes from Fanals Beach, a hotel particularly well equipped for children, who have their own pool, a playground, specially organised entertainment and separate meals. The large swimming pool for adults still does not seem big enough when the hotel is full. 374 rooms on 7 floors (3 lifts).

Flamingo★★★ Frigola★★ adjoining hotels sharing facilities, which include two swimming pools, but with 504 rooms between them, the sun terrace can be extremely crowded. The Flamingo, which has its own disc[o] is the better of the two, unless you are given a room overlooking the extremely busy and noisy main road into Lloret. However the Flamingo does have 287 rooms to choose from, on 7 floors (2 lifts).

Montanamar★ on the main road to Tossa, but far enough back to avoid most of the traffic noise. This hotel is more than 1½ miles from the centre, at least 10 minutes from the beach, with a small pool and an uninspiring restaurant. What rescues it from mediocrity is its sports facilities, which include three squash courts and a gymnasium. 38 rooms.

150 THE GOOD RESORT GUIDE

COSTA BRAVA

OTHER RESORTS

BLANES

Only four miles from Lloret, the Costa Brava comes to an abrupt halt here, together with the railway line from Barcelona, which fortunately impinges very little on the resort. The narrow streets of the old quarter, full of cursing motorists, lead down to a colourful harbour and a charming promenade. The beach, inevitably not sand but fine stones, is far from safe at the Los Pinos end, where it shelves sharply into the sea. In mid-summer, however, the population does tend to be swelled with campers, who pitch their tents outside and come into town for a good time rather like cowboys at the end of a trail drive. Transfer time: 45 minutes from Gerona, twice as long from Barcelona or Reus.

CALELLA DE PALAFRUGELL

First, check your brochure. Are you looking at Calella de la Costa, which is on the Costa Dorada (see page 156) 30 miles north of Barcelona? It could be no mean mistake. Calella de Palafrugell is north, not south of Lloret, and usually served by Gerona airport (1½ hours) although occasionally, and confusingly, by Barcelona airport as well. The Palafrugell version is greatly superior, based on a small and friendly fishing village. The beaches are equally small and attractive, but energetic swimmers should beware the presence of underwater rocks. Abundant windsurfing and sailing, but apart from a few bars, nothing to do at night.

ESTARTIT

Twenty miles to the north, 27 miles east of Gerona, another quiet resort particularly popular with families. Its main attraction is a long, flat beach, with real sand. Children are particularly safe here, except on rare days when the sea is whipped up by strong gusts of wind. You can learn to windsurf or sail at Estartit, but the outstanding attraction is a glass bottomed boat through which you can watch shoals of exotic fish below on the way to Las Medas, an island nature reserve. Transfer time: 1¼ hours from Gerona, twice as long from Barcelona or Reus.

TOSSA DE MAR

North-west of Lloret, but all too close for the day-trippers to pile off their coaches and swamp the bars and restaurants during the height of the season. Prudent holidaymakers actually staying in Lloret abandon the main beach, coarse sand in a picturesque location at the back of the bay, in favour of Menuda Beach, half a mile north-east. However when they

Tossa de Mar coastline

THE GOOD RESORT GUIDE 151

COSTA BRAVA

return in the evening, Tossa is quiet again, and its open-air restaurants have an enchanting air after dark. Fortunately for Tossa, the encroachment of developers is frustrated by its position: hills surround three sides of the town, and a medieval wall bars the fourth. Transfer times: 1 hour from Gerona, 1½ hours from Barcelona and Reus.

LLORET FACTS

Your journey

To Gerona	Hours
From Gatwick, Luton	2
From Birmingham, Bristol, Cardiff, East Midlands, Stansted	2¼
From Leeds, Manchester, Newcastle	2½
From Glasgow, Belfast	2¾

To Barcelona or Reus	Hours
From Gatwick	2
From Birmingham, Cardiff, East Midlands, Luton	2¼
From Manchester, Newcastle	2½
From Edinburgh, Glasgow	2¾

Shopping
Most shops open around 0900 to 1330 and 1630 to 2100.

Shopping in the old quarter of Lloret can be extremely congested, especially on Tuesdays, market day, when careless visitors should beware pickpockets and plausible street salesmen.

Money matters
Banks open 0900 to 1400 Monday to Friday, closing 1 hour earlier on Saturdays. Closed Sundays.

Most banks are closed on January 1, January 6, Good Friday, May 1, Corpus Christi (June), July 25, August 15, October 12, December 8, Christmas Day.

Bureau de change tend to offer slightly better exchange rates than most banks. Only the more expensive hotels, restaurants and shops will admit to accepting credit cards and some shops will not even accept travellers' cheques.

Plugs
Some older hotels have 110 volt plugs and sockets, which may result in problems for appliances usually running on 220 volts.

Weather

Averages	Jan	Feb	Mar	Apr	May	Jun	Jul	Aug	Sep	Oct	Nov	Dec
Temperature	56	57	61	64	70	77	82	82	77	70	61	57
Sun hours	5	5	6	8	8	10	10	10	8	6	4	4
Rain days	3	4	5	4	5	4	2	4	5	7	4	5
Sea temp.	55	55	55	57	61	68	72	73	72	68	61	57

Lloret is extremely hot in high season, with many solid days of sunshine but, it must be said, more cloudy or even wet days than southern Spain. The temperature is at its most comfortable in May and October, but October can be a conspicuously wet month. The winters, in comparison with the Costa del Sol, are really quite cold.

Transport
A circular shuttle bus service operates between the two main parts of the resort, Lloret proper and Fanals, linking the beaches and the principal hotel areas to the town centre. It is cheap and frequent but in the summer months long, disorderly queues build up at bus stops.

Duty-free
Most spirits and international brands of cigarettes are cheaper in the duty-free shop at the airport. Perfume and fortified wines, such as Martini and Campari, are cheaper in large local supermarkets.

COSTA DORADA

Where the Costa Brava ends, the Costa Dorada begins, stretching from Malgrat down to Salou, one of the most popular destinations for British tourists. But Salou and possibly Sitges apart, this is not an area of conspicuously pleasant resorts, as much of the coast is marred by an inconveniently close railway line and by the urban sprawl of two big cities, Barcelona and Tarragona. 'Dorada' means 'golden', a slightly romantic reference to the long sandy beaches, but alas nothing to do with prospecting for nuggets.

SALOU

Before the package tour industry reached its height, Salou was a quiet and slightly pretentious weekend watering-hole for the upper-class families of Reus, the provincial capital that has become familiar to British visitors through its modest airport. It seems difficult to believe it now, but Salou once had only two hotels, and one of those closed for the

Salou

THE GOOD RESORT GUIDE 153

COSTA DORADA

winter. Now it has 30 mainly large hotels in a sprawling jigsaw of interlocking resorts, which vary so much in character, that what may be appealing to one holidaymaker may be appalling to the next.

Of the five separate sides to Salou, the most hotels per square mile are to be found opposite the Playa Capellans, an agreeable sandy beach limited by pine trees to the back and rather too small for the number of potential visitors. The way to the beach is down a flight of 43 steps, which can be so jammed with people in high season as to be positively dangerous. However, the hotels are better placed for the best shops on the Avenida Andorra, the heart of Salou's commercial centre.

West of Playa Capellans is the first of Salou's main beaches, Playa Levante, splendid sand but extremely crowded. It is divided by the harbour from Playa Poniente, more gently sloping sand, but slightly narrower and if it were possible, busier still.

Behind the two big beaches a broad, attractive promenade with neat flower beds, tall palm trees, and a large, floodlit fountain, leads into Salou's old town. The main street, Calle Barcelona, sweeps down to the harbour. In September 1229, when King Jaime of Aragon launched from here an expedition to reconquer Majorca for Christendom, it took a week to embark his army of 15,000 men and 1,500 horses.

Going east from the harbour, just past the Playa Capellans, more hotels have been built overlooking the small cove of Cala Font. Fringed by woods, this beach is slightly less crowded than the rest in midsummer, but because of its sheltered position, it can be intolerably hot after lunch.

Further east still, Playa de Pineda marks the fifth identifiable portion of Salou. Already a long way from the centre, this beach becomes increasingly untidy the closer it runs to Tarragona's ugly industrial quarter. However, for all its shortcomings, Playa de Pineda is infinitely superior to the fully fledged resort of Pineda del Mar (see page 157). As the Pineda beach in Salou is 66 miles south of Barcelona, and Pineda del Mar is as far north as you can go from Barcelona and remain on the Costa Dorada, they should not be confused; but every year some holidaymakers go to Pineda del Mar based on what they have read about Playa de Pineda and are sadly disappointed.

For beach amenities, Playa Levante and Playa Poniente have the best sailing and windsurfing, and are conveniently placed for impulsive boat trips from the nearby harbour.

In the resort itself, children will like the funfair beside the promenade near the old town, which compensates in atmosphere what it lacks in extravagant machinery. You can also try go-karting, ten pin bowling, mini-golf and tennis; but if you hire a bicycle, do check the brakes.

For eating out, travel west of Salou for three miles to the fishing village of Cambrils, which has a line of open-air restaurants during the summer months. It is just as well they can put the tables outside, as many of the buildings with houses are so tiny, there is barely enough room for the kitchen; the washing-up is sometimes done in the back yard.

Salou's most popular night club is Galas, which does most of its business on an inclusive ticket for the floor show and half a bottle of champagne. However, despite a wide cross-

Beach at Salou

THE GOOD RESORT GUIDE

COSTA DORADA

Fisherman with his catch, Tarragona

section of bars and discos, Salou has nothing to compare with the bright lights and dynamism of Benidorm or Lloret de Mar.

Excursions

As the Costa Brava leads directly into the Costa Dorada, many of the excursions detailed in that section (see page 147 - 148), including Barcelona and Montserrat monastery, are equally accessible. Montserrat however is only one of three interesting monasteries in the mountains, and the others require a less arduous journey. Poblet, past Reus, is more like a fortress, a reminder of the days when bandits preyed upon unsuspecting travellers in the passes. The monastery at Sante Creus, off the main Zaragoza to Barcelona motorway, is now essentially a museum. On a triangular trip, after the junction with the Zaragoza route, a short diversion from the motorway towards Reus will bring you to a safari park.

Only seven miles north east of Sitges is Tarragona, a large industrial town with a fascinating medieval quarter surrounding the

THE GOOD RESORT GUIDE 155

COSTA DORADA

SPAIN

huge gothic cathedral. Among its maze of little streets is a restored Roman fortress, for this was a flourishing city in Roman times. Like Barcelona, Tarragona has its Ramblas, a series of tree-lined streets with outdoor cafés, where the world watches the world go by.

To the south lies Pensicola, a famous old town dominated by its huge medieval castle above the fishing harbour. Some of the nearby restaurants that take the fishermen's wares are quite superb. However, enthusiasts for souvenir shops will have an even better day out.

Roman aquaduct at Tarragona

SALOU HOTELS

Augustus Park★★★ directly on the Playa Poniente, south-west of the harbour, so you can flit between the swimming pool or the sun terrace and the sea, which can make it difficult to keep an eye on children. Particularly attractive restaurant overlooking the sea, but of the 324 rooms, only those at the rear have a full sea view. All of them, however, have a balcony (5 floors, 2 lifts).

Cala Font★★★ the small sandy cove of that name is a few minutes' walk by way of the hotel filter road, but with the centre of Salou a good two miles away, local amenities are sparse. Two restaurants, both air-conditioned. Children are particularly well catered for, with early meals, high chairs, separate swimming pool and baby sitting available. Do not, however, expect peace and quiet here. 318 rooms on 8 floors (2 lifts).

Cap Salou★★ seems singularly uninspired, but its position is outstanding, behind almost a private beach east of Cala Font in a deep, secluded bay. The dining room looks out on a large swimming pool, which can be covered in for use in the chillier months. One snag: Salou's centre is almost 3 miles away, and the nearest bus stop to the hotel is at the top of a steep hill which older guests may find arduous. 325 rooms on 6 floors (2 lifts).

Delfin Park★★ a spacious, central hotel just off the Calle Mayor, well placed for the shops, but at the same time an easy 5 minutes' stroll to the Playa Levante. The restaurant provides separate meals for children, who also have a separate swimming pool. Not the place for a relaxing holiday. 244 rooms on 6 floors (2 lifts).

Donaire Park★ leads directly on to Playa de Pineda but otherwise extremely inconvenient: the nearest shops in the Pineda suburb are 15 minutes' walk, and older people could take an hour to walk into the centre of Salou. However, the hotel is ideal for children, who have a delightful separate swimming pool, organised games and shows, and separate meals. Everyone else also has to settle for a set menu, though. Two discos close by, sports centre opposite. 426 rooms on 9 floors (4 lifts).

OTHER RESORTS

CALELLA DE LA COSTA

Another potential brochure mix-up, as there is another Calella, the greatly more attractive Calella de Palafrugell on the Costa Brava (see page 151). Visitors to Calella de la Costa do not all come by air, arriving at Gerona, a 1 hour transfer, or at Barcelona, 1½ hours; many come by coach direct from the UK, a journey of between 24 and 28 hours, depending on the route. It follows that after that kind of experience, the drawbacks of the actual resort may seem trivial by comparison. The principal

156 THE GOOD RESORT GUIDE

COSTA DORADA

...sadvantage is the railway line, which runs between the hotels and the beach, restricting access to a number of tunnels which inevitably may be far from a convenient way to cross. Indeed so many visitors used to take dangerous short cuts over the line itself, that the authorities have now erected a wire fence along its complete length; but even that has been penetrated in places. The dangers to children are not limited to the line: the beach, much of it rather painful shingle, shelves steeply into the sea. But many single people or young couples on a budget holiday will not find the unpretentious hotels and will think the night life terrific.

MALGRAT
The problems of Calella de la Costa are magnified here. At Malgrat the railway line is entirely unprotected, so the temptation to cross direct from beach or hotel or vice-versa is almost irresistible. The beach, another mixture of sand and shingle, shelves just as steeply and a breakwater is an added danger in parts. Nor is the night life as good as at Calella de la Costa, so this resort is really not recommended.

Transfer time: 45 minutes from Gerona, 1½ hours from Barcelona.

PINEDA
An agreeable little town just north of Calella, whose hectic night life is just a short train ride away. In other respects, however, the railway is once again a huge disadvantage, barring the way to the sea. The beach is largely shingle, and drops sharply to the sea. Given the wide choice usually available on the Spanish Costas, this resort is scarcely recommended. Transfer time: 1 hour from either Gerona or Barcelona.

SANTA SUSANA
This resort sits uneasily between Pineda and Malgrat, lacking the vigour of one and the inactivity of the other. A new promenade has been built but nothing has been done to reduce the effects of the inevitable sea-front railway line, which is almost entirely unprotected. Like Calella, Pineda and Malgrat, all blighted by the railway, the line at Santa Susana is given only a passing mention in many of the big brochures, and simply drawn disingenuously on the resort map. Not recommended.

SPAIN

Beach at Sitges

COSTA DORADA

SITGES

Like Salou, Sitges rescues the Costa Dorada from complete disaster. Unlike Salou, it does have a prominent railway, but fortunately it runs nowhere near the sea. As a consequence, the principal sandy beach of Playa d'Oro, fringed by a line of palm trees and a sparkling promenade, is particularly attractive. The beach narrows further west where the posh villas have been built, but the original coarse shingle has been submerged in tons of Saharan sand, imported from Morocco. The town itself has few amenities, but at least it has succeeded in resisting high-rise development; most of the hotels are small and relaxed, run by the same families for generations. Unfortunately at weekends the peace of the place is shattered when the Spanish day-trippers turn up from Barcelona, an hour away on the train. Around here, the railway line always wins in the end. Transfer time: 45 minutes to Barcelona Airport.

Sitges stre...

SALOU FACTS

Your journey

To Barcelona or Reus	Hours
From Gatwick	2
From Birmingham, Cardiff, East Midlands, Luton	2¼
From Manchester, Newcastle	2½
From Edinburgh, Glasgow	2¾

To Gerona	Hor
From Gatwick, Luton	2
From Birmingham, Bristol, Cardiff, East Midlands, Stansted	2
From Leeds, Manchester, Newcastle	2
From Belfast, Glasgow	2

Transfer time from Reus is 20 minutes to the centre of Salou, 30 minutes to some of the outlying hotels. Transfers from Gerona take a great deal longer, 2½ hours, and from Barcelona, 1¾ hours.

Weather

Averages	Jan	Feb	Mar	Apr	May	Jun	Jul	Aug	Sep	Oct	Nov	De
Temperature	56	57	61	65	71	77	82	82	77	71	61	57
Sun hours	5	5	6	8	8	10	10	10	8	6	4	4
Rain days	3	3	5	5	5	4	2	4	5	6	4	5
Sea temp.	53	53	54	55	59	66	71	71	70	66	60	55

Salou is hot, though far from oppressively so, in June, July, August and September, but not entirely free from risk of rain. July is the driest month with practically guaranteed sunshine, but curiously the next driest are January and February, though they are rather cold. October is the wettest month, but much drier than the Costa Brava to the north.

Shopping
Most shops open 0900 to 1330 and 1630 to 2100. Monday is market day.

Money matters
Banks are open 0900 to 1400 Monday to Friday 0900 to 1300 on Saturdays, not at all on

THE GOOD RESORT GUIDE

COSTA DORADA/COSTA BLANCA

…ndays. Most banks are closed on January 1, …nuary 6, Good Friday, May 1, July 25, August …, October 12, December 8, December 25.

Bureau de change give a better rate than …any banks for sterling travellers cheques, because some banks charge extra commission on sterling cheques to encourage holidaymakers to arrive with cheques in pesetas. Credit cards are widely accepted.

…ransport

…om Salou's station in the old town, about ten …ains daily run to Barcelona and Tarragona. In summer buses run every half an hour from Tarragona to Cambrils south-west of Salou until late at night.

COSTA BLANCA

The resorts of the Costa Blanca, the central stretch of Spain's eastern coastline, are served predominantly by Alicante with …hts, both scheduled and charter, from more …n a dozen United Kingdom airports. The …hite coast', a name derived from its brilliant …ite sand, runs from Denia in the north to …zarron in the south, more than 150 miles of …aches backed by vivid mountain scenery.

BENIDORM

…lieve it or not, the first coach arrived in …nidorm, the great symbol of the Spanish …rist industry, as long ago as 1868. True, it

…ante Beach, Benidorm

SPAIN

THE GOOD RESORT GUIDE 159

COSTA BLANCA

had only four horse-power — literally, four horses — and was a stage coach operated by an enterprising local businessman from Valencia, designed to attract the more adventurous Spanish gentry into the unknown. Given that sun-bathing and sea-bathing were then desperate remedies prescribed by doctors at their wit's end to satisfy demanding and ailing patients, it was not altogether surprising that the venture failed. In those days Benidorm had a single, flea-ridden inn, which had fallen on hard times following the blowing-up, in 1812, of the local fort with the cream of the French garrison inside it ... their hostelry bills unpaid. A far cry from the boom which began in the 1960s that has left Benidorm with hotel rooms for 35,000 tourists, and ten times that many in flats and houses in the immediate vicinity.

Above all, Benidorm has a beach — not the miserable strip of sand that can masquerade as such in some Mediterranean resorts. Called the Playa de Levante (levante being 'sunrise' in Spanish), it is ideal for children because there is enough room, even at the height of the season, behind the lines of loungers for energetic games without the risk of landing in someone's lap. The sand slopes gently into the sea, making bathing equally safe. A pity then, as many of the most popular hotels are only a few minutes' walk, that nothing has been done to make that brief journey less precarious. For while the narrow sea road is easily crossed, the same cannot be said of the Avenida del Mediterraneo, a dual carriageway on which the traffic flows furiously from morning to night.

Benidorm, coastal view

COSTA BLANCA

Benidorm old town

The Playa Levante runs roughly west as far [as] the original village, a mesh of miniature [st]reets that reach to the top of the headland, [w]hitewashed houses with neat little balconies [an]d lovingly cultivated window boxes.

Just inland is less beautiful Benidorm, the [R]incon de Loix district, populated by smaller, [bo]x-like hotels and cheap apartment blocks. [A]ny semblance of Spanish flavour is [co]mpletely submerged here in a brash [in]ternational scene. The Germans have their [bi]erkellers, with German beer; the British their [pu]bs, with British beer and even British [m]easures, plus the added advantage (or [di]sadvantage, depending on your viewpoint) of [no] licensing hours; the Scandinavians, [di]scouraged from drinking at home, seem to [us]e any bar where the alcohol is dispensed [wi]th a minimum of delay.

Only the noise of the traffic outdoes the [ja]zz in downtown Benidorm, especially [fu]rther west, where the second of Benidorm's [bi]g beaches, the Playa de Poniente is backed by [on]e of the main routes between Alicante and [Va]lencia. Until recently, it was the only route, [bu]t a new by-pass has marginally reduced the [vo]lume of vehicles.

Poniente, or 'sunset' beach has a solid cliff [fa]ce to the rear, restricting both new [de]velopment, and the tanning space available [to] existing hotels, many of which cast [di]sagreeable shadows on each other for much [of] the day. The beach, if you survive crossing [th]e road, is much narrower than Levante and [in]evitably much more crowded in high season.

At its south-westerly end, the main road at last leaves the beach on the way to Alicante, and the Poniente beach widens in front of the up-market headland of La Cala, which has its share of large hotels and, mainly hidden behind high walls, many beautiful villas. If you are determined to get a tan without risking claustrophobia, this is the part of the beach to choose.

The final choice of beach is offered by Cala Finestrat, a small fishing village whose tiny beach in a sandy cove lacks amenities and, unfortunately, no longer lacks visitors. It is still less crowded than Poniente or Levante in the summer months, but only just.

The two main beaches offer a great deal for the water enthusiast, including pedaloes, windsurfing, snorkelling, sailing, scuba-diving (previous experience necessary) and waterskiing by means of a cable-ski course around the bay. For water activities better suited for children, go to Aqualand, just outside Benidorm, with one of the longest water chutes in Europe.

Benidorm old town

SPAIN

THE GOOD RESORT GUIDE 161

COSTA BLANCA

SPAIN

Even if you never go near the water, Benidorm has a huge range of other activities, including riding (horses and donkeys), tennis, ten-pin bowls and a huge go-kart circuit.

However, at night Benidorm really comes alive. From the top of the old town, sunset can be a romantic experience, watching the sun slip behind the distant escarpments, then turning to see the moon glittering on a motionless sea. Below, visitors stroll arm in arm along the promenade between the palm trees, or sit quietly in the bars of the old quarter listening to the penetrating sounds of a Spanish guitar.

In the centre, the music is more like a force of nature, bringing shabby streets to life. Even the tour reps lose count of the number of bars and discos, which change hands, and reputations, with startling regularity. Those worth trying include Bacchus Garden, Black Sunset, Blinkers, Harrods, the Pig and Whistle, Rumples, Vanity, Viking and the White Horse.

For something different, El Corral is a roller disco complete with its own swimming pool. Benidorm rivals the best for sophisticated sound equipment, but if you want live entertainment, some of the bigger hotels have regular shows (befriend a resident), go to the Silver Bullet or one of the two leading nightclubs, Benidorm Palace or Granada. Coach trips are arranged more or less every night to the Castell Comte d'Alfaz for a medieval banquet, including some impressive jousting; to the Rancho Grande, for a barbecue with (almost) as much wine as you can drink; and for those who fancy a flutter, the Costa Blanca Casino.

Excursions

For real train enthusiasts, the sheer delight of narrow gauge railway that runs from Benidorm into the foothills. Called the Lemon Express after the fruit trees that line much of the track the ancient engine with equally ancient drive

Benidorm nightclub

162 THE GOOD RESORT GUIDE

COSTA BLANCA

Benidorm

atters its way to Gata, noted for its
[wi]ckerwork. Not far away, to the north-west, is
[th]e safari park of Vergei, with, for those who
[lik]e that kind of thing, performing dolphins.

About six miles north-east of Benidorm,
[th]e Moorish village of Altea survives largely
[in]tact, with nearly 300 steps from the main
[st]reet to the oldest quarter. On Sundays the
[lo]cals play pelota, bouncing the ball off the
[w]alls; Tuesday is the best market day, although
[in] summer it is staged all week for the benefit
[of] coach parties: try the local bus and get there
[ea]rly.

Excursions also run to Javea, said to be the
[su]nniest spot on the Costa Blanca; Elche, with
[th]e largest palm grove on the Continent of
[Eu]rope; and to Alicante, which some would-be
[vi]sitors may unwisely select as their resort.

[B]ENIDORM HOTELS

[Ca]mbel★★★★ the building is impressive, the
[lo]cation, midway along the sea road opposite
[th]e Levante beach, outstanding; but the pool is
[poo]ky. The restaurant is no longer quite as far
[ah]ead of other Benidorm hotel restaurants as it
[on]ce was; and it, like the hotel, is expensive.
[29]4 air-conditioned rooms.

Don Pancho★★★★ on the far side of the busy Avenida del Mediterraneo, 5 minutes from Levante beach, with swimming pool on a rather cramped first floor roof. First-class restaurant. Not really suitable for children. 251 rooms, surprisingly few sea views considering that the hotel has 18 floors (4 lifts).

Dalmatas Sol★★★ close to Levante beach, but located in the Rincon de Loix district which may not suit some tastes. Self-service restaurant may also be a disadvantage. Children's playground, substantial swimming pool, but not much sun gets through the adjacent tower blocks. 270 air-conditioned rooms on 22 floors (4 lifts).

Fenicia★★ close to the harbour, handily placed to sample the atmosphere of the old quarter, and convenient for Poniente beach. The swimming pool is surrounded by a terrace which makes sun bathing almost impossible. Good restaurant. 274 rooms on 7 floors (4 lifts).

Ocas Sol★★, **Pelicanos Sol**★★ adjacent hotels in the Rincon de Loix quarter, 5 minutes from Levante beach, and sharing the same facilities. They include a large pool and for children, a separate pool and a playground. Ocas, with 329 rooms, is the quieter; Pelicanos, with 476 rooms, is both large and noisy.

Reymar★★, **Riviera**★★ adjacent hotels two streets behind the Avenida del Mediterraneo, 5 minutes from Levante beach. They share indoor, outdoor and children's pools. Children's facilities, breakfasts and evening entertainment particularly impressive. Some noise. Reymar has 198 rooms, Riviera 200.

Rio Park★ tucked away inconveniently far from the sea, Levante beach 20 minutes. Large, jolly, rather noisy hotel with a particularly generous swimming pool including separate children's section. 464 rooms on 14 floors (3 lifts).

OTHER RESORTS

ALICANTE
Alicante is an airport. At least, that is all most visitors see of it. Although Alicante proper (only 15 minutes transfer time) does have a

SPAIN

THE GOOD RESORT GUIDE   163

SPAIN

COSTA BLANCA

Sunset on the harbour, Calpe

promenade liberally punctuated by palms, the beach is like a yellow ant-hill in summer and the town, apart from an ancient castle, dull and dreary. However, the principal town on the Costa Blanca is a shopping centre, not a resort, whatever the brochures may claim for it.

CALPE
Not the place for grandmother with a heart murmur to sample the shops, as the main stree is steep enough to tax an Olympic athlete out of training. But an even more demanding clim is provided by Pinon de Ifach, a huge volcanic pillar that rivals the Rock of Gibraltar, which towers over the town. It also bisects the beaches, both of which have water sports, but otherwise are completely different: one, more

THE GOOD RESORT GUIDE

COSTA BLANCA

Pinon de Ifach, rock at Calpe

accessible, is narrow and saturated in summer; the other, much broader, has more than its fair share of minor rocks and pebbles. The fish auction in the harbour, not quite, but almost, timed for the arrival of the day trippers, is the leading attraction. However, the real charm of Calpe is to amble along the promenade after dark, watching the bars and discos gathering momentum. Transfer time: 1½ hours from Alicante, 2½ hours from Valencia.

DENIA
The Roman legionnaires were once brought here north of Calpe for rest and recreation, a long march no doubt from Hadrian's wall in full armour. Their fort has largely survived, perched high above the cluster of narrow streets around the harbour. Many self-catering holidays are centred on Denia, whose fine, sandy beach leads into shallow water, a safe spot for children. Transfer time: 2 hours from either Alicante or Valencia.

LA MANGA
Seventy miles south of Alicante, a transfer of nearly 2 hours, La Manga was once a purely Spanish resort, lacking in facilities. However, now it has a fine holiday centre with a first-class hotel and a village of smart apartments, with no fewer than three swimming pools, and two outstanding golf courses close by. The actual resort, though, is situated on a narrow sandbar, with the beaches, all on the Mediterranean side, of soft white sand rather spoilt by frequent rough seas. To swim safely you often have to cross the promontory to the calm waters of an almost land-locked gulf, which has many sailing boats for hire.

BENIDORM FACTS

Your journey

Flight times to Alicante or Valencia	Hours
From Bristol, Cardiff, Gatwick, Heathrow or Luton	2¼-2½
From Birmingham, East Midlands, Leeds	2½-3
From Manchester, Newcastle	2¾
From Edinburgh, Glasgow	3

Transfer to Benidorm from Alicante Airport is 45 minutes by motorway, 1 hour by coast road, more in busy periods. Valencia Airport is much further, at least 2½ hours.

Shopping
Most shops open around 0830 until 1300 and 1630 to 2100 on weekdays; many are open all weekend as well.

Money matters
Banks open 0900 to 1400 Monday to Friday, 0900 to 1300 Saturdays, closed Sundays.

Most banks are closed on fixed public holidays, which are Jan 1, Jan 6, Good Friday, May 1, July 25, August 15, October 12, second Monday in November, December 8, December 25.

Most shops accept one or more of the major credit or charge cards. Many will accept Eurocheques or sterling (or, for that matter, any other major European currency or dollars) — but do check the exchange rate. Hotels and travel agents will change sterling or travellers

THE GOOD RESORT GUIDE 165

COSTA BLANCA/COSTA DE ALMERIA

cheques but there are a great many exchange offices. Banks do not necessarily have the best rate of exchange and some charge a higher commission — in particular, beware changing small value travellers cheques one at a time.

Plugs
Continental two-pin plugs are standard but note that some newer hotels have sockets with a protruding earth pin so a plug or adaptor capable of accommodating this pin will be needed. The voltage is 220.

Weather

Averages	Jan	Feb	Mar	Apr	May	Jun	Jul	Aug	Sep	Oct	Nov	Dec
Temperature	61	62	66	70	75	82	88	88	84	77	68	62
Sun hours	6	6	6	8	10	10	12	10	8	7	6	4
Rain days	4	4	4	5	4	2	1	1	4	5	4	4
Sea temp.	57	57	58	61	62	69	70	74	69	64	62	57

Benidorm is extremely hot and dry during July and August with practically guaranteed sunshine. May and October have a more pleasant temperature but the risk of rain is considerably higher. The temperature remains high by UK standards from late March to late November (although the nights are cold in those months and during the winter).

Transport
Benidorm has four interconnecting bus services, with a uniform fare. A shuttle bus service operates along the sea front. Taxis are cheap and plentiful. Local car hire firms undercut the international companies by a substantial margin. In theory, rather than in practice, an International Driving Licence is required.

Duty-free
Alicante airport has an excellent duty-free shop whose prices for leather goods and local souvenirs compare favourably with central Benidorm. However, most high quality Spanish-produced alcohol (which to most tastes is largely indistinguishable from, for example, spirits produced abroad) and cigarettes can be purchased more cheaply in local supermarkets.

COSTA DE ALMERIA

The Costa Del Sol is popularly supposed to extend the full length of Spain's southern coast. In fact at the eastern end, beyond Castell de Ferro, it becomes the Costa de Almeria, taking its name from the prosperous provincial capital. Almeria has its own airport, with charter flights from more than half a dozen UK departure points, a climate that makes the Costa del Sol seem positively damp, and one attractive resort close to the remarkable hilltop village of Mojacar.

MOJACAR

The sea has evidently receded gradually over the years, for 3,000 years ago Mojacar was a Phoenician port. A series of violent

COSTA DE ALMERIA

Mojacar

earthquakes led it to be temporarily abandoned, recovering its prosperity only when the Moors seized, and occupied, southern Spain. However, Mojacar was always an isolated community, perched on a hillside in a part of Spain little short of a desert, where once a traveller would be foolhardy to venture without a large, and expensive, supply of water. Its Arab traditions survived for so long, that it became known as the 'Village of the Covered Faces' a reference to the fact that Mojacar women continued to wear the veil. Even today the older women instinctively hide their faces when strangers approach, and many houses carry the sign of the Indalo, an ancient totem god whose mission was to root out and destroy evil spirits. It is said that witchcraft continues to be practised in Mojacar, but as a form of white, rather than black magic. Either way, it is wise not to enquire.

Mojacar's little white houses were clearly not designed to double as bars and boutiques, though some of them do. However, most of the village, tucked away in tiny alleys that eventually all find thir way to the huge fountain in the village square, is unspoilt by commercial pressures. Fortunately for the atmosphere, Mojacar is simply too far for most excursions from the Costa Del Sol, and since the failure of one hotel, the pressure for further development

THE GOOD RESORT GUIDE 167

COSTA DE ALMERIA

seems to have disappeared.

Not surprisingly, most of the amenities belong to the hotels, including night clubs and discos, although some of the beach bars have an independent spirit. The Pavilion Club at the Indalo Hotel has three substantial swimming pools and a number of tennis courts. Riding is available at the Cortijo Blanco Ranch, 15 minutes drive from the village, once you know the way. The hotels by the sea provide sailing and windsurfing, and have arranged particularly expert instruction for visitors without previous experience. Mojacar is now about 1¼ miles from the mixed sand and pebble beach, which is tidy and attractive opposite the large hotels and self-catering complex, but ruined by rubble and rubbish elsewhere. Unfortunately the proliferation of camp sites and individual villas has left the seashore perilously close to pollution.

Excursions

Although Mojacar is far from ideally placed for excursions to the inland cities of Andalucia, the most important, Granada, is fortunately the nearest (see page 174). Rather closer, located to the west, in every sense, is the village of Tabernas, whose rugged canyons have been a setting for several westerns. Indeed such a cinematic conveyor-belt has been created, that its film-set facade stays perpetually in place, waiting for the next director to call for action. You will be lucky to find a Clint Eastwood lookalike striding down the main street, but the paralysing afternoon sun is authentic enough. Due north of Mojacar, a favourite excursion visits Almanzora with its gipsy cave-dwellings, and returns via Garrucha, where there is usually time for a swim off one of the nearby rocky beaches before watching the fishing fleet returning home with the day's catch.

In the opposite direction, but still along the coast, the village of Salobrena looks bizarre from a distance, like a model on a marzipan cake: in fact it is perched on a rock surrounded by stalks of green sugar cane. This excursion invariably also takes in Almeria, once a Moorish stronghold and later a precarious outpost of Christendom, indicated by the heavily fortified cathedral that dates back to the 16th century, when a black sail on the horizon could herald the arrival of the Barbary pirates.

MOJACAR HOTELS

Reyes Catolicos ★★★ relaxed, tasteful parador, or government-owned inn, where

Beach at Mojacar

168 THE GOOD RESORT GUIDE

COSTA DE ALMERIA

Almeria

OTHER RESORT

ROQUETAS DE MAR
Roquetas is a sad little village with no apparent interest in the artificial resort constructed a mile away on windy salt flats. Perhaps the villages are more discriminating than they have been given credit for, as modern Roquetas de Mar, a single street of rather scattered hotels, has little to offer. The beach of coarse sand, shelving steeply into the sea, is unsuitable for young children: it is difficult to resist the temptation of concluding that the one-horse town, apart from some stimulating discos, is equally unsuitable for adults. Not recommended. Transfer time: 1¼ hours from Almeria airport.

profit does not seem the paramount consideration. That is an advantage as far as the rooms are concerned, as the size and furnishings are exceptional. Almost all of them have a formidable sea view, as the hotel is just off a rather scruffy beach. The food, however, is inconsistent and the hotel runs down conspicuously during the winter months. The village of Mojacar is 1¼ miles up the hill. 48 bedrooms, on two floors.

El Moresco ★ ★ designed in Moorish style, less than 5 minutes from the village square, but pressure of space made it inevitable that the rooftop pool would be inadequate and the sun terrace a bottleneck of bodies. Shuttle bus to the sea, or nearly half an hour's walk. It is as far as it looks from the 147 rooms.

Indalo ★ ★ it would be difficult to get much closer to the beach, which is outside the windows, or much further away from Mojacar, 1½ miles distant, making the shuttle bus essential. Two swimming pools, including one for children, but a restaurant that is open only at night. Visitors can use the self-catering village of Pueblo Indalo the rest of the day, but that is two miles away, a long hike for lunch. 308 rooms on eight floors.

Mojacar ★ ★ easily the most central hotel, close by the main square, absorbing the village atmosphere. Rooftop swimming pool makes up in scenery what it lacks in size. The views of the Sierra Cabrera mountains from most of the 98 bedrooms takes one's breath away.

Zoraida beach at Roquetas de Mar

THE GOOD RESORT GUIDE

COSTA DE ALMERIA/COSTA DEL SOL

MOJACAR FACTS

Your journey

To Almeria	Hours
From Bristol or Cardiff	2½
From Birmingham, East Midlands, Gatwick, Luton	2¾
From Manchester	3
From Glasgow, Newcastle	3¼

Transfer time to Mojacar: 1¾ hours, more when the roads are crowded.

Shopping
Shops open 0930 to 1300 and 1600 to 1930 in the village, but for visitors with transport or a lot of patience, the supermarket and adjoining shops in the Pueblo Indalo complex stay open much longer hours in season.

Money matters
Credit cards are not conspicuously welcome in Mojacar, but the Indalo and El Moresco hotels operate an ingenious credit system of their own. On arrival, guests are given vouchers for the meals included in their package, which can be used to buy meals, snacks or drinks at any of the restaurants or bars run by the group. As you can buy extra vouchers at reception, they take on the status of a kind of currency, and have been known to change hands in beach poker.

Weather

Averages	Jan	Feb	Mar	Apr	May	Jun	Jul	Aug	Sep	Oct	Nov	Dec
Temperature	62	62	65	71	77	84	88	89	84	76	67	64
Sun hours	6	6	7	8	10	12	12	12	10	8	6	6
Rain days	3	2	1	0	0	0	0	0	1	2	2	3
Sea temp.	59	58	59	61	63	70	73	75	71	65	63	68

Even in winter, there is very little rain, less than eight inches on average in a year, making the Costa de Almeria one of the driest regions in Europe. In other respects, its climate is similar to that of the Costa Del Sol, although in Mojacar itself, evenings tend to be significantly cooler out of season.

Transport
A major snag in Mojacar is the complete absence of public transport. A free shuttle bus service for guests connects the Hotel Indalo, the Pueblo Indalo, and the Hotel El Moresco in the village of Mojacar. It operates every half hour between 10.00am and midnight. However, a good deal of queuing can be involved at high season.

COSTA DEL SOL

What was once southern Spain's greatest liability is now her biggest asset: high temperatures and sustained sun. Cloudless summer skies, warm tireless waters and a backcloth of rugged mountain scenery have made the Costa del Sol the height of fashion. Not simply for the international set, tucked away in secluded luxury villas or on yachts worth more than most people's houses; but for family holidays on modest package tours, with direct flights to Malaga from more than a dozen airports the length and breadth of the United Kingdom. East of Malaga, the resorts escape the consequences of mass tourism: to the west, the numbers trip off the planes and names trip off the tongue: Fuengirola, Marbella and Torremolinos. But if their night life is relentless and exciting, the beaches are a little disappointing, largely consisting of dark unappealing sand. Some of the big resorts have made epic architectural blunders in the scramble to meet the growing need for accommodation, and are scarred for life. Their blunders become all the more

COSTA DEL SOL

Gardens of the Alhambra Palace

obvious to visitors who take the superbly attractive excursions inland. The cities of Granada (whose Alhambra Palace is truly one of the wonders of the world), Cordoba and Seville have superb architecture and great character; and the mountain villages of Andalucia still possess that mysterious vitality of the real Spain, land of the siesta and the flamenco.

TORREMOLINOS

Time has no meaning in Torremolinos, where many of the temporary inhabitants are just going to bed, or dispensing with sleep altogether, just when most of us are usually thinking about getting up. Which is why they think nothing of dancing to disco music at maximum volume at breakfast time, especially in the bars around the pedestrian precinct south-west of Plaza San Miguel. The noise is so enormous, that it is sometimes impossible to distinguish between the dozen different languages being spoken around the outdoor tables, often piled high with empty bottles that have grown in number, if not in weight, since the night before. By midday, the ranks of the revellers have thinned out, some feeling their way the few yards back to their high-rise hotel, constructed so close to the next that many of the rooms, and sometimes even the swimming pool, exist in a zone of perpetual twilight. Of course most of the visitors here are young, fancy free and perpetually short of money. As

Torremolinos

THE GOOD RESORT GUIDE

COSTA DEL SOL

SPAIN

Torremolinos and its neighbouring resorts offers them a chance for cheap foreign travel, they love the atmosphere and gloss over the shortcomings. However, someone looking for a relaxed, sophisticated holiday, with anything above the most basic accommodation, is strongly advised to go elsewhere.

The whole of the town centre is on a low plateau. The nearest beach to the massed ranks of hotels is El Bajondillo, rather grubby in appearance, and difficult to reach. A lift is supposed to take visitors up and down, but as it is slow, frequently out of action, and closed at night to stop people fooling around and falling out, the only reliable route is provided by a steep, and by no means secure, cliff path.

At an imprecise point, the Playa El Bajondillo becomes the Playa del Lido, which runs north-east into the more subdued district of Playamar. The hotels and high rise apartments, and therefore their inhabitants, continue undiminished for miles, to be

Torremolinos

172 THE GOOD RESORT GUIDE

COSTA DEL SOL

replaced finally by individual hotels with wooded surroundings. Unfortunately as the sun-bathers thin out, the beach becomes progressively unappetising. Back in the centre, a rocky headland leads into La Carihuela, once a distinct and tiny fishing village, with fish restaurants on the quayside but an extremely narrow and crowded beach. The traffic from the main road behind keeps up a continuous roar, and only at the extreme western end does the road disappear inland, allowing space for a few hotels to be built directly behind a much wider part of the shoreline.

Beyond a largely dry river bed, Torremolinos becomes, almost imperceptibly, Benalmadena Costa, which has all of the characterless concrete of Torremolinos but none of the its compensations. The beach may be of brighter sand, imported from Africa, but it fails to conceal groups of uncomfortable and inconvenient rocks. Though it scarcely seems credible, the night life is more down market. Many of the hotels, skyscrapers of the most uninspired architecture, are on the wrong side of the busy main road. Unfortunately, some of the better hotels are also in this area, giving the holidaymaker an individious choice between disagreeable accommodaton and disagreeable surroundings. A small compensation is that all the beaches do have exceptional water activities, including waterskiing, yachting, windsurfing and, for the less adventurous, pedaloes. More suitable for the children, but just outside the resort, is the Atlantis acquapark. However, for a truly remarkable day out, visit the Tivoli World Pleasure Gardens in the village of Arroya de la Miel, midway between, and to the rear of, Benalmadena and Torremolinos. Though hardly Copenhagen, home of the original Tivoli, this huge amusement centre stretches over 20 acres, and includes some formidable rides ranging from the Big Dipper to the Ferris Wheel. The best time to go is early evening, when the temperature cools and the complex is less crowded.

Also outside Torremolinos, La Colino has a splendid riding stables, while inside the resort there are facilities for squash, billiards, snooker, ten-pin bowling and hard court tennis. Golfers are particularly well catered for, with one 18-hole course just outside Benalmadena, and another in Torremolinos itself, the Campo de Golf, the oldest course on the Costa del Sol.

For those who like to dress up and are

Casino at Torrequebrada

preferably not on a tight budget, the casino in Torrequebrada, just beyond Benalmadena, offers a sophisticated evening out. Men must wear jacket and tie, ladies something formal; if you want to go in the gaming rooms, bring your passport. No one will expect you to spend a fortune. Win or lose you can eat in the casino restaurant and watch the show at the luxurious La Fortuna night club.

Less expensive clubs with a good reputation include Gatsby and Number 1. The Montemar district has a virtual monopoly on superior discos, or you can drop in for a drink at Willies, Snoopy, Onkel or Champagne Charlie without much risk of being disappointed. If you come back in the morning, a lot of the bars serve churros, an elongated deep-fried doughnut liberally scattered with sugar. That is the moment when you know whether you had one too many the night before.

For serious eating, a few seaside restaurants in El Bajondillo may fit the bill, but for a really good meal, sample the fish restaurants in La Carihuela. Their specialities include fritura malaguena, mixed fresh fried fish, if you can say it in Spanish or English; and espetones, sardines turned slowly over a fierce charcoal grill. As a starter, order gazpacho, a chillingly cold soup made with tomato, onion and cucumber, topped with breadcrumbs.

Excursions
Even if it means paying twice over for your bed, a three-day, two-night trip to the three great inland cities of Andalucia, Granada, Seville and Cordoba, will be both a memorable and moving experience.

THE GOOD RESORT GUIDE

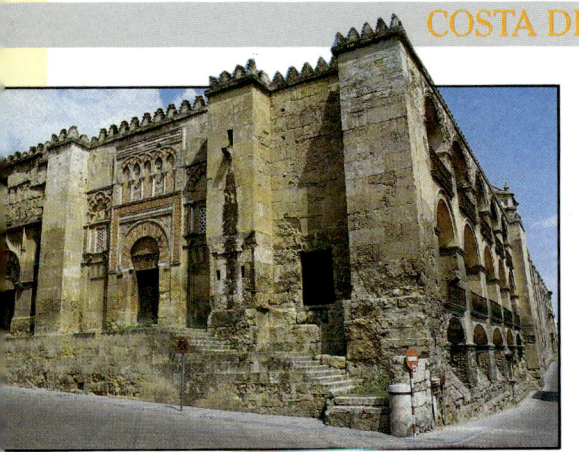

COSTA DEL SOL

La mesquita Mosque, Cordoba

Cordoba's heyday was ten centuries ago, when the Moors built La Mesquita, the great arched mosque that stuns the senses. Resist proposals for an organised tour and take an independent stroll through the Jewish district, where little fountains play in private, cool patios beside the claustrophobic, cobbled streets.

Seville, 150 miles north-west of Torremolinos, can be visited by air from Malaga but is otherwise definitely a two-day excursion at the very least. Here too, the restless energy of the Moors has manifested itself in superb architecture. The Giralda, an exquisite minaret tower, was so superb that the Christian conquerors could not bear to pull it down. The cathedral boasts arches so huge that it is surpassed only by St Paul's in London and St Peter's in Rome. In April, during the week-long celebrations of the Spring Fair, the city truly comes alive.

Granada is possible as a day trip and the one excursion that no visitor to the Costa del Sol can afford to neglect. The Alhambra, a delicate Moorish palace that according to tradition was supposed to die with its royal creator, is one of the great wonders of the world. Unfortunately it also attracts tourists on a colossal scale that can ruin the spectacle unless you stay overnight and arrange an early evening visit.

Back on the coast, Malaga is an agreeable city with a fine cathedral and lovely gardens, best seen from a plush seat in a horse and carriage. In the summer, Malaga also provides a circus, funfair, flamenco dancing and in August a fair, though it scarcely compares with that of Seville in colour or excitement.

Malaga is also the departure point for a hydrofoil trip to Morocco, which takes 35 minutes, providing a choice between three destinations. At Ceuta, you can clamber around the formidable city walls; at Tetuan, visit the atmospheric old quarter; and at Tangier, be outmanoeuvred by shopkeepers in the bazaar. If Tangier appeals to you, for more information turn to page 29.

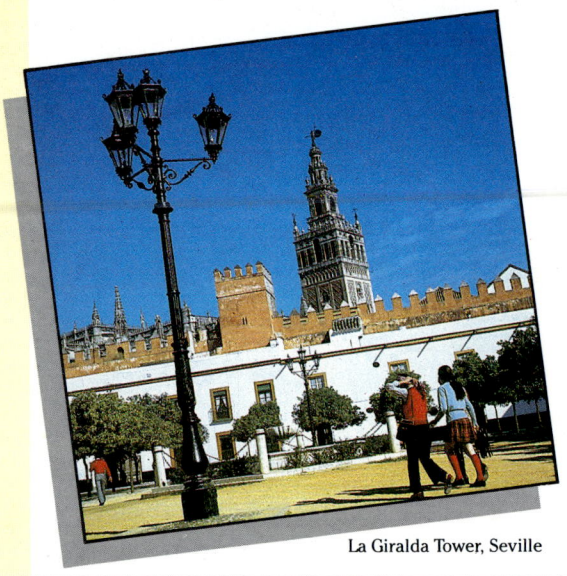

TORREMOLINOS HOTELS

Castillo de Santa Clara ★★★★ good location, on a headland west of the El Bajondillo Beach, with a lift down to the sea. Promising restaurant, separate pool for children, but for them the only concession. Drinks are hugely expensive. The main hotel has 224 rooms, all air-conditioned, on eight floors.

Triton ★★★★ probably the best, and most expensive hotel in the resort, 2½ miles from the centre just over the invisible demarcation point from Benalmadena. Its great asset is its situation, seawards of the busy main road and set well back, with exotic gardens leading directly to the beach. No fewer than four swimming pools, including two for children, and massive poolside lunches. Spacious public areas. 196 rooms, each air-conditioned, on seven floors (4 lifts).

La Giralda Tower, Seville

174 THE GOOD RESORT GUIDE

COSTA DEL SOL

Aloha Puerto Sol ★★★ consists of three tower blocks grouped around a big swimming pool, with uninspired gardens leading down to a narrow, but sandy beach. However the hotel, located near Benalmadena marina, where the resort merges with Torremolinos, is a long walk from the centre. 420 rooms, each with the considerable asset of a terrace and separate sitting area.

Cervantes ★★★ an outstanding rooftop swimming pool with exceptional view, which is just as well, considering the logistical problem of getting down to the El Bajondillo beach directly below. 397 rooms on eight floors (4 lifts).

Don Pablo ★★★ opposite the El Bajondillo beach, a rather over-organised hotel with a disco and seven tennis courts whose floodlights give the place an uncanny resemblance to Colditz. 443 rooms on five floors. Shares three swimming pools with the adjoining Don Pedro.

Don Pedro ★★ fewer facilities and less attentive service, like its sister hotel a taxing uphill walk into the centre, but nevertheless a charming atmosphere. Traditional Andalucian architecture. 290 rooms on five floors.

Principe Sol ★★ huge hotel, divided into three sections, located midway between El Bajondillo and Playamar quarters, with a 20 minute walk to the centre. Sun terrace tends to dwarf inadequate pool, though children have one of their own, as well as a playground, a club, and special meals. Air-conditioned disco and restaurant. 577 rooms, all with sea view, on 11 floors.

Club Torremolinos ★★ a long way from the centre, at least 25 min walk, located in the Playamar district. Particularly well suited for children, with nursery, separate pool, playground, early suppers; the food for their mothers and fathers, however, is far less popular. 400 rooms, some particularly large and ideal for families.

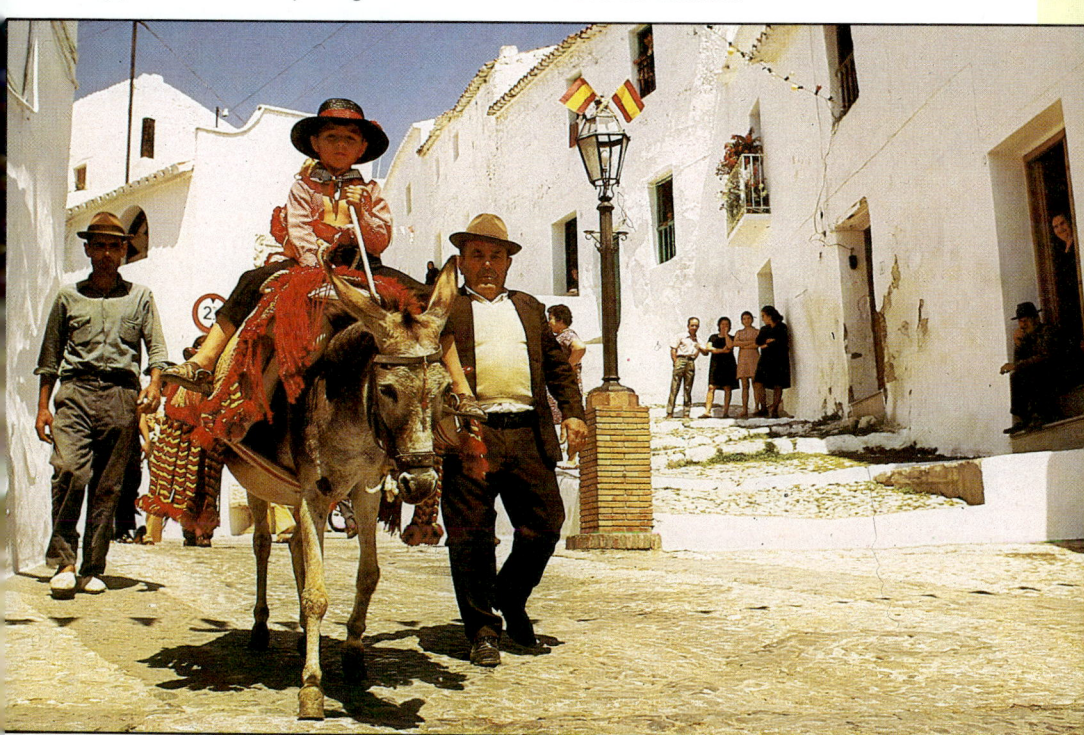

SPAIN

Torremolinos, local colour

THE GOOD RESORT GUIDE

SPAIN

COSTA DEL SOL

OTHER RESORTS

ESTEPONA
Visitors who have come here in the knowledge that this resort, the most westerly on the Costa Del Sol, has escaped the attention of some of the major tour operators, may find the new promenade and increasingly affluent marina an ominous sign that mass tourism is on the way. For the moment, packages linked to Estepona almost all use hotels or apartments which are as near to Marbella, perhaps because the narrow beach of grey sand, backed by a busy main road, is hard to sell. However, sooner or later, Estepona's single, delightful square and placid harbour will have more than a few cafés with a table or two warming in the sunshine.

At night, it is still possible to sit out in the open air undisturbed by disco music. Enjoy it while you can. Transfer time: 1½ hours from Malaga airport.

FUENGIROLA
A sprawling resort with no clearly defined beginning and end, like neighbouring Torremolinos, but with the added disadvantage of the absence of an obvious centre. Perhaps as

Yacht marina at Marbella

176 THE GOOD RESORT GUIDE

COSTA DEL SOL

a result the bars and discos seem strangely half-hearted, encouraging younger visitors to hop on the electric railway, which operates from Torreblanca station every few minutes until long after midnight, an easy journey to the hot spots along the coast. High rise hotels, across a narrow but hectic sea road, continue to spring up; but for the moment they are still outnumbered by apartment blocks with permanent residents. The beach is outstanding, four miles of slightly greyish sand either side of a tiny harbour, with congenial fish restaurants beckoning on the quay. Transfer time: 30 minutes from Malaga Airport.

MARBELLA
Not so much a resort, more an idea — the concept of the international jet set that in reality abandoned Malaga, with its rather claustrophobic beach of imported sand, long ago in favour of secluded villas. One sign of their affluence is open to view: the row of multi-million yachts in the marina at nearby Puerto Banus, an expensive and impossibly snobbish haunt of the rich but not so famous. Remember that the best hotels are several miles from both Marbella and Banus and stay put on your particular beach. Transfer time: 1 hour from Malaga Airport.

TORREMOLINOS FACTS

Your journey

To Malaga	Hours
From Bristol, Cardiff	2½
From Birmingham, East Midlands, Luton, Gatwick, Heathrow	2¾
From Leeds, Manchester	3
From Belfast, Edinburgh, Glasgow, Newcastle, Teesside	3¼

Transfer time to Torremolinos is between 15 and 30 minutes, depending on the location of your hotel, a reflection of the level of traffic on the coast road.

Shopping
Shops open 0930 to 1330 and 1630 to 2000, except in summer, when shops catering for tourists often stay open much later.

Money matters
Most banks open 0930 to 1330, Monday to Saturday, but close on Sundays.

Banks close on January 1, January 6, Good Friday, May 1, July 25, August 15, October 12, December 8, December 25.

Exchange bureau generally offer as favourable a rate as the banks. Hotels will change sterling and travellers' cheques but at a much poorer rate. Most shops and hotels accept credit cards willingly.

Weather

Averages	Jan	Feb	Mar	Apr	May	Jun	Jul	Aug	Sep	Oct	Nov	Dec
Temperature	62	62	65	70	76	83	87	88	84	76	67	64
Sun hours	6	6	6	8	10	11	12	11	9	7	6	5
Rain days	6	5	6	5	2	0	0	0	2	6	5	5
Sea temp.	59	58	59	61	63	70	70	75	70	65	63	58

Torremolinos has practically no rain in summer, long hours of sunshine, and extremely high temperatures. In April, May, October and early November it is still warmer than many Mediterranean resorts can boast in mid summer. Even in winter the temperature is warm with a good deal of sunshine; but with an appreciable risk of rain.

Local transport
As many hotels are actually located several miles outside the principal resorts, bus services are an economic means of getting about. They are also surprisingly reliable and frequent: with more than 30 buses a day linking Marbella to Malaga and almost as many Fuengirola to Torremolinos, despite the equally frequent electric railway.

THE GOOD RESORT GUIDE

PORTUGAL

Algarve	180
Estoril Coast	187

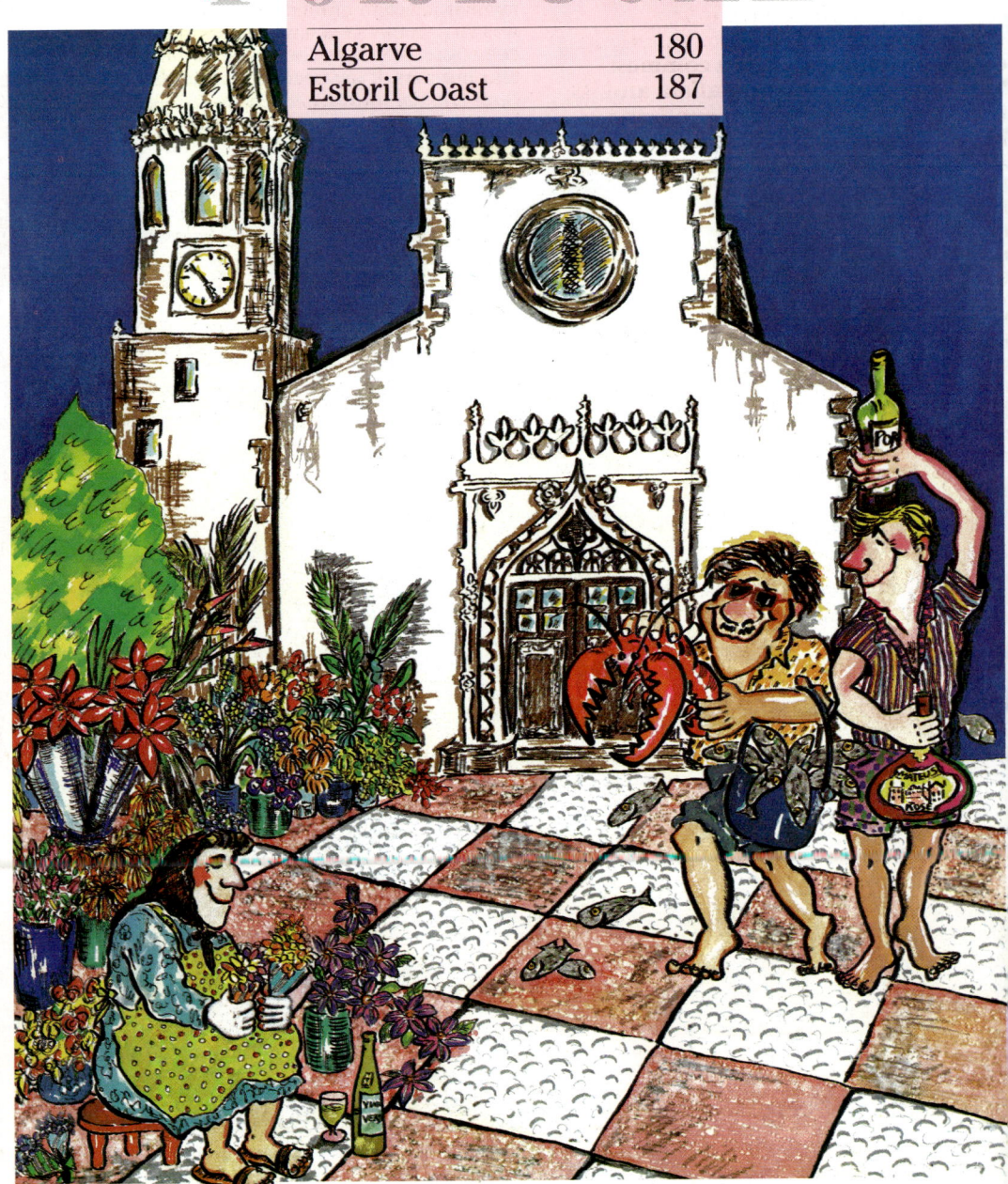

178 THE GOOD RESORT GUIDE

PORTUGAL

Portugal, by rights, should be a Mediterranean country. Its people are Latins by temperament if not exactly in origin; its language has a common bond with Spanish and Italian; and its temperature is typical of southern Europe, hot and dry in summer, mild and unpredictable in winter. Unfortunately, due to some geographical accident, Portugal's coast lies completely on the Atlantic ocean, making the water cooler and rougher; and the high mountains that slope westwards towards the sea have left her natural boundaries entirely with Spain, ensuring that Portugal would be both fiercely independent and a political backwater. An apparent contradiction sustained in Portugal's celebrated record of being Britain's oldest ally, over more than six hundred years. For should you ask a historian in how many of those years the Portuguese actually fought on the British side, he might be hard pressed to come up with six.

The Algarve, once too far removed from familiar pleasure grounds of Europe, when it was visited only by a few intrepid motorists, has been transformed by the arrival of the package tour business. It has become a major holiday centre, to the unconcealed astonishment of the local population, who hitherto eked out a precarious living based largely on the local fishing industry. For this reason, the pace of life remains doggedly slow, and visitors who expect fast service, fast roads and fast reactions will return home disillusioned. Anticipation has no place in the Portuguese vocabulary: if someone has not asked for the bill, then it is concluded that they do not want it. If a motor car, or a refrigerator, or a television has not actually broken down, it is deemed to be in perfect condition. This is part of the charm of the Portuguese way of life and the sooner holidaymakers adjust to it, the more enjoyable their visit.

Praia sao Rafael

THE GOOD RESORT GUIDE 179

ALGARVE

ALGARVE

You can still fish on the Algarve, or indeed indulge in any or every form of water sport, on a coast that offers more than 100 miles of superb beaches and breathtaking views. It is particularly popular for golfing holidays, as the non-playing spouse (should there be one) can sample the delights of the seaside, a short drive away, sometimes even in both senses of the word, from the player who has five championship courses at his or her disposal.

Golf at Vilamoura

ALBUFEIRA

The Algarve consists of a series of predominantly quiet, unsophisticated resorts with only Albufeira comparing remotely with the larger package tour destinations in neighbouring Spain.

Unlike the rest of the Algarve, Albufeira does still earn more money from fishing than tourists, which gives it a slightly superior air, and a reluctance to make concessions that in turn helps to preserve its original character. On the hill above the sea, twisting cobbled streets weave back and forth between decrepit Moorish cottages, of whom an unkind observer once remarked that they had been painted by the Moors but never since. Local colour comes not out of the paint pot but from a whole string of markets, for fish of course, but also for flowers and appealing souvenirs. Some of the town centre hotels are close by, convenient when you walk back with your purchases, but unbelievably noisy early in the morning. The fish market, too, provides an unmistakeable aroma which lingers disagreeably in the rooms.

If you want somewhere cleaner and quieter, there are some smaller hotels tucked away in the west of the resort, but the uphill walk back from the beach will tax all but the very fittest.

In the centre, Albufeira has largely solved the problem of the slope by constructing a bizarre tunnel, which runs from the shopping precinct at the end of the main street down to the beach. Here, in summer, expect to be cheek by cheek with other visitors, for while Albufeira's main beach is agreeable and sandy, it does become incredibly crowded, and completely impossible around high tide. Nor, because of the active presence of fishing boats, is it as clean as more fastidious holidaymakers would like.

180 THE GOOD RESORT GUIDE

ALGARVE

PORTUGAL

Albufeira

ALGARVE

Two miles further east, the Praia da Oura beach is equally crowded in summer but in many ways more attractive. Water sport enthusiasts are particularly well catered for; less so, those who want simply to while away the hours eating and drinking in the sunshine. Behind the beach, up a formidably steep hill, lies the Albufeira suburb of Sao Jao, linked on an extremely bumpy road by a shuttle bus service which, because of the queues and the traffic, can take 20 minutes or so in either direction.

However Sao Jao does have a night life in its own right. Albufeira's most invigorating club, Michel's, is close to the huge Montechoro hotel complex (see page 184). on high ground behind the suburb, while Kiss, the pick of the discos, stands close to the Hotel Auramar (see page 183), on a headland above the Praia da Oura. For those who prefer drinking to dancing, the Fastnet and Twist bars offer plenty of atmosphere, provided, that is, you do not suffer from claustrophobia. The Ancora is rather more relaxed and can seem positively romantic when the crowds thin out in the early hours of the morning. However it must be said bluntly that while Albufeira rightly claims to be the liveliest resort on the Algarve, that is only relative, not a recommendation for young people looking for action.

Nor is Albufeira a centre of culinary excellence, although it does offer one superb speciality called caldeira, a stew of mixed fish saturated with pepper and garlic, and served with tomato, onion and potatoes. As a welcome relief from grilled sardines, the Rancha da Orada, on the outskirts of town, serves healthy portions of barbecued chicken and chips to supplement a lively evening where the wine flows cheaply, if not exactly for free.

Although you can order Mateus Rose, you may find it rather drier than the export version, and probably no cheaper; for better value, try vinho verde, the so-called green wine which is Portugal's true speciality. Vinho verde does not come in green bottles, nor is it green except in the sense of a 'green' youth, lacking in maturity. Vinho verde can be white or red, and while the white is the more popular, the red is usually cheaper, and packs a powerful punch.

Excursions

Although the cost of car hire has risen since Portugal's entry into the EEC and the introduction of VAT, holidaymakers looking for more secluded beaches will welcome the independence provided by their own transport. Excursions are also more satisfying the fewer the numbers, especially to Silves, the old Moorish capital; the walled market at Loule; Monchique, the highest point in the Algarve; the Cape St Vincent, the most south-westerly place on the Continent of Europe.

Rising nearly 250ft above the sea, Cape St Vincent was once believed to be the end of the world. For many sailors so it proved: if not sunk by gales then by gunfire, for just off the cape in the space of a century nearly 100 English, French, Spanish and Dutch ships were sent to the bottom. The most noted survivor was Christopher Columbus, whose birthdate and birthplace (claimed by Genoa and Majorca) remain a matter of some argument but who, in 1470, was washed ashore from a sinking galley clinging to a plank.

Columbus stayed in Portugal for a further 14 years but could find no-one willing to sponsor his dream of crossing the ocean to the East Indies and departed to see the much more receptive rulers of Spain. For Portugal, his accidental arrival was too late, a decade after the death of Prince Henry the Navigator, who had founded at nearby Sagres a School of Navigation, whose discoveries made possible the voyages of Colombus, Magellan and Vasco da Gama (both taught at Sagres) to the New World and beyond.

ALGARVE

Portugal fell under Spanish dominance and relied almost entirely on her navy for defence. After the disastrous defeat of the Armada this proved somewhat unwise, especially in 1596 when the second Earl of Essex, better known as a favourite of Queen Elizabeth I, sacked the Algarve capital of Faro. He made such a thorough job of it that few of its historical buildings remain, and visitors have to settle for what is largely a shopping trip.

On a really long day, and better as an overnight, Lisbon is a much more attractive excursion (see page 188). For those with this sort of stamina, Seville (see page 174) is not too far either. Or you can visit Gibraltar on a three-day, two-night trip, and note how while the British army no longer guards the frontier, on the Spanish side, the soldiers are still in place. However Gibraltar and the three Spanish towns of Seville, Granada and Cordoba are much more easily visited from a base on the Costa del Sol (see page 170).

ALBUFEIRA HOTELS

da Balaia★★★★ stands on its own at the far end of the Praia da Oura, so guests rely mainly on the hotel bus to take them in and out of Albufeira, almost 5 miles distant. However for many there is little incentive to go into town, as the hotel has marvellous grounds, abundant sports facilities, a large swimming pool and (down some steep steps) its own small sandy beach. Air-conditioned restaurant, disco, live entertainment. 193 rooms, many with sea view.

Auramar★★★ on a headland above the Praia da Oura, half an hour's walk from Albufeira, which is also served by a none too regular hotel bus. Large swimming pool, attractive beach, but the climb back is more breathtaking than the view. One rather nice touch: most rooms have a kitchenette where you can prepare your own breakfast from

left: green tiled house, Albufeira

Beach at Albufeira

PORTUGAL

ALGARVE

ingredients, including fresh bread daily, supplied by the hotel. 287 rooms on four floors (7 lifts) in four blocks, two of them set back from the main part of the complex.

do Cerro★★★ a Portuguese estalagem or inn, family-run, with a congenial, intimate atmosphere. Located in the upper part of Albufeira, 15 minutes from the beach (double the time back), with a small open-air swimming pool which is heated outside the summer months. Not much room for sun bathing. 83 rooms on four floors but other, taller buildings restrict the view of the sea.

Montechoro★★★ in the Sao Jao suburb, three miles east of Albufeira proper, large complex with many amenities, including tennis courts, squash courts, and a gymnasium. Children are particularly well catered for, with a playground, separate meals, and their own swimming-pool. However the main pool is still not large enough, given that Praia da Oura beach is 25 minutes' walk. 410 rooms, all air-conditioned, on eight floors (3 lifts).

Sol e Mar★★★ directly overlooking Albufeira beach, built into the cliffs with the rear entrance rather oddly at beach level and the main entrance to the town from the top floor. Small indoor pool but most guests use the sun terrace that leads straight on to the beach. Restaurant usually serves only breakfast and dinner but the hotel owns several restaurants in the town and provides a popular voucher system for eating out. 74 rooms on five floors (2 lifts).

OTHER RESORTS

ALVOR

A village atmosphere retained despite the huge influx of tourists, with a charming cobbled street clattering down to the sea. Its superb beach, Tres Irmaos or Three Brothers, named after three huge perpendicular rocks, is unfortunately crowded in high season. Torralta, a high-rise hotel and shopping complex, lies two miles east of the centre — not far enough away for some. Transfer time: 1 hour, 20 minutes

Alvor beach

THE GOOD RESORT GUIDE

ALGARVE

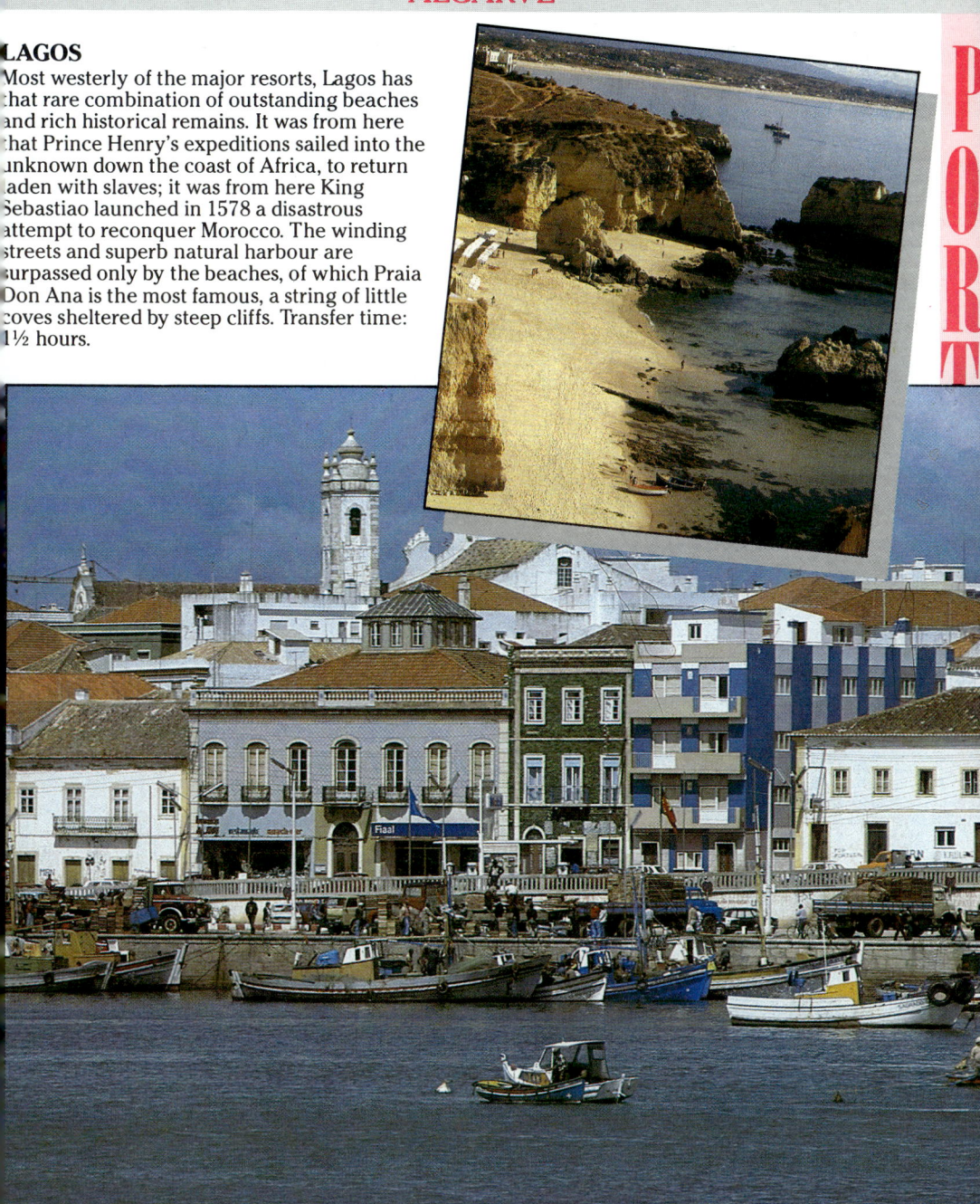

LAGOS

Most westerly of the major resorts, Lagos has that rare combination of outstanding beaches and rich historical remains. It was from here that Prince Henry's expeditions sailed into the unknown down the coast of Africa, to return laden with slaves; it was from here King Sebastiao launched in 1578 a disastrous attempt to reconquer Morocco. The winding streets and superb natural harbour are surpassed only by the beaches, of which Praia Don Ana is the most famous, a string of little coves sheltered by steep cliffs. Transfer time: 1½ hours.

Portimao harbour Inset: Praia don Ana

THE GOOD RESORT GUIDE 185

ALGARVE

MONTE GORDO
Barely in Portugal, three miles from the border with Spain, at the eastern end of the Algarve. Long, lovely sandy beach, where inexplicably most visitors crowd together in front of the rather uninspired shops and hotels. Night life is equally uninspiring, despite two discos and a casino. Transfer time 1¼ hours.

PORTIMAO/PRAIA DA ROCHA
Attractive harbour makes the main town, narrow streets beset by heavy traffic, a decided anti-climax. Portimao remains principally a canning centre, not a tourist resort, which is left to Praia da Rocha, two miles away, with its wide if windy beach and startling rocks. Transfer time: 1¼ hours.

VILAMOURA
Essentially a yachting marina, from where you can go on fishing expeditions far out to sea, or take part in every conceivable water sport. A fine beach stretches in both directions, backed by an extremely demanding golf course, a casino and a cinema. Little night life outside the hotels, and Faro is 27 miles away. Transfer time: 30 minutes.

Portimao fishermen

Vilamoura marina

THE GOOD RESORT GUIDE

ALGARVE/ESTORIL COAST

ALBUFEIRA FACTS

Your journey

	Hours
From Bristol, Cardiff, Gatwick, Luton, Stansted	2¾
From Birmingham, East Midlands, Manchester	3
From Glasgow, Newcastle	3¼

Transfer time to Albufeira from Faro airport: 50 minutes.

Shopping
Most shops open 0930 to 1300 and 1500 to 1900 Monday to Friday, 0830 to 1300 Saturdays; closed Sundays.

Money matters
Banks open 0830 to 1145 and 1300 to 1430 Monday to Friday; closed weekends.

All banks are closed on January 1, February 15, Good Friday, Easter Monday, April 25, May 11, June 10, August 15, October 5, November 1, December 8, December 25. When banks are closed, many exchange bureau remain open, including at weekends. A better rate is given for most travellers' cheques.

Weather

Averages	Jan	Feb	Mar	Apr	May	Jun	Jul	Aug	Sep	Oct	Nov	Dec
Temperature	61	61	63	68	72	76	82	82	79	76	66	62
Sun hours	5	6	7	8	10	12	12	11	9	7	5	5
Rain days	9	9	11	6	4	1	0	0	2	5	8	9
Sea temp.	59	59	59	61	63	66	70	70	70	68	64	61

Outside the summer season, wet weather can never be ruled out. Rain is extremely rare in July and August, when the temperatures are reduced by sea breezes. Dry, sunny summers inevitably give way to unsettled, much cooler winters.

Local transport
Local buses are cheap and reliable, but rather slow on the many rough roads. Taxis are obliged to show passengers a list of fares, in English, if you ask them; it can result in a much lower fare.

ESTORIL COAST

Outstanding weather, agreeable beaches, and some grand hotels explain why the Estoril coast has been the natural choice of more affluent holidaymakers for nearly a century. However the existence of the largest casino in Europe, with more than 200 croupiers spinning a wheel of chance or dealing a card at its peak, is really a legacy of Estoril's past. By and large its clientele is no longer drawn from the aristocratic families of Europe, returning after an evening's gaming, win or lose, by chauffeured limousine to an opulent villa in the

ESTORIL COAST

PORTUGAL

hills. But if its grand promenade and grander buildings are a reminder of better days, it remains a little oasis for British expatriots, as witnessed by the existence of an English Library and a thriving bridge club.

The railway, too, was built with the help of British engineers, in an era when access to the beach was a secondary consideration to the easy lie of the land. The commuter line into Lisbon detaches Estoril from the sea with limited crossing points and ugly viaducts, and at one point bisects the beach itself.

ESTORIL

True, this does not seem to deter the Portuguese day trippers, who at weekends pour into Estoril from the capital and make the beach akin to Blackpool on a Bank Holiday. Nor do all of them come by train: the gloomy tunnels may make it safe to cross the tracks, but they do not extend under the main road, where the traffic at weekends flows fast and furious. Add to the noise and the crowds a high level of pollution, and it must be said that the mere presence of a sandy beach does little to make Estoril the ideal choice for a seaside holiday.

Away from the sea front, Estoril has the air of a Torquay or Eastbourne, quiet and respectable, with gardens that look as if every blade of grass has been trimmed one by one. Only the casino, complete with a splendid floor show, gives Estoril a suspicion of excitement: the occasional bars and discos seem to be fighting a losing battle.

Cascais, two miles to the west, has rather more life. The night clubs make up in stamina what they lack in size. The Wednesday market provides colour and bustle, and occasional bargains. If you do not trip over the fishing tackle on the beach, there is plenty to do: sailing, waterskiing, windsurfing and a scuba diving school.

Excursions

For a taste of the real Lisbon, take the commuter train which runs every 15 or 20 minutes on the short journey to the capital. Most of the workers head for their offices, but

Church of Sao Vicente, Lisbon

more than a few men disappear immediately into cafés. Just as in Greece, they are used as cheap centres of commerce, tables with a telephone within reach. In the gloom at the back sit other men doing business or simply doing nothing. After nightfall, they move on to narrow, sweaty restaurants, waiting for the arrival of the singer of the *fado*, the haunting song that captures both the indecision and the melancholy of the Portuguese way of life.

Out of doors, the Moorish gardens beside St George's Castle offer a wonderful respite from the sun. From its paved terrace the view of the River Tagus is breathtaking, with what look like Dinky cars crossing the April 25th bridge, the longest in Europe, towards a statue of Christ in Majesty reminiscent of Rio. Beneath the castle, the Alfama, a maze of cobbled streets and cul-de-sacs, is the oldest and most evocative part of Lisbon.

Beach at Vila do Conde

188 THE GOOD RESORT GUIDE

ESTORIL COAST

PORTUGAL

Alfama, Lisbon

ESTORIL COAST

PORTUGAL

Discoveries Monument

On the way back, alight at Belem, whose high tower and guns once made the Tagus a secure harbour. Nearby is the Monument to the Discoveries, a tribute to Henry the Navigator, with spectacular carved likenesses of the men who first sailed out of sight of land.

Many excursions operate from Lisbon, Estoril and Cascais. Among the most popular destinations are Sintra, the summer residence of the Portuguese nobility, with its Disneyland castle dominating the skyline; Evora, a perfectly preserved walled town; and the fortified convent belonging to the Knights of Christ at Tomar. Each can be reached comfortably in a single day.

ESTORIL HOTELS

Palacio ★★★★ exceptional position, set back from the railway and Estoril's main sea-front road, overlooking the Casino gardens. The public rooms are quite magnificent, the hotel has a disco, a sauna, a hairdressing salon and a restaurant of great repute. The swimming pool is huge, the tennis courts well maintained and guests have the run of the golf course a few minutes' away. 167 rooms on six floors (2 lifts).

Albatroz ★★★ in Cascais, on a promontory overlooking both the town and the beach, which is both sandy and within easy reach. Th

THE GOOD RESORT GUIDE

ESTORIL COAST

...batroz was once a private villa, and in the ...venings when a pianist plays softly in the bar, ...ou could almost be the house guest at an ...egant soiree. More energetic guests splash ...out in the sea water swimming pool before ...aking up the sun on the terrace. Particularly ...nvenient for the shops. 40 rooms, the best ...d most expensive with a sea view, on four ...ors (3 lifts).

...tlantico ★★★ in Monte Estoril, the ...idpoint between Estoril and Cascais, right on ...e sea front, but rather too close for comfort to ...e railway line which runs between the hotel ...d the shore. Large salt water swimming pool, ...ildren's paddling pool, and a tunnel under ...e railway to the Tamariz beach. 175 rooms on ...ven floors (3 lifts).

...ido ★★ lacks the grandeur of older Estoril ...otels, but it has an unpretentious charm and a ...articularly quiet location, on a hill in the ...sidential area. The beach, however, is a good ... minutes' walk and the swimming pool by no ...eans huge. Not much to do in the evenings. ... rooms, all with balcony (1 lift).

...enith ★★ in Monte Estoril, closer to Cascais ...an to Estoril casino, overlooking public ...rdens. The sea is less than five minutes' walk, ...ough to reach it, you have to use a passage under the railway. The hotel, which is friendly and relaxed, has a swimming pool, but there are no special facilities for children. Rooftop garden. 40 rooms (lift).

Market at Funchal

ESTORIL FACTS

...our journey

	Hours
...atwick, Luton	2½
...anchester	2¾

The transfer time to Estoril/Cascais is 1-1¼ hours from Lisbon airport.

...eather

Averages	Jan	Feb	Mar	Apr	May	Jun	Jul	Aug	Sep	Oct	Nov	Dec
Temperature	57	59	63	68	70	77	81	82	81	70	63	59
Sun hours	5	7	7	9	10	11	12	12	9	7	6	5
Rain days	6	6	7	4	2	1	0	0	3	7	6	7
Sea temp.	59	57	57	59	63	64	68	68	68	66	63	59

...ith more than 3,000 hours of sunshine each ...ar, the Estoril coast is, like the Algarve, ...nong the sunniest parts of Europe. It also compares very favourably with the Algarve both in air and sea temperatures.

PORTUGAL

THE GOOD RESORT GUIDE 191

CHANNEL COAST

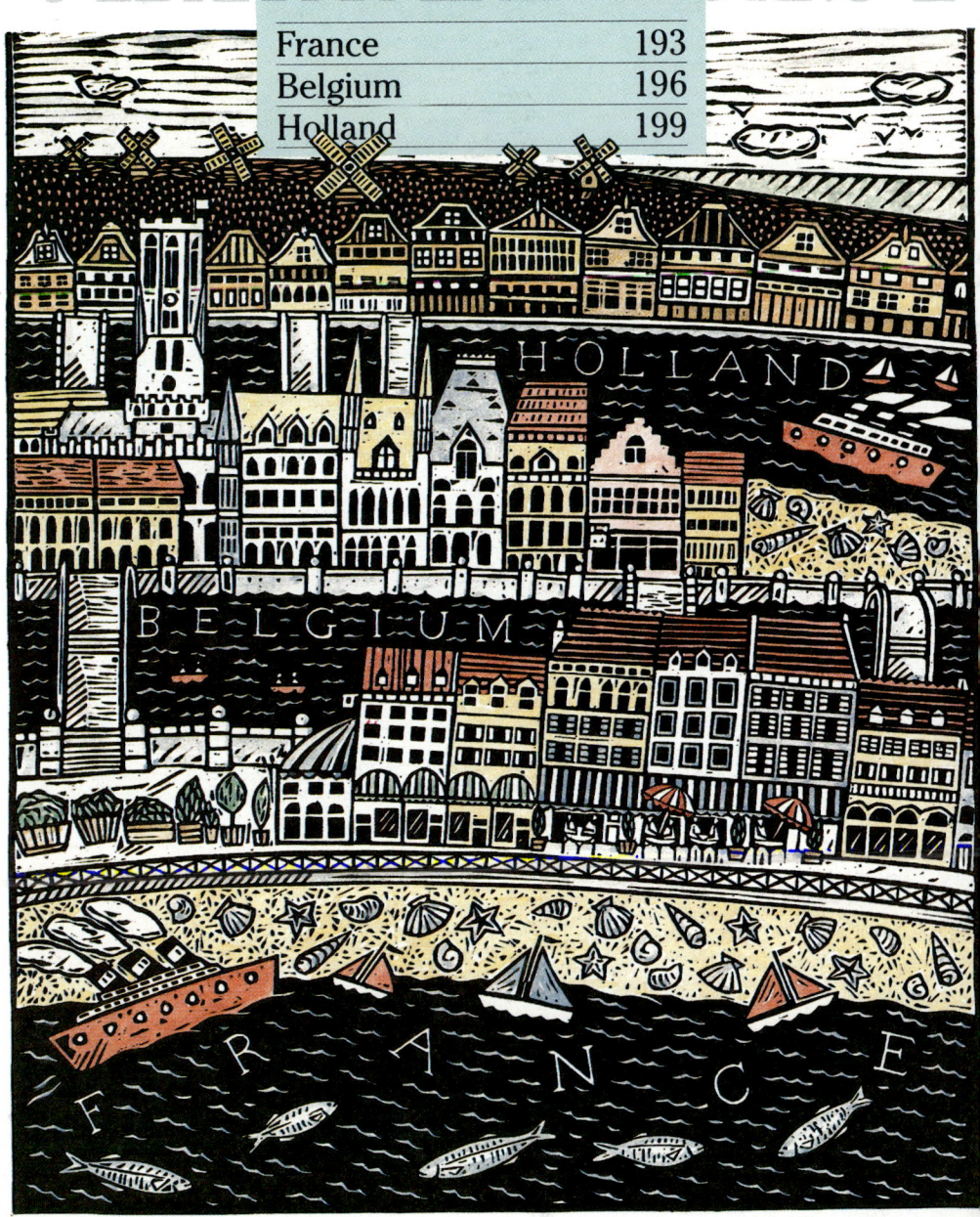

France	193
Belgium	196
Holland	199

192 THE GOOD RESORT GUIDE

FRANCE

CHANNEL COAST

The British may have invented the seaside, but the foreigners made it fun. Striped awnings, beach umbrellas, and naughty double wicker recliners all had their origins just across the Channel. By the middle of the last century, local businessmen were dipping their hands in their pockets to pay for a promenade and in some places, like Scheveningen in Holland, even for a pier. But the Continentals still regarded the hardy British practice of actually immersing themselves in the sea with complete consternation: paddling was supposed to be a last desperate measure for invalids, not a source of amusement. As for sun bathing, that was simply for lunatics: sane people sat in the shade. But it was not long before those immoral foreigners realised that both activities were a splendid excuse for taking their clothes off in public and in mixed company. It took the arrival in numbers of the

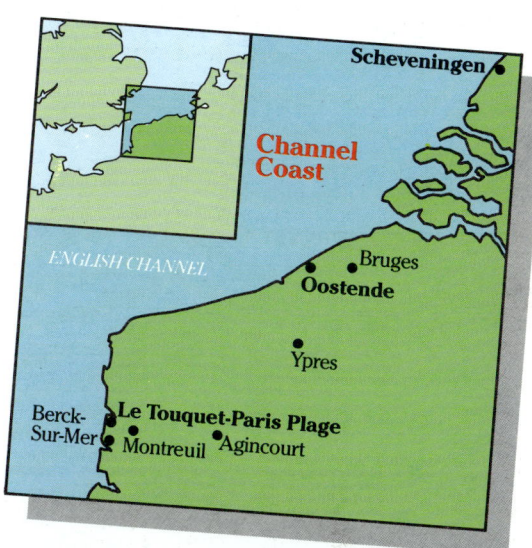

Scheveningen

THE GOOD RESORT GUIDE 193

FRANCE

CHANNEL COAST

Le Touquet

puritanical British, complete with one piece bathing suits and even private bathing machines, to stop the beaches at Oostende and Le Touquet from looking like the exclusive premises of a nudist colony. Over the years of course attitudes have changed and in particular beach costumes have become briefer, much briefer, and meanwhile the British have gone further afield in search of endless sunshine; but on the Continent these resorts are no less fashionable and remain hugely popular, especially for families. However, by using ferries from Dover, Folkestone, Harwich, Hull, Newhaven, Ramsgate and Sheerness, or flying to Holland from any one of 25 airports, a package deal out of the UK is perfectly possible.

LE TOUQUET-PARIS PLAGE

The finest beach in France, mile upon mile of firm sand and shallow water, although when the tide goes out you may need a pair of binoculars to keep your eye on the kids, as it can be easily half a mile to the sea. A lot of summer activities for children, including riding, sand sailing, and trampolines. The promenade, decked out with wonderful flowers for much of the season, is equally superb and so very British. The view is sacrosanct so the Boulevard de la Mer is allowed to have buildings — mainly hotels and smart boutiques — only on the far side of the street, which sometimes resembles a film set that is slightly behind schedule. There is certainly nothing quite as frantic anywhere as the bargain house of fashion, Griffmode, where the changing rooms can be in such chaos that would-be clients have been known to pick up and even pay for the clothes other people arrived in. At weekends the smart set arrives from the French capital — this is, after all, Paris Plage — to pack out the discos and the night clubs. Most famous is Flavio's Club de la Fôret, with

194 THE GOOD RESORT GUIDE

FRANCE

reathtaking food, and breathtaking prices to atch. The adjoining casino attracts nternational stars throughout the summer onths.

xcursions

or children, the best is Bagatelle, a formidable nusement park, whose reputation has xtended the length and breadth of France. ocated between Le Touquet and Berck-sur- er, another bathing extravaganza to the uth, it extends in all over 55 acres. Note, owever, that it opens only between Easter and e end of September.

For children and adults, see the sites of two mous English victories, or rather English and 'elsh, as Wales provided many of our best hting men in the Middle Ages, the era of gincourt or Crecy. You can stand on the spot uth-west of Le Touquet on the edge of the lley of the Somme where, in 1346, the Prince Wales won his spurs aged 16 and 1,300 ench knights died in what became known as e battle of Crecy. Due east of Le Touquet lies gincourt where, in 1415, Henry V's heavily utnumbered army had an even more aprobable success. You can still see the ooded copse where the French knights, ammed together in the mud, were unhorsed d massacred to a man.

Also to the east but much closer to Touquet is the walled town of Montreuil-sur- er, although the sea deserted it long ago. The arrow, cobbled streets are circled by a perfect t of ramparts, from where the views are aperb: the walk takes about an hour.

Montreuil overlooks the left bank of the ve Canche, one of three river valleys — the hers are the Authie and the Course — taking languid route through fields and meadows. ollowing them for a few miles can provide a re relaxing day out. They are so well hidden, at few French tourists have ever discovered em, a region remote from the cares and omentum of everyday life.

E TOUQUET HOTELS

anoir ★★★ 3 miles south of Le Touquet, eal for golfers, right next to a demanding ourse, but a fine terrace and swimming pool r those who don't play. Country house mosphere with slight touches of a Whitehall rce, young maids with long legs and short irts stretching to dust suits of armour. The

food, unfortunately, does not match the price. 45 rooms, including some ideal for families. Closed early January to early February.

Novotel-Thalamer ★★★★ a modern hotel at the extreme, southern, end of the promenade, so near enough to take in the action, but quiet and relaxing in itself. Splendid views of the sea, and a swimming pool if you do not fancy the rollers. Agreeable restaurant. 104 rooms.

Le Plage ★★ unpretentious hotel offering bed and generous Continental breakfast, but with so many restaurants to choose from, this is scarcely a disadvantage. A bigger snag may be a bar licensed for aperitifs and wine but not spirits, so forget the cognac before you turn in. Given the hotel's position on the sea front, surprisingly few of the 26 rooms have a proper sea view. Closed mid-November to mid-March.

Beach at Le Touquet

THE GOOD RESORT GUIDE 195

CHANNEL COAST

BELGIUM

OOSTENDE

The Queen of Belgian beaches, with miles of sand and shallow, safe bathing, prides itself on its facilities for families. Oostende (if you drop an 'o' the locals do not like it) has more than 100 registered hotels, most of them catering for modest incomes rather than the top end of the market. While the buckets and spades are mainly wielded by young Belgian sand-castle constructors, British visitors who abandon Brighton or Bognor for a year will find plenty to do. All along the beach there are facilities for fishing, sailing and windsurfing; a miniature railway (if railway it can be called, running as it does on the tarmac roads) circumnavigates the town; horse-drawn cabs trot up and down the sea front; the marine aquarium is worth a separate day trip in itself; and the view from Europanorama, 340ft high, the tallest building overlooking the English Channel, is superb on a clear day. A large indoor swimming pool is located west of the Casino, which prides itself on the quality of its high season entertainment.

Oostende racecourse, 2 miles to the west, has several important flat meetings during the summer. The fish restaurants on the Visserskai provide spectacular dining out.

If you arrive in Oostende on the first weekend in March, do not be surprised to find half the town made up as clowns, and as the night runs on, to the constant crackle of fireworks, a glittering lantern procession, culminating in a giant bonfire. This is the Oostende Carnival, which has as its climax the Ball of the Dead Rat, nothing to do with the menu, but called after an infamous Parisian nightclub of the turn of the century.

Excursions

Bruges, half an hour away by rail, and not much more by road, is the outstanding excursion. Between the 12th and 16th centuries Bruges was one of the richest and most powerful cities in Europe, with a population of more than 200,000. Its buildings emphasize just how rich it was: a huge Belfry with a carillon of 47 bells, two great squares, and row upon row of marvellous houses

Old harbour, Oostende

THE GOOD RESORT GUIDE

BELGIUM

adjoining the network of canals, spanned, incidentally, by more than fifty bridges. The best way to see Bruges is by boat, or perhaps by horse-drawn carriage, whose hay refuelling stop is the beautiful beguinage, the home of widows of the crusaders, in a marvellously peaceful setting. The Gruuthuse Palace, with its glimpse of medieval life in the city; and Groeninge Museum, which houses masterpieces of the great Bruges School of painting, are worth a day all to themselves.

A rather longer trip is to Ypres, due south of Oostende near the Belgium border, where during the First World War 55,000 British soldiers gave their lives. Every evening at eight o'clock, the Last Post is still played in their memory: their graves, and those of the allies and the enemy, lie in 170 military cemeteries in the surrounding district. Ypres itself, of course, has been rebuilt, but you can have a snack at the Brasserie Central in the main square which used to be the Café de Miroir where the Tommies (or at any rate, the officers) drank back in 1914. The Salient Museum nearby is a fascinating account of this sector of the front. However for a real taste of the trenches, visit Hill 62, three miles away, where the back door of another café opens out into a genuine section of the 1916 British trenches. You will need wellingtons, for the mud is still there.

OOSTENDE HOTELS

Ambassadeur ★★★ in the central square, ideal for the shops, reliable service and reassuringly comfortable. However the only public room is a rather expensive tea shop. As Oostende traffic wardens make our own look like the Salvation Army, it is just as well that the Ambassadeur guarantees a parking space to anyone who reserves one of its 23 rooms.

Andromeda ★★★★ in the prime sea front position, next to the Casino and the beach (although you do have to cross a busy road), a rather characterless hotel where guests speak in hushed voices as though in some gentlemen's club. Definitely not the place for children. However, its restaurant, the Cafe Gloria, has outstanding seafood specialities and some of the bedrooms overlooking the beach are truly superb. 56 rooms.

Prince ★★ bright, cheerful, if modest hotel in an exceptional position, one of the very few

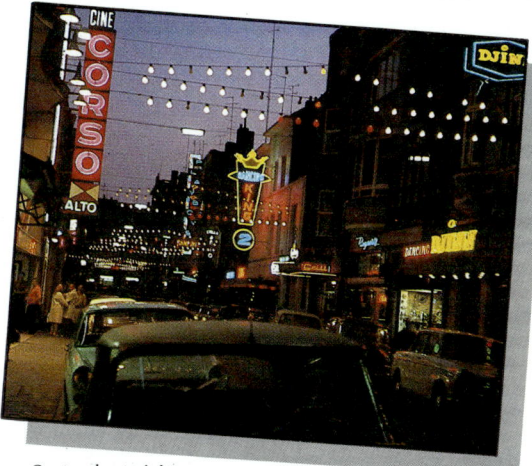

Oostende at night

hotels overlooking the seaside promenade. Ideal for families. Its 46 rooms are surprisingly well-furnished and many have a glorious view of the sea.

Cathedral at Oostende

THE GOOD RESORT GUIDE 197

BELGIUM

CHANNEL COAST

Bruges, canal cruisers

HOLLAND

SCHEVENINGEN

The seaside resort of the Dutch capital The Hague, Scheveningen was a popular bathing place as early as 1836. Perhaps popular is not the most apt description, as a Scottish doctor, Arthur Granville, wrote a scathing letter home to his wife about 'invalids who had come for benefit of the sea water who instead were dying of boredom'.

There is certainly little danger of that in modern-day Scheveningen, where the biggest problem for visitors is pronouncing the name. Indeed during the Second World War, the ability to pronounce the name correctly was the Dutch Resistance's infallible test to establish whether someone who claimed to be Dutch was in fact genuine.

One major benefit of the last war is the modern pier, replacing the one wrecked during the fighting. It extends 400 yards into the sea and has four satellites, looking rather like a space station which has spun out of orbit. On the four 'islands' are a restaurant, shops, an amusement arcade, a cinema, an underwater wonderland, a sea aquarium, and a watch tower rising high above the waves.

Scheveningen beach is undoubtedly the best on the Dutch coast, firm clean sand stretching for miles, though perhaps lacking the space of Oostende or Le Touquet. However at the Kurhaus (see hotels, see page 200), is a remarkable all-weather centre that includes a huge swimming pool with a surf action which connects directly with an open air pool. Alongside are jacuzzis, a sauna, a solarium, a huge shopping arcade and several restaurants, making it possible to spend an agreeable day entirely under cover whatever the weather. The seaside resort, known as Scheveningen Bad, is the north of the town. To the south lies Scheveningen Haven, the nucleus of the old fishing village, with an old church tower. However none of the buildings dates back before 1570, when the original village, built further out to sea, was swamped in a storm with great loss of life, and subsequently abandoned. The present harbour's south-east quay is the departure point for sea cruises and fishing trips, invariably watched by the older inhabitants whose clothing seems to have changed little in half a century. Nearby the marine museum has a remarkable collection of more than 25,000 sea shells. Beyond the

Scheveningen beach

harbour, Scheveningen gives way to Kijkduin, The Hague's second seaside resort, with fewer amenities but particularly popular for family holidays.

Traditional windmills

THE GOOD RESORT GUIDE

HOLLAND

Amsterdam by night   Inset: Madurodam miniature city

Excursions

Scheveningen is in effect a suburb of The Hague, the Dutch administrative centre, home of their parliament buildings, and of Queen Beatrix. However for children the highlight must be Madurodam, a city in miniature, to a scale 1/25th of real life, with many of the most famous buildings drawn from the whole of Holland. There are many working models, including a railway, a harbour and an airport, while at night the whole city is illuminated with thousands of little lamps.

No visit to Scheveningen would be complete without an excursion to Amsterdam, less than an hour away. A canal trip, unashamedly for the tourists, is certainly the best way to take in the city, to see on the quayside row after row of quaint, narrow buildings with architecture spanning several centuries. Amsterdam is in fact a collection of some 90 small islands, held together by hundreds of quaint bridges, delightfully lit by lanterns after dark. Apart from by canal, the only sensible way to get round Amsterdam is on a bicycle: they can be hired in several parts of the city. The museums are world famous: Vincent Van Gogh has one entirely dedicated to his works, while the Rijksmuseum gallery contains one of the largest collection of paintings by Rembrandt, including 'The Night Watch'. But for many the most moving visit will be to an unfashionable canalside house where a 13-year-old Jewish girl, Anne Frank, hid from the Nazis; and before her discovery wrote the diary that touched everyone's heart.

SCHEVENINGEN HOTELS

Kurhaus ★★★★ founded exactly a century ago, the Kurhaus has been enlarged and modernised to such good effect, that it must now compare with any seaside hotel in Europe in terms of amenities and sophistication. Outstanding restaurants, one located in a huge arcaded salon, casino and adjoining surfpool (see above). The hotel leads directly down to the beach at the centre of the resort. 250 rooms.

Carlton Beach ★★★★ on the seafront, a modern, luxurious hotel directly opposite what is probably the best part of the beach. Two first-class restaurants, open air dining in good weather. Large indoor swimming pool and health club. 181 rooms with splendid sea views.

200 THE GOOD RESORT GUIDE

CHANNEL COAST

CHANNEL COAST FACTS

Your journey

Amsterdam's Schipol airport is the nearest international airport to Scheveningen, with flights from 25 different UK airports; the journey time from Gatwick or Heathrow is as short as one hour. There are no regular direct flights from the UK to Oostende or Le Touquet, although both towns have an airport.

The nearest ferry port to Le Touquet is Boulogne:

	Hours
From Folkestone	1½
From Dover	1¾

Oostende has a direct ferry and jetfoil service:

	Hours
From Dover (jetfoil)	1¾
From Dover (ferry)	3½
From Folkestone (ferry)	4

Scheveningen has one direct ferry service:

	Hours
From Great Yarmouth	8

Otherwise the shortest routes are:

	Hours
Dover-Oostende (see above)	3½
Dover-Zeebrugge	4
Sheerness-Vlissingen	7
Harwich-Hook of Holland	7

Shopping

In France, from Tuesday to Saturday, most food shops open 0730-1200, 1500-1900 or even later; on Sunday, 0800-1130; but may close part or all day Monday. Other shops open 0930-1200 and 1500-1900 Monday to Saturday. Department stores open 0930-1800 Monday to Saturday. Hypermarkets 0900-2200, Monday to Saturday. In Belgium, shops open on similar lines to France but in Oostende there is no uniform closing day. Small shops stay open late at night, especially on Fridays.

In Holland, shops open 0830 or 0900 to 1730 or 1800, Tuesday to Friday, often closing earlier on Saturdays; on Mondays, only 1300-1730 or 1800.

Money matters

In Northern France, most banks open 0900-1200 and 1400-1700 Monday to Friday, very occasionally in rural areas, on Saturday mornings. Beware the large number of public holidays when banks are closed. In Belgium, banks open 0900-1200, 1400-1630, Monday to Thursday, closing later on Friday. In Holland, banks open 0900-1600 Monday to Friday, occasionally in the evening.

Credit cards and Eurocheques are widely accepted in hotels, restaurants and shops.

Weather

Averages	Jan	Feb	Mar	Apr	May	Jun	Jul	Aug	Sep	Oct	Nov	Dec
Temperature	43	43	48	52	61	64	68	70	64	57	48	45
Sun hours	2	2	4	6	8	7	7	6	4	2	1	1
Rain days	12	10	11	12	10	11	11	11	10	12	12	13
Sea temp.	38	38	43	47	52	57	63	63	61	52	43	40

The weather does not suddenly improve once you cross the Channel.

Le Touquet, Oostende and Scheveningen have similar conditions to the UK, that is, extremely unpredictable. However the sea temperature, under the influence of the Gulf Stream, is slightly higher.

Local transport

All three resorts have good rail connections but Oostende has an outstanding service to Bruges, Gent and Brussels.

THE GOOD RESORT GUIDE

DENMARK

202 THE GOOD RESORT GUIDE

DENMARK

Denmark, the land of Hans Christian Andersen, the prince of fairy-tale tellers, is truly a child's paradise. It offers two of the greatest attractions for children anywhere in the world: the wonderful Tivoli Gardens in Copenhagen and, in the middle of the Jutland peninsula, the equally compelling Legoland, an entire town of plastic building bricks. Add to this matchless fantasy a universal atmosphere in which children are not simply tolerated but encouraged and indulged, and a coastline more than 4,500 miles in length, and Denmark has some of the essential ingredients of an outstanding family holiday.

Unfortunately for the aspirant holidaymaker, Denmark, like France, does not cater for the air package market. There are no charter flights to most of Scandinavia and air fares are expensive. Economic package tours

Tivoli Gardens

THE GOOD RESORT GUIDE 203

DENMARK

therefore are largely confined to rail, an overnight trip from London to Copenhagen usually by way of Oostende, or by car using the modern DFDS ferry from Harwich to Esbjerg on the west coast.

Unlike many summer destinations, a car in Denmark is an asset, not a liability. It is possible to drive from one end of the country to the other in a single day; traffic, other than in and out of Copenhagen at peak hours is remarkably light; and the road system is quick and modern with many motorways.

Indeed for the family that wishes to make the best of a Danish holiday, to visit both Legoland and the Tivoli, a car is really an advantage. For in Denmark, where everything seems a little smaller than true life, part of its essential charm, there are no big seaside resorts: no Benidorm or Torremolinos. Some of the finest beaches are at the end of a country lane, cleverly unsignposted, with not so much as an ice-cream salesman in sight. There are no rows of unsightly concrete skyscraper hotels: indeed, outside Copenhagen, hotels with more than 50 rooms are something of a rarity. Many are simply a local inn or 'kro', with appealing old architecture and sometimes with appealing old retainers.

Although the prices of some accommodation may seem high, most of the country inns operate a voucher system offering a standard, discounted charge per person per night. Nearly 400 restaurants also provide a two-course Danmenu, lunch or dinner, consisting of local specialities, at a fixed price inclusive of services and taxes. However, avoid the born-sandwich or children's snack: most British children will not like them.

Be prepared for several ferry trips. If you intend to visit Copenhagen, whichever way you arrive in Denmark with a car, you must make a crossing of around one hour, and none too cheap a crossing at that. However, apart from peak weekends in summer, when half the country seems to be leaving Copenhagen and the other half going there, advance booking is not necessary. The ferries run as frequently as 30 times a day and take

Nyhavn

204 THE GOOD RESORT GUIDE

DENMARK

several hundred cars. At the Knudshoved-Halsskov ferry, on the main link from Esbjerg to Copenhagen, little mobile petrol wagons come along the queue in the car park to fill you up while you wait. Using this route, the journey between Esbjerg and Copenhagen can be accomplished in five hours.

Denmark is ideal for the energetic. Honeycombed with islands and fjords, it offers almost perfect conditions for sailing and windsurfing; and yet the beaches of the west coast, and of the large islands of Funen and Sealand are sandy and safe. Rich green countryside beckons the walker and the cyclist, for the highest hill in Denmark would in Switzerland be scarcely recognised as a slope.

Excursions

Two days in Copenhagen, including one at the Tivoli Gardens, are the bare minimum to acquire even a superficial taste of the capital's charm. Although the canal and harbour tour hardly matches Stockholm or Venice, it provides an effortless means to see the oldest section of the city; boats leave from Gammel Strand, but unlike Amsterdam, most are fully open to the elements. However you will have a better view of the Little Mermaid statue, based on Hans Christian Andersen's fairy tale, from the port promenade, the Langelinie. The old harbour, Nyhavn, is worth a second visit, especially on summer Sundays, when improvised jazz bands on the quayside make lunch a noisy but colourful affair.

Not far from Nyhavn is Amalienborg Palace, the home of the Danish Royal Family, incidentally the oldest in Christendom. The guard marches from its barracks close to Rosenborg Castle (where the Crown Jewels are on display) and changes daily in Amalienborg's splendid square, accompanied by a band when the royals are in residence.

At weekends, toy, or rather boy, soldiers dressed in red and white uniforms like the Queen's Royal Life Guard, march through the Tivoli Gardens with a military precision worthy of the royal guard itself. There is strong competition to be part of one of the 109 detachment of soldiers and sailors, complete with gun crew and a royal coach carrying a make-believe miniature prince and princess.

The Tivoli has been going strong for more than 150 years, and a visit is a momentous occasion for most children. In the nicest possible way, however, it is also an endurance

Little Mermaid statue, Copenhagen

test; expect to stay for eight or nine hours and possibly twelve. Take push chairs, changes of clothing, snacks and drinks for the children. The Tivoli does not accept credit cards for admission or rides but will change more or less any recognised currency into kroner. Admission is relatively modest, rides relatively expensive. However the all-day unlimited rides ticket or 'Tur-pass', which is fixed to your wrist to stop others sharing it, is only a good investment for indefatigable children and then only if you arrive early, around midday. Later, the queues for rides can be substantial, making it extremely difficult to receive value for money from the unlimited pass. Experience shows that the boating lake and the junior dipper (still

THE GOOD RESORT GUIDE 205

DENMARK

Tivoli at night

quite formidable) attract the longest queues, so head for these at the start. Twice during the afternoon, there are free shows, including top-class circus acts and even symphony concerts, at the open air theatre; stake an early claim for a seat. Most of the 26 restaurants do take credit cards, and range from inexpensive self-service to grand luxury. However when darkness falls, and the 110,000 Tivoli lights twinkle in the sky, casting mystic shadows over old fountains and fresh flowers on warm summer nights, the meal is far too romantic for you to remember the price.

From Nyhavn the hydrofoil whisks visitors across from Copenhagen to Sweden in a mere forty minutes but only to Malmo, Sweden's third largest town and undoubtedly its dullest.

If you fancy a trip to Sweden, the even shorter crossing to Helsingborg from Holsingør, a few hours north of Copenhagen, is much more promising. Just outside Helsingør, better known as Elsinore, the narrow streets are dominated by Kronborg Castle, immortalised by Shakespeare in Hamlet, Prince of Denmark. A performance of Hamlet in English on the floodlit castle walls adds an unforgettable fresh dimension to one of Shakespeare's greatest plays.

At Odense, the midpoint between Sealand and Jutland, the birthplace of Hans Andersen has been turned into a museum, which traces the story of his humble origins — his father made shoes, his mother washed clothes — and how, aged fourteen, he set off for Copenhagen,

THE GOOD RESORT GUIDE

DENMARK

his one spare shirt tied to his back, to seek his fortune; almost a fairytale in itself. You can hear his stories, including 'The Princess and the Pea' and 'The Tinderbox' read by famous actors, including even Sir Laurence Olivier; the ultimate accolade. And see an incredible collection of books in literally dozens of languages, all bearing the name of Hans Christian Andersen, a rare kind of immortality. Less easy to find is the house where he spent his childhood in real poverty, with rooms scarcely bigger than a broom cupboard.

Odense is on Funen, strictly speaking no longer an island, as the waters separating it from Jutland are spanned by a colossal motorway bridge, worth a visit in itself. But in central Jutland, just outside Billund, budding engineers are constructing even bigger (at any rate, bigger to scale) bridges entirely of Lego. This is the home of Legoland, a summer adventure park like no other, where children's fantasies come to life. Here you can stroll around an entire town made of Lego bricks, past working cranes, vibrating trains and moving ships; see Nyhavn and Amsterdam in miniature and a busy airport and a rocket launch site with the briefest turn of the head. A Lego train runs around the site; a Lego tower takes you high in the air where the town takes on a stunning authenticity, as though thousands of feet below. Children can ride the monorail, take an authentic driving test, or pan for gold at the mine next to the wild west Legoredo Town. And if the weather is unkind, there is ample to do indoors: marvellous exhibitions of toys, dolls (and the ultimate dolls' house, Titania's Palace), and amazing Lego models; a huge Lego playroom where children can build and create to their heart's content. Separate from the entrance fee, discount cards can be bought which give access to eight different rides (or, knowing some children, to eight turns on the same ride), a much fairer system than the Tivoli. Legoland is however overwhelmingly popular and not as spacious as Tivoli; to avoid the crowds, go in the second half of August after Danish children are back at school.

Jutland's rich, rolling countryside stretches from north to south with only the clusters of working windmills to interrupt the skyline. Cosy farms and quaint villages abound, none quainter than Ebeltoft in a sheltered eastern bay. Ebeltoft has hardly changed since the fourteenth century because its inhabitants were never rich enough to pull down their houses and build again. Their poverty has preserved a wonderful cobbled street like the pages of a storybook, so perfect that you have to peer round corners to satisfy yourself that it is not simply a facade. Outside the town, "Jylland", an eighteenth century warship is preserved. You can clamber from deck to deck, sit in the officer's cabins, pretend to roll out the guns, and marvel at the tons of granite ballast deep in the ship's bowels below.

Ebeltoft is not, however, Denmark's oldest town. That distinction goes to Ribe in the extreme south-west, where the Vikings once brought their plunder across the marshes. A nightwatchman still does his rounds past half-timbered old houses and tells tales of Ribe's fascinating past. From the top of the 14th-century Red Brick Tower, an exhausting climb up wooden staircase after wooden staircase, the tidal flats stretch for miles down to the sea. You can visit the tiny island of Mandø, whose one hundred inhabitants are cut off every day when the waters rush across the ebb road. However take the tractor bus: some motorists who thought they could beat the turn of the tide did not survive to tell the tale in Mando's lonely little inn.

Barges on Nyhaven

THE GOOD RESORT GUIDE 207

DENMARK

Legoland

DENMARK HOTELS

Munkebjerg ★★★ on the east coast of Jutland, located in deep woodland high above the Vejle fjord, within easy reach of Legoland. Large indoor swimming pool with safe children's area; splendid children's playground. Comfortable rooms, exceptional service. Two restaurants, one with panoramic views and special children's menu, the other with a prodigious wine cellar where, if you win the pools, you can order a bottle of wine as old as 1890. 148 rooms.

Kommandorgarden ★★★ on the island of Rømø in the south-west of Denmark, reached by a causeway, a modern complex principally of self-catering apartments constructed around indoor and outdoor swimming pools and close to an outstanding sandy beach. Children's playground, restaurant with seafood specialities. A ferry from nearby Havneby harbour crosses in 50 minutes to the West German island of Sylt. 12 rooms in hotel, 80 apartments.

Molskroen ★★★ at Ebeltoft on the Djursland peninsula in eastern Jutland. Overlooking the sea and within 100 yards of an exceptional beach of white sand. Family rooms, children's

208 THE GOOD RESORT GUIDE

DENMARK

playground, but no swimming pool. Agreeable restaurant. Unless you like billiards, not much to do in the evenings. 23 rooms.

Menstrup Kro ★★★ 200-year-old inn near Naestved in south Sealand, not much more than an hour's drive from Copenhagen and within easy reach of the island beaches of Mon, Falster and Lolland. Charming restaurant, indoor swimming pool, but shallow area unsafe for small children. 70 well furnished rooms, many suitable for families, with the quietest, and best, in an exceptionally agreeable annexe.

Nyhavn ★★★ strictly speaking 71 Nyhavn, the harbour district of Copenhagen. Former 19th century warehouse on the Nyhavn Canal, delightful atmosphere, outstanding restaurant, half price meals for children. Many of the rooms are extremely small and far from soundproof, making the free camp bed for children something of a challenge for both the occupants and their neighbours. Talking of neighbours, a Mr. H. C. Anderson once lived next door. 82 rooms on 4 floors (1 lift).

DENMARK FACTS

Your journey

To Billund	Hours
From Southend	2

To Copenhagen	Hours
From Gatwick, Heathrow, Manchester	1¾
From Newcastle	2¼
From Birmingham	2½
From Leeds	3
From Aberdeen	3¼

The transfer time from Kastrup airport, Copenhagen, is 30 minutes to the city centre.

The drive-on, drive-off DFDS ferry service between Harwich and Esbjerg takes 19 hours and runs daily in the summer months.

Shopping

Shops are free to decide their own hours, which vary from town to town. However the majority of shops open from 0900 to 1730 Monday to Thursday, some staying open until 1900 to 2000 on Friday. On Saturday most shops close by lunchtime (1400 in Copenhagen), except at holiday resorts. A few food shops open Sunday mornings. At Copenhagen Central Station, some shops stay open until nearly midnight.

Money matters

In Copenhagen, banks open 0930 to 1600 on weekdays, except on Thursdays when most remain open until 1800. Banking hours vary substantially elsewhere.

Credit cards and Eurocheques are widely accepted at hotels, shops and petrol stations. VAT on many purchases will be refunded at departure ports provided that the shop completes the necessary forms. The customs office at Copenhagen Airport will also refund VAT on purchases in Sweden and Norway.

Weather

Averages	Jan	Feb	Mar	Apr	May	Jun	Jul	Aug	Sep	Oct	Nov	Dec
Temperature	35	35	41	50	61	66	72	70	64	54	45	39
Sun hours	3	5	4	5	8	8	8	7	5	3	2	2
Rain days	9	7	8	9	8	8	9	12	8	9	10	11

Rapid changes of weather must be expected in Denmark. The wettest month, surprisingly, is often August, when, however, the sea temperature is at its highest, around 64 degrees. June and July are particularly sunny along the coasts. With the highest hill only 560 ft, strong winds are common.

Local transport

Vehicles must carry a warning triangle. Drivers under 25 may experience considerable difficulty in obtaining a hire car in Denmark.

THE GOOD RESORT GUIDE 209

INDEX

Adriatic Riviera	92-96	Cala Santa Galdana	134-136
Agadir	25-29,32-33	Cala'n Porter	134,136
Aghios Nikolaos	56-60	Calella de la Costa	153,156
Agincourt	193,195	Calella de Palafrugell	146,151
Agrigento	103,105	Caleta de Fuste	21
Albufeira	180-184	Calpe	159,164
Alcudia	129	C'an Picafort	127,131
Algarve	180-187	Canary Isles	6-23
Alghero	99,100	Cannes	117,123
Alicante	159,163	Canoni	69,72
Almanzora	166,168	Cape St Vincent	180,182
Almeria	166	Capri	88,89
Altea	159,163	Carthage	35,38
Alvor	180,184	Cascais	187,188
Amalfi	88,89,90-91	Castelsardo	99,102
Amsterdam	200	Cattolica	92,95-96
Andalucia	171	Cavouri	51,55
Andorra	149	Cefalu	103,105,106-7
Arena d'en Castell	134,136	Chania	57,60
Arroya de la Miel	173	Channel Coast	192-201
Arta	127,129	Chaouen	25,31
Ayia Napa	43,46	Ciudadela	134
Baia Sardinia	101	Comino	113-114
Barbagia	102	Copenhagen	203,204-206
Barcelona	148,153	Cordoba	171,174,183
Barumini	99	Corfu	68-73
Becici	78-79	Corfu Town	69,71
Belgium	196-198	Corinth	55
Benalmadena Costa	173	Corralejo	21
Benidorm	159-163	Costa Blanca	159-166
Benitses	69,71	Costa Brava	146-152
Berck-Sur-Mer	193	Costa de Almeria	166-170
Betancuria	21,22	Costa Del Sol	170,171-177
Billund	207	Costa Dorada	153-159
Blanes	146,147,151	Costa Smerelda	101
Bled	80,83	Crecy	195
Brela	76,79	Crete	56-62
Bruges	193,196	Curium	43,45
Budva	75,76,78-79	Cyprus	42-47
Bugibba	113	Dalmatian Riviera	76-80
Cagliari	99,102	Dassoudi	45
Cala Mayor	127,131	Denia	159,165
Cala Millor	127,131	Denmark	202-209

210 THE GOOD RESORT GUIDE

INDEX

Drach	129	Helsingor	203,206
Dubrovnik	76-78	Heraklion	57
Ebeltoft	203,207	Holland	199-201
El Arenal	127,131	Hyères	123
El Djiem	35,37	Ibiza	137-143
El Golfo	18,20	Ischia	89
El Medano	8,12	Istrian Riviera	80-85
Elche	159,163	Italy	86-107
Elounda	57,60	Janubio	20
Elsinore	206	Javea	159,163
Erice	103,105	Jutland	207
Es Cana	137,141	Kairouan	35,37
Es Pujols	143	Kalithea	53
Esbjerg	205	Kamiros	63,65
Estartit	146,151	Kassandra	53
Estepona	171,176	Kassiopi	69,72
Estoril	187-191	Kastoria	51,53
Etna	103,105	Kebili	35,37
Evora	190	Knossos	57,59
Eze	123	Kolocep	77
Faliraki	63,67	Kolossi	43,,45
Faro	180	Kotor Bay	76
Florence	92,95	Kykko	43,45
Formentera	137,143-145	La Carihuela	173
Fornells	134,135	La Manga	159,165
France	116-125,193-195	Lagos	180,185
Fuengirola	171,176	Lanzarote	18-21
Fuerteventura	21-23	Lapad Peninsula	77
Funen	205,207	Lardos Bay	63
Gabes	35,37	Larnaca	43,45
Garrucha	166,168	Las Palmas	9,14,15
Ghajn Tuffieha Bay	110	Le Touquet	193,194-195
Giardini	103,107	Lefkadia	51,53
Gibraltar	31,183	Levant	123
Giens	123	Lido	92,94
Glyfada (Corfu)	69,71	Lido di Jesolo	92,97,98
Glyfada (Greek mainland)	51,55	Limassol	43,45
Golden Bay	110,113	Lindos	63,67
Gomera	8,9-10	Lisbon	187,188
Gouvia	69,72	Ljubljana	83
Gozo	109,110,111-112,115	Lloret de Mar	146,147-150
Gran Canaria	9,14-18	Lokrum	77
Granada	166,171,174,183	Lopud	77
Greece	48-73	Los Cristianos	8,9
Hague, The	200	Los Lobos	21,22
Halkidiki	51-56	Loulé	182
Hammamet	35,39	Magaluf	127,128-131
Hania	57,60	Mahon	134,135
Haniotis	53	Majorca	127-133
Helsingborg	203,206	Malaga	174

THE GOOD RESORT GUIDE 211

INDEX

Malgrat	153,157	Palma Nova	127,128-131
Malmo	206	Paphos	43,46
Malta	108-115	Pella	51,53
Mando	203,207	Pensicola	156
Marbella	171,177	Pesaro	92,96
Marrakesh	25,28	Petaloudes	65
Marsalforn	115	Pineda	153,157
Marsaskala	109,113	Piran	80,82
Maspalomas	14-18	Playa D'en Bossa	137,141
Mdina	109,111	Playa De Las Americas	8-13
Medulin	80,83	Playa Del Ingles	15
Mellieha Bay	110	Poblet	155
Menton	117,125	Pompeii	88,89-90
Messina	107	Porec	80-83
Messonghi	69,72	Porquerolles	123
Minorca	133-137	Port-Cros	123
Mirador Del Rio	18	Port El Kantaoui	35,36-39
Mljet	77	Port Grimaud	117,119-120
Mojacar	166-169	Portimao	180,186
Monaco	117,121-123	Portinatx	137,142
Monastir	35,40	Porto Cervo	99,101
Monchique	182	Porto Conte	101
Monte Carlo	121-123	Porto Heli	51,55
Monte Gordo	180,186	Portoroz	80,82,84
Monte Toro	134,135	Portugal	178-191
Montreuil-sur-Mer	193,195	Positano	88,91
Montserrat	153,155	Praia Da Rocha	186
Moraitika	69,72	Puerto Banus	177
Morocco	24-33	Puerto De Alcudia	127,132
Mostar	76,77	Puerto De La Cruz	8,11-12
Mycenae	55	Puerto De Pollensa	127,132
Naestved	208	Puerto De Soller	127,132
Naples	88,89,90	Puerto Del Carmen	18,19-21
Naxos	107	Puerto Del Rosario	21
Neapolitan Riviera	88-91	Puerto San Miguel	137,142
Nice	117,123	Pula	80,82
Nicosia	43,45	Qawra	113
Nora	99,102	Ramla Bay	110,115
Nyhavn	205,206	Ravenna	95
Odense	206	Rethymnon	57,61
Oostende	193,196-197	Rhodes	62-68
Opatija	80,83	Rhodes Town	64-66
Pag	76	Ribe	203,207
Paguera	127,131	Riccione	92,96
Palamos	146	Rimini	92,93-95
Pals	146,148	Rome	90
Paleokastritsa	69,70,73	Roquetas de Mar	166,169
Palermo	107	Rovinj	80,82,84
Palma	127,128-130	Sa Calobra	127,129

212 THE GOOD RESORT GUIDE

St Julian's Bay	109,112	Valldemossa	127,130
St Maxime	117,121	Valletta	109,111,112
St Paul's Bay	109,113	Venetian Riviera	97-98
St Raphael	117,121	Venice	92,93-94
St Tropez	117,118-119	Vergei	159,163
Salobrena	166,168	Vesuvius	88,89,90
Salonica	51,53	Vilamoura	180,186
Salou	153-156	Villa Carlos	134,136
San Antonio Abad	137,138-141	Vouliagmeni	51,55
San Feliu	146	Vulcan	105
San Marino	95	Ypres	193,197
Santa Cruz	8,9,10	Yugoslavia	74-85
Santa Marguerita di Pula	102	Zurrieq	109
Santa Susana	153,157		
Sante Creus	153,155		
Santo Tomas	134,136		
Sarajevo	76,77		
Sardinia	99-103		
Scheveningen	193,199-201		
Sealand	205		
Senj	82		
Seville	171,174,183		
Sicily	103-107		
Sidari	69,70,73		
Sitges	153,158		
Sithonia	53		
Solano	76,79		
Sliema	109,112		
Sorrento	88-90		
Sousse	35,36-39		
Spain	126-177		
Split	76		
Stromboli	105		
Su Nuraxi	102		
Sweden	206		
Syracuse	103-104,105		
Tabernas	166,168		
Tangier	25,29-33		
Taormina	103,104-106		
Tarragona	153,155-156		
Tenerife	8-13		
Tetouan	31		
Thessaloniki	51,53		
Tomar	190		
Torremolinos	171-175		
Tossa de Mar	146,151		
Trieste	80,82		
Tunis	38		
Tunisia	34-41		

CREDITS

Publisher
PUBLISHED BY PICKFORDS TRAVEL SERVICE LTD BY ARRANGEMENT WITH BBC PUBLICATIONS, A DIVISION OF BBC ENTERPRISES LTD

Introduction
ROGER MACDONALD, EDITOR, BBC BREAKAWAY

Design and Production
DAVID DAVIES LTD IN ASSOCIATION WITH HEADSTART MARKETING LTD

Picture Research
SALLY HODGSON

Illustrators
CANARY ISLES; PHIL DOBSON
MOROCCO; PAUL ROBINSON
TUNISIA; CORALIE WALKER
CYPRUS; JULIA ROWNTREE
GREECE; KEVIN O'KEEFE
YUGOSLAVIA; ELIZABETH KERR
ITALY; JOANNA CIECHANOWSKA
MALTA; STEWART WALTON
MEDITERRANEAN FRANCE; ANDY BYLO
SPAIN; SIMON THOMPSON
PORTUGAL; MARY FERRILL
CHANNEL COAST; NANCY ANDERSON
DENMARK; TONY WATSON

Photographs
ACE; ART DIRECTORS; ASPECT; EXPLORER; SPECTRUM; TESSA TRAEGER; ZEFA

THE GOOD RESORT GUIDE 215

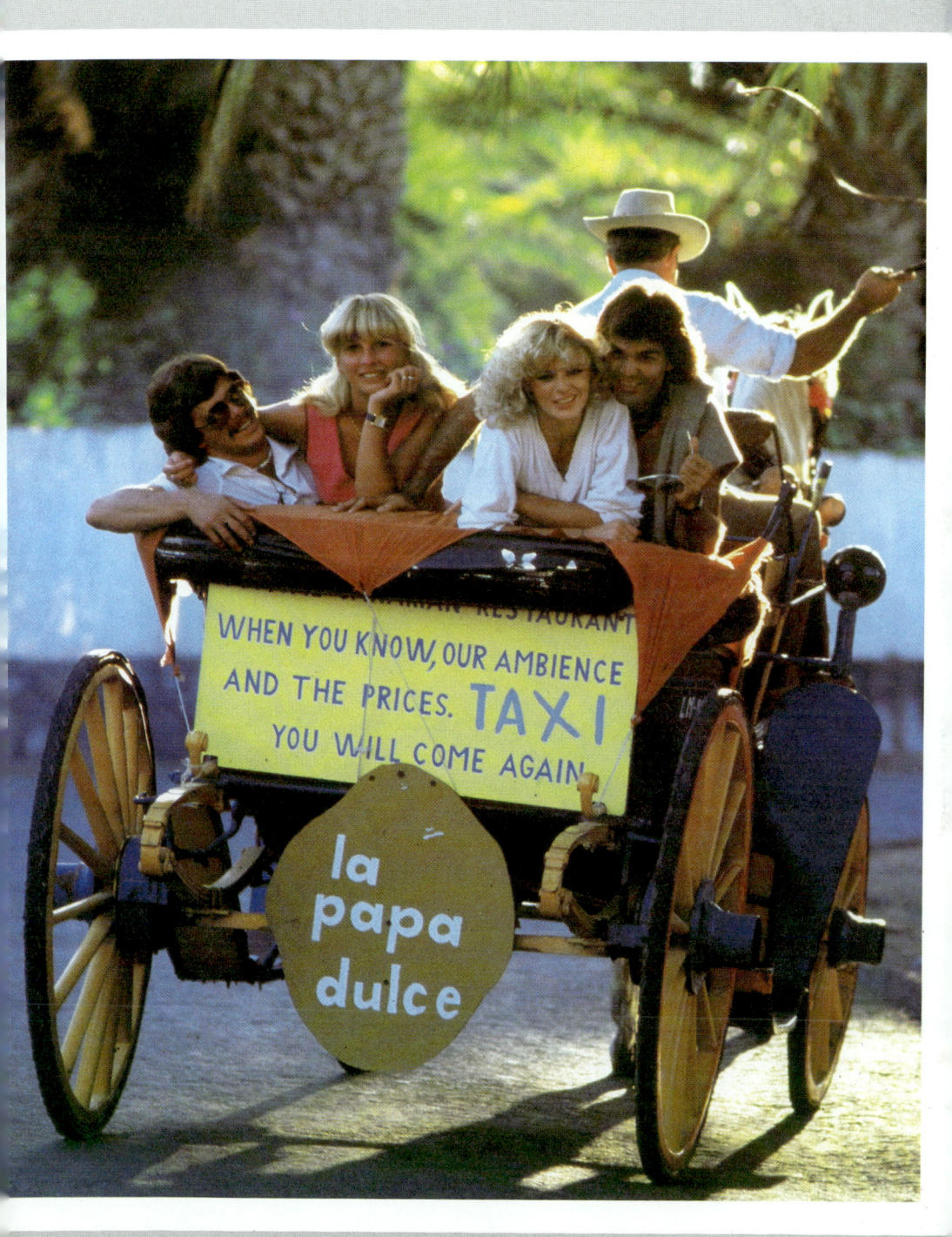